BREESE'S GUIDE TO MODERN FIRST EDITIONS

COMPILED BY MARTIN BREESE

First published in Great Britain by
Breese Books Limited
164 Kensington Park Road, London W11 2ER, England

First Edition

First published 1993

ISBN: 0 947 533 36 2

Typeset in Gill Sans and Bembo by
Ann Buchan (Typesetters), Middlesex
Printed and bound in Great Britain by
Itchen Printers Ltd., Southampton

CONTENTS

PUBLISHER'S FOREWORD

Some time ago, I approached a well-known figure in the world of book collecting and commissioned him to produce a guide for book collectors. The brief was to concentrate on the most collectable authors and to give comprehensive information wherever possible rather than provide brief information on a wider range of authors. The writer agreed to produce the text but insisted that he (for very good reasons) should remain anonymous. The book has now been expanded and a number of additional chapters have been contributed by other specialists.

A few dealers and collectors have seen sections of this book and already there is a fierce debate regarding the prices listed for some of the authors. It is clear that, on publication, the debate will continue and the arguments for higher or lower values will be put forward.

The author writes at length in his introduction about the system used for establishing values for all the books that are listed. I have taken every possible step to ensure that these values are in line with reality and have found that each expert that I consult has his or her own ideas of a book's value. In particular the Ian Fleming chapter was seen by a dealer and he considered that all the values quoted to be far too low — the values were then increased in line with his suggestions. Another expert saw these revised values and thought them to be far too high. He provided a modified set of values and these proved to be almost exactly the same values as set originally!

It is very clear that values and prices are really just a matter of opinion. Values offered here can and do change substantially within days — they can increase or drop overnight without any understandable reason. One dealer may ask high prices and have the ability to hold on until such prices are achieved. Another with less capital has to ensure that his books are sold reasonably quickly and consequently he asks what one might consider to be fair prices.

The price guide listings are for a book of average condition taking into consideration the age of that book. A book in above average condition will be worth more and the converse will also apply.

So many authors, book collectors, dealers and enthusiasts have helped with this book that it is impossible to name them all individually but I would like to thank everybody who has assisted. In particular I am really grateful to James Lay. He is a close friend who has been a constant help with information and who has been the one person to guide me in the right direction with my own growing collection. Kevin Nudd and James Pickard have answered numerous questions and three experienced enthusiasts have extended this book's scope with extra chapters: Stephen Francis Clarke on Henry Williamson, Peter Foord on Simenon and Chris Martin on A.A. Milne.

The living authors in this guide (all but one or two) have been kind enough to read and correct their own chapters.

INTRODUCTION

Over the last twenty years the growth of interest in modern first editions has been staggering. All types of books have been collected — illustrated books, children's literature, sci-fi, detective fiction — all have enjoyed a boom of varying degrees but at the moment the hot money is in modern firsts. Books published just a few years ago (early works by writers like Martin Amis, Salman Rushdie and William Boyd for example), can sell for around ten times or more their original published price. Forget investing in Van Gogh's *Irises*, original Penny Blacks or even the latest privatisation; when a copy of Stephen Spender's first, privately produced collection of poems *Nine Experiments by S.H.S.* (1929) fetches as much as nearly £40,000 as it did at auction in 1990 (and sets a record price for any book published this century), you can see just how lucrative this business can be. Spender's book wasn't one of those huge, sumptuously illustrated volumes bound in elephant skin and sack-cloth and signed by its author, illustrator and publisher's aunt. It was a plain, modern first edition. Don't be put off by that price, though. There were very good reasons why that particular title fetched so much — not least because it was the first book by a major twentieth-century literary figure, printed by himself on his own press in his own dining room in Hampstead.

Most books that we term modern first editions are very affordable indeed. What this book sets out to do is to explain some factors to consider if you decide to collect modern firsts, and then provides an introduction to collecting some of the 'most collectable' authors around. The choice of authors surveyed isn't arbitrary — they have been picked to provide a good indication of who's 'in', why they're in, and what their books are currently fetching on the open market. All the giants are here — Agatha Christie, P.G. Wodehouse, Graham Greene, Dick Francis — also those whom we think merit a place among the top twenty-five or so. No doubt many collectors and dealers will resent the omission of *x* or *y*, but that can be rectified in future editions. For now we present this choice of authors, based on years of collecting modern firsts, scouring second-hand bookshops, and studying those items which make reading the morning's post such a delight — the bookseller's catalogue.

Foremost among this book's objectives is to provide a *practical* guide to collecting modern first editions. In various other books and magazines covering the subject, efforts have been made to assess the availability and value of books which no one has ever seen, or if they have, they're so rare it's impossible to put a fixed value on them. No one expected Spender's hand-printed pamphlet to fetch a tenth of what it did — the item is unique. How then, can you value a first edition of Agatha Christie's first novel complete with fine dust-jacket, or a mint copy of Graham Greene's *Brighton Rock* similarly attired? Copies of these books surface once in a lifetime, if at all, and any attempt to value them should take this into account.

But this principle doesn't apply to these elusive volumes alone. Numerous modern first editions by collectable authors from the 1930s, 40s and 50s can be very hard to find in fine condition for numerous reasons — this, too, should be taken into account. As a result, we have decided to steer clear of giving them an all-embracing value for a given book (invaluable as this practice has been in the past). Instead we have tried to assess a book's value in two ways: in a general second-hand state without a dust-jacket (the least desirable); and in good or very good condition *with* a dust-jacket but with *all the defects one would expect in a book of that age*. It's barely possible to stress those words in italics enough. It is absolutely futile to ignore the book's age, and the prices given in the second column of the bibliographies should be read with one eye on the publication date. The prices given for books published in the 1930s and 40s are for copies in slightly bumped or knocked or frayed condition (ie *with all the defects one would expect in a book of that age!*). This, we hope, will reflect the *real* circumstances of book collecting. If a guidebook says a particular title is worth £100, how can the ordinary collector determine the right price for a very good copy in a chipped dust-jacket, with the spine a little faded through standing in the sun too long, and with the previous owner's ugly inscription scribbled on the title page? *That* is the real state of searching for modern first editions; that is the real world and any guide should take it into account. I hope this offering goes some way to doing just that.

Modern First Editions

The term *first editions* usually applies to the first publication of any book or volume of material that hasn't been published before in book form. That is its intrinsic appeal to collectors. Book collectors are spoilt for choice in the amount of material they can acquire — from sumptuous limited editions to cheap paperback reprints. Most collectors like to have some sort of basis upon which to build their collection and the first appearance of any favourite book in a published form is the most obvious and the ideal starting point.

There's little doubt that there is something special about buying, owning and handling a first edition, particularly one in pristine condition. Reprints, paperbacks, even signed limited editions all have their own merits, but a first edition represents the very first appearance of a favourite book (perhaps an important literary work) and it shows how the book first appeared to an unsuspecting world; how it was when first placed on bookshop shelves by assistants; and how it might have been handled (who knows?) by the author him or herself. Imagine a world without your favourite Jeeves title or *Brighton Rock* — then imagine how that world was changed by the appearance of that book. The first edition of that book you so admire may have changed the world of literature. It was that copy, or a copy just like it, that the publisher sent to its author and to reviewers, and it was that edition that eager readers bought to make it into literary history. The appeal is obvious to all but the most insensitive!

Despite the awe and trepidation with which most collectors view modern first editions, they are really very easy to identify. Most publishers this century have adopted the habit of dating their publications (either on the title page itself or its reverse), and a glance at this should tell you whether or not your book is a first. If it has just the date of publication and nothing else then it's fairly safe to assume it is a first. If, on the other hand, the date is followed by any other information such as 'Second Impression, May 1946', then it is clearly not a first.

Different publishers adopt different methods of course, so it might be worthwhile showing how some of the major publishers present this information. Most books issued by Heinemann have 'First published in —' on the reverse of the title page; while Chatto & Windus make do with a dated title page. Early titles from Gollancz have dated title pages, but from around 1947 they also carry copyright notices; and first editions from Faber and Faber usually tell you in which month and year they were first published. A recent development in publishing (and one which baffles many collectors and dealers, although almost all publishers are using it), is a little row of numbers, from 1 to 9 or 0 under the publishing history on the reverse of the title page. It has only been used for the past two or three years. If any of your books has this make sure that the sequence begins with the number 1: this means there is absolutely no doubt that the book is from the very first print-run. If the sequence begins with 2 or 3 it's from a later batch. The variations are enormous, but the general rule applies. This set of numbers should not be confused with the ISBN system. Avoid any book cluttered up with history of reprints, editions etc.

Despite the fact that a second or third impression can contain new or revised text, collectors are generally interested in only the first impression of a title. When collectors and dealers mention the term 'first edition', they really mean first impression; the first batch of books run off from a single block of type (in the days of letterpress printing). This type was usually kept safe, and if demand dictated a reprint a second, third or even fourth impression could be printed. Eventually, though, when the book was allowed to go out of print the text was broken up. A new edition appeared when the text was actually re-set and then reprinted. Nowadays, of course, almost all books are printed using litho printing techniques and the basic text is kept on film and on litho printing plates. Usually the plates are destroyed and the film is used to make new plates prior to a reprint.

Another thing to look out for and avoid are book–club editions. Dating from the late 1920s and typified by Alan Bott's The Book Society, these volumes were usually published simultaneously with the standard trade edition but at significantly reduced prices. Quite often they are almost identical to the standard edition, although they may have a declaration such as BCA on the book's spine or 'Published in Association with the Book Society' on the reverse of the title page. Occasionally (but not always) these editions are printed on slightly inferior paper. There are no standard rules. The one major difference between regular first editions and book–club editions is that the latter are not collectable (at least for the time being). Although there is a slight 'snob' element at play here, the main reason is that the print-run of these club editions can often be ten times that of the regular. The more copies, the more availability, the less collectability and less value.

A word or two about the 'modern' part of modern first editions. Just what is modern? Generally speaking most dealers and collectors think of any book published after 1900 as modern, although it is not quite that simple. As you will see, we have included some books published before 1900 (eg some Sherlock Holmes titles) — these titles are *seen* to be part of the modern first edition scene unlike other books by, for example, Oscar Wilde and Thomas Hardy published at the same time. We are just reporting what actually hapens in the world of modern first edition collecting; we don't make the rules. After ferreting around the modern firsts scene you'll soon realise what is considered modern and what isn't.

What to Collect

As with all areas of collecting, the only real guideline one can use is to follow your individual taste — collect what you like. Modern first editions are prone to changes in fashions and writers who were ignored a few years ago are now very popular. On the other hand, highly collectable authors from ten years ago are now falling out of fashion. Fifteen years ago nobody seemed to collect books by Ian Fleming or P.G. Wodehouse, but nowadays everybody's after their books, and the same can be said for writers like Ruth Rendell or P.D. James. The collectable giants of two decades ago like George Bernard Shaw, H.G. Wells and Arnold Bennett seem to be totally forgotten. Whether Fleming and Wodehouse's vogue is a result of publications like Joseph Connolly's *Modern First Editions* and *Book and Magazine Collector*, or whether those guides simply reflect the trends is difficult to ascertain, but there can be little doubt that both have awakened a large interest in collecting modern first editions. Certainly Fleming and Wodehouse titles are very highly sought after. This can only be a good thing. Neither writer can be said to produce great literature, but collectors have decided to collect what they enjoy, leaving the market to follow suit. Without the snob factor, book collecting can be a highly enjoyable pastime.

Of course, some great writers are very collectable today. Virginia Woolf, Iris Murdoch and Graham Greene not only produce great literature but their first editions are also some of the most sought after this century. The important point is that being great literature doesn't necessarily mean that a book will be collected, nor does being low-brow popular fiction mean that collectors will ignore it. A book or a writer only becomes collectable when collectors decide — no amount of manipulating or promoting will change that. And that is just how it should be, of course. There is one story of an American collector who deliberately bought up all the copies he could find of a particular Hank Janson book to make it collectable — inevitably he failed. Not enough people were interested in Janson's work.

Don't be afraid to follow your tastes. If you want to acquire first editions by Harold Robbins, Jackie Collins or an entirely unknown writer do so — it's your money — and don't be put off by sneering replies when you ask your bookseller if he has anything in stock. Most people laughed when Mr Connolly included the works of P.G. Wodehouse in his guide, and look what happened! Collectors who acquire for investment purposes only don't deserve vilification, only slight pity because they'll never really appreciate the joy of buying, owning, handling, or reading a copy of their favourite book in its original format — they are too busy scanning auction notes to see what sort of return their investment will bring. That isn't book collecting, it's commodity fetishism; the privilege of the rich who can afford to take their pick of auctions but who will never know the joy of finding a cherished long-sought volume after hours, days or even years of trudging around second-hand bookshops throughout the country. The idea of spending so much money on a book and not even reading it, is quite ludicrous. These 'collectors' don't affect the rank and file of committed book collectors too much. They tend to operate at the top end of the market, an area sadly remote from most. Collect those authors and those books you enjoy, regardless of fashions or values. The worst that can happen is that the demand for your particular favourites slump and you suddenly find your previous volumes are worthless — *in monetary terms*. But so what? You'll still have them to enjoy.

If you are just starting out on your quest for modern first editions we hope we will be able to give you some ideas in the main part of the book. Many collectors like to concentrate on their favourite authors but increasingly collectors are turning to *themes* or *genres*. Some concentrate on spy novels (hence the essay on Deighton and le Carré) or great American novels. Others want to acquire important one-offs (see the chapter covering novels like *The Ginger Man* and books such as *The Naked Civil Servant* — a few people collect all of Quentin Crisp's books but no good collection of modern firsts is complete without his seminal title). Others still might be interested in the works of the 'angry young men'; novels like *Saturday Night and Sunday Morning* and *Live Now, Pay Later* which represented a new movement in literature. The choice is yours.

Rarity and Values

If you do want to collect for investment purposes (and there's nothing intrinsically wrong with that), there are so many factors to take into account. The most important rule to remember is that just because a book is rare doesn't necessarily mean that it's *valuable*. A book only becomes valuable and collectable when its *scarcity is combined with a high demand*. It's a straightforward case of supply and demand. You may possess the only remaining copy of Toby Tootle's *Memoirs*, but if nobody want to buy it at any price then the book is valueless. If, on the other hand, you want to sell your copy of the first trade edition of, say, T.E. Lawrence's *Seven Pillars of Wisdom* it doesn't matter that the print-run was in its thousands and that there are always several copies floating around. The demand is greater than the supply, and it stands to reason that when it comes to determining a price the vendor is at a distinct advantage. *Caveat emptor*.

Valuing modern first editions is a minefield, and any sensible publisher of a book like this would steer clear at all costs. To value a particular book can't be done with any confidence or accuracy because, like all objects, a book is worth only what someone else is willing to pay for it. It can't be put any simpler than that. A dealer trying to sell for £300 a book that most people would pay around £50 for is deluding himself, until somebody comes into his shop and pays that £300. To that collector, at least, the book was worth £300. As another writer has commented, all values are arbitrary, mutually agreed levels reflecting the balance between demand and scarcity. The only fixed rule is that there are no fixed rules. If a dealer offers you a book at a high price and you can't obtain it elsewhere, consult your bank manager and your heart and ask yourself whether you can live without it. Then consult your bank manager again. If the asking price is O.K. for you (and you alone) then that is what the book is worth. Simple as that!

The value indicated in this book will give a guide to a book's rarity — the true value is what you are prepared to pay! If value is a very personal thing then, how can one produce a book like this attempting to set standard values for so many collectable titles? It's tempting to suggest it can't be done and give up here, but it's important to try to *standardise* prices, to suggest what the normal bookseller with normal overheads in a normal town would charge a normal customer for a good clean collectable copy of the book. We don't want to say a book is worth *that*, and that's final, but we think collectors and dealers will find it useful to see within which price range the book generally sells *at the moment*. That way, nobody will be cheated or disappointed. But, again, it must be emphasised that a book's value is personal and should be determined between the dealer and customer. All that has been done here is to provide some kind of loose guide, based largely on years of browsing through shops, catalogues and (least realiable of all) book auction records. If you know what a copy has been priced at before, it might help to value the same book now. We'll leave the haggling to you — that's part of the fun. By the way, when you see a dash like this – in the checklist it means the book in that condition has no intrinsic value as such. For example, Iris Murdoch's most recent novels are so common in virtually mint condition that a collector would be a fool to buy copies with or without jackets in a less than fine state.

Condition and Dust-Jackets

Apart from scarcity and demand, the most important factor to take into account in valuing a book is its condition, hence the different prices listed in this book. Nothing affects the value of a book more than condition. Generally speaking, in an ideal world all collectors would like to acquire a first edition of their favourite book in a condition as close as possible to how it was originally published; they want their copy to be fine in a dust-jacket. Copies of any book with missing pages are to be avoided at all costs, regardless of its scarcity (who, after all, would buy a Chippendale desk with only three legs?) Books are made to be read and handled so acquiring copies in absolutely mint condition is almost impossible but, if you can, avoid copies with bumped corners, stained covers, sprung spines and all the other defects one associates with well-loved books. It is important to be realistic when offered an imperfect copy of a book you want. Assess the chances of finding a bright, clean, almost perfect copy. Are they good? You might want to accept this copy now, always keeping on the look-out for a better example in the future. Collecting modern first editions is an exercise in patience and compromise. Only the rich can afford to buy complete sets in fine condition from auction houses, but, again, that isn't collecting at all. Most of the fun of collecting comes from the hunt for *exactly* what you've been looking for. One of the more alarming trends both collectors and dealers are commenting on at the moment is the growing scarcity of even relatively modern titles in truly fine condition. Some of the battered and bumped offerings on sale at book fairs in particular don't deserve the shelf space given to them. For titles published in the 1970s and 80s this is unforgivable, and they should be bought in the absence of any other copy.

The most radical and controversial development in collecting modern first editions in recent years has been the importance of dust-jackets. It's hard to emphasise just how important the presence of a complete clean jacket is to a book's collectability and value today. It's best to illustrate with an example. Iris Murdoch's first novel, *Under the Net*, can sell for as much as £200 complete with a clean dust-jacket on today's market. Without this flimsy, ephemeral piece of paper, dealers would be hard pressed to get £10 for the book. Over the past few years dealers have found it increasingly difficult — almost impossible — to sell recent modern first editions (those published after around 1950) without a clean jacket, unless the book or the jacket is exceedingly scarce.

Why the importance of dust-jackets? To put it bluntly, collectors (and, thus, dealers) have at last come round to the way of thinking that the dust-jacket is an integral and vital part of the whole book. As *Under the Net* shows, it is often much more important than the book itself from a collecting point of view (I have even seen people trying to sell copies of jackets by themselves, without the books!) From a purely aesthetic sense, a row of books with their attractive dust-jackets standing against each other is much more pleasing to the eye than a row of dull-coloured cloth spines, particularly as those spines are so prone to fading in the light. Furthermore, many jackets have been designed by artists collectable in their own right. Artists like Val Biro, Edward Bawden, Michael Ayrton, Barnet Freedman, Edward Ardizzone, Lynton Lamb and Mervyn Peake, for example, all illustrated dust-jackets during the 1930s and 40s (the golden age of dust-jackets).

Apart from the purely aesthetic, there is another good reason why the presence of a jacket should affect a book's value so much. For many years they were immediately discarded by the book's new owner. It might be worthwhile outlining the history of the dust-jacket here. Although little information is available on the subject, it is generally accepted that the first dust-jacket was issued by Longmans in 1833 for *Keepsake*. Because it really was meant as a dust cover to protect the book in the shop until its purchaser took it home, the jacket was a dull buff affair printed in red. On the front was the book's title and the publisher's imprint, on the book was an advertisement for three other Longmans titles. For the next eighty or so years dust-jacket design developed little (in fact only a fraction of books were issued with jackets even up to around 1910), and it wasn't until just before the First World War that it became the norm rather than the exception to issue books in jackets. Many were still rather plain, usually used to advertise the publisher's other offerings. Gradually, though, publishers realised that the jacket could be used to market and promote the book. The accepted wisdom was that an attractive dust-jacket attracted purchasers.

Even so, collectors and readers continued to regard the jacket as ephemeral and it was usually discarded. Perhaps readers felt uncomfortable holding a book with a loose piece of paper around it (I still take off a book's jacket before reading it, only to replace it carefully before restoring the volume to the shelves), or perhaps they just didn't like them. Whatever the reason, it was with very good reason that an exhibition of dust-jackets organised by David Alexander in Oxford in 1983 was called 'Saved from the wastepaper basket: British Book-Jackets 1925–1955'. So many jackets suffered this fate (and still do) that it's hardly surprising collectors consider them so important today. People still deliberate about dust-jackets, pointing out that the book was meant to be read, not looked at, but the fact remains the same — a first edition without a jacket and published after the Second World War is worth, at best, a fraction of the price a complete copy would fetch and at worst, nothing. If the presence of jackets or otherwise matters nothing to you, fine! I think that you'll find yourself in the minority. However, you'll also find yourself acquiring a large collection for very little outlay.

Sources of Modern First Editions

Tracking down those elusive modern firsts is part of the fun, and there are numerous channels you can explore. Each one has its advantages and disadvantages, normally to do with the quality of material on offer and price. The most obvious source, of course, is the second-hand bookshop, but even here you will soon become aware of the difference in quality. Some are little better than junkshops, stocked full to the rafters with tatty reprints and little else. This is great if you want tatty reprints — we don't. Most collectors will find though that they aren't too far away from a reputable dealer in modern firsts and, if you take the time to cultivate a friendship you could reap the benefits for years. He or she will accept your wants lists and track down those elusive titles on your behalf, with surprisingly successful results. But beware, because the dealer is in a strong position. He knows you want the title, and he will know how much you are prepared to pay for it. There will be very few bargains from this source, particularly if you are dealing with London dealers who have to cover high rents, business rates and other overheads. Essentially you are trading ease of acquirement for a higher price. It's often worth it.

Unfortunately, the days of finding pristine copies of James Joyce's *Pomes Penyeach* or Wodehouse's *The Great Bat* in the local charity shop or jumble sale are long gone (though there are occasional exceptions) — even these dealers or organisers have wised up and anything even suspiciously valuable-looking is taken to the local bookseller for valuation. It's no secret that antique dealers and the local bookseller fraternity are invited to scour many jumble sales long before Joe Public is admitted.

Again, this book is attempting to portray the real world of book collecting; not a pipe-dream of how romantics would like to see it. If you really want to acquire fine copies of good quality modern firsts you simply must fall back on the higher-brow sources. Magazines such as *Book and Magazine Collector* are a wonderful source (around eighty pages of good titles offered for sale every month at reasonable prices), as are modern first specialist shops. Booksellers' catalogues are another good source. Get yourself on several dealers' mailing lists to ensure a regular supply of these catalogues — it's often surprising just what choice items do appear in these lists. I have several in front of me as I write. Between them they offer a complete set of Anthony Powell's *Dance to the Music of Time* sequence, several early titles in jackets from William Golding, Iris Murdoch's first novel

Under the Net in a mint jacket, and two signed Virginia Woolfs. You will never find these in jumble sales. But again, you have to pay a price for the convenience.

In Britain, book fairs (such as those organised by Book Fairs Ltd and the P.B.F.A.) have a growing influence on the second-hand bookmarket, and most towns and cities stage at least one such event a month, often much more frequently. These are normally attended by a couple of dozen dealers from all over the region, and many offer a respectable number of modern firsts (although they also cater for the general book-collecting public looking for illustrated items and other interest areas). They are not usually cheap (the more prestigious and popular the fair, the more you'll pay), but they provide wonderful opportunities to make new contacts with more dealers who might be able to provide worthwhile items in the future.

Another excellent source is the book auction. Most towns have an auction house which holds occasional book auctions. You can rest assured that any book offered for sale at these places will be exceptional — it just isn't worth their time to auction rubbish. Again, the more prestigious auction houses like Sothebys, Christies and Bloomsbury Book Auctions in London offer the best items but you will have to pay high prices. It is from these places that the real scarcities are bought: author's first pamphlets and signed limited edition issues. Other auctions are less exclusive, and many offer boxes of books (from house clearances for instance) in which scarce titles may be found. Although you will often find yourself bidding against more knowledgeable book dealers, these places are great fun. Go along, and enjoy the thrill of the bid. It's addictive.

Caring for Your Books

Given that condition and dust-jackets are so important, what is necessary to maintain your collection in anything like reasonable condition? Books are, after all, made of paper and paper is very prone to tearing, burning, discolouring and many other hazards. The most obvious advice is to be sensible and handle them with care and remember that they are fragile. If you can, always keep books standing upright on shelves and try to avoid standing them at an angle like tired sentries — this will warp them. Keep them fairly close together, but not too tight as this can lead to split spines when you try to pull a book out. Try to avoid housing your collection in a glass-fronted bookcase, particularly one in the direct sunlight. This may look attractive but books, like all perishables, need air to breathe and the sun is one of a book's worst enemies. Exposing a book to sunlight for even a few hours can fade its colour and there's nothing worse than seeing the all-too-common sight of a nice bright dust-jacket spoiled by a sickly faded spine. For some reason red, yellow and orange are particularly prone to this fading, so Gollancz collectors beware! One of my most regular purchases is rolls of transparent plastic sheeting which can be folded over the jacket to protect it from stray coffee mugs, sweaty fingers and all kinds of harm. This is particularly important for dust-jackets published up to the late 1960s before jackets were ruined by having an awful plastic laminate put on them. The irony is, of course, that it's only those titles from the 1930s to the 1960s which need protecting by plastic — those superbly designed jackets printed on rough textured paper. Why jackets should be laminated today when they are invariably photographic, I have no idea. Some collectors don't like having their Ardizzone, Lamb et al jackets covered in a protective wrapping, objecting that it creates a harsh glare.

If you do feel that a jacket needs repairing, *don't* use sellotape. Ensure that all the materials you use to repair, cover or enhance a book are acid-free and designed for archival purposes. Sellotape may look O.K. to start with but within a year or so it dries, discolours the area affected, and makes it even more fragile than before. There are some new archival-quality tapes on the market which are safe, but jackets with tape on their reverse do nothing for a book's value. If you must get a book repaired, go to a professional. The same goes for repairing torn binding, removing unwanted inscriptions and getting rid of *foxing*; those unsightly light brown spots which form at the edges of old pages. If your particular book is valuable enough to warrant treatment from a trained expert, it's worth spending money getting the job done well. You'll hate yourself if you ruin your precious book.

The Rest of this Book

There have been a lot of changes in collecting modern first editions in recent years. It's my intention to cover today's most collectable authors in this volume. A quick look shows that there seems to be a distinctive swing towards more modern authors in this volume than there are in similar books. People still collect the two Lawrences' and Ezra Pound but these seem to be at the top end of collecting — it's my distinct feeling that more and more collectors are turning to writers like Ruth Rendell, Dick Francis and the old favourites like Wodehouse, Christie and Greene. This is partly because their books are more accessible, and they are all so wonderful to read. It's also interesting to see that almost all the books of the authors featured here are 'normal' books — books which were issued in standard octavo format with dust-jackets — rather than the privately printed, asbestos-bound, triple-signed, super limited editions so beloved by some. This is important for collectors. It may take a lifetime to complete your collection, but most of the books covered here were issued commercially and there are copies out there somewhere. They are not all in private collections or prestigious public libraries.

Each entry has fairly extensive biographical information, together with comments on problems you are likely to find with particular books. I've tried to describe as many of the more important books as I can. The bibliographies are as complete as possible but please take into account that some authors are particularly prone to issuing tiny pamphlets of obscure texts now and again just for the sheer hell of it. It is almost impossible to trace all these. John Fowles and Graham Greene are two that spring to mind. However, the bibliographies do include all the commercially produced titles. And before leaping into print yourself do remember that the value of a book can change overnight. Ruth Rendell's books in one dealer's catalogue have astronomical asking prices — the asking price is not always the selling price! Please remember, the values are meant to serve as a guide, not as gospel. So, with that exclusion clause firmly embedded in your consciousness, let us begin . . .

KINGSLEY AMIS

Kingsley Amis is an intriguing writer to collect. While his early works remain frustratingly elusive and expensive, his more recent titles can be found for not much more than their publication price. Many collectors like to benefit from this 'duality'. A combination of scarcity and accessibility generally keeps collectors on their toes without discouraging them too much. And few authors are as rewarding as Kingsley Amis. His books, particularly his marvellous, sardonic and amusing tales are sure to live on well into the next century. They are comic classics of our time and Sir Kingsley Amis (as he is now) is, in every way, one of the Grand Old Men of English Letters.

This transformation into a literary establishment figure is interesting because in his early years he was part of the Angry Young Man school of writing, a doctrine seemingly espoused in his most favous novel *Lucky Jim* which was based loosely on his friend, the poet Philip Larkin. Jim Dixon an academic grammar schoolboy determined to let as little work as possible interrupt his drinking and womanising, was seen as an entirely realistic hero. He was totally unlike any other character then created — so it's small wonder that a first edition of *Lucky Jim* forms the cornerstone to any collection of modern fiction. Be warned though, fine copies are notoriously scarce and you might have to make do with a less-than-perfect example.

Recently Kingsley Amis's life story has been admirably told in his autobiography, *Memoirs* (Hutchinson, 1991) — a frank and controversial book which is sure to become a classic. When it was published reviewers were up in arms at what they saw as its amorality; how dare Amis tell such stories about his fellow writers? This is sheer nonsense of course. A more realistic question is why shouldn't he tell such stories, if they are true? If, as Amis claims, Dylan Thomas appeared to be an unpleasant man with a propensity to behave badly particularly when he was a house guest there is no reason why this should not be written about. In revealing as well that Philip Larkin, his great friend, had a penchant for girlie magazines perhaps he was attempting to explain that literary giants are not gods but talented people with human foibles. Amis's autobiography is well worth reading.

Kingsley Amis was born in London on 16 April 1922. When he was eleven a teacher inspired him to embark on a blank verse epic and from then on he wrote continuously, although in his own words his efforts were 'abnormally unpromising'.

In 1947 Fortune Press published a collection of early verse entitled *Bright November* and this is probably his scarcest title — so scarce that some bibliographies do not record it at all. This was followed by another collection of verse *A Frame of Mind* which was published in 1953 by the Reading School of Art in an edition of 150 copies and at Amis's own expense. Very good copies have been known to sell for around £150–£200. *Frame of Mind* was issued without a jacket and the soft covers are prone to tear or fray. *Bright November* was issued in a jacket

— don't be tempted to believe that it wasn't if you are offered one without.

These two collections of verse are Amis's scarcest titles but they are by no means his most valuable. That tribute is reserved rather predictably for *Lucky Jim*. This is just one instance of where scarcity doesn't necessarily mean extortionate value. *Lucky Jim* is expensive today because it combines those two essential ingredients, scarcity *and* desirability. The publishing history of *Lucky Jim* is particularly interesting because Victor Gollancz chose to issue it in 1954 in the month of January (it is dated 1953 on the title page), a month when traditionally very few novels are published. The book was, as a result of this tactical publishing ploy, ensured extensive media coverage but it was the book itself rather than the publicity that surrounded it that guaranteed that it would become a best-seller. The wily Gollancz even manipulated the details of the reprinting of *Lucky Jim* to give the impression that the book was a bigger best-seller than it actually was. With each successive printing Gollancz would halt the presses (after every thousand or so copies) to insert news of a further impression on the verso of the title page. This could mean for example that a copy from the so-called seventeenth impression probably isn't exactly that — it is more likely to be one of the many interruptions of an earlier reprinting!

The very first impression of *Lucky Jim* was bound in green boards and issued with Gollancz's standard yellow dust-jacket with Stanley Morrison's distinctive typography. Like many famous Gollancz novels (John le Carré's *The Spy Who Came in from the Cold* is another example), the first edition of *Lucky Jim* was unusual in that it carried a reader's recommendation on the front of the jacket. This often causes confusion among collectors, who are more used to seeing reader's and reviewer's tributes on second and later impressions. Looking back now, though, C.P. Snow's comments are faint praise rather than a glowing eulogy. He wrote: 'It is humorous, self-mocking, hopeful, endearing. For promise and achievement combined it is the best first novel I've read in the last two years.'*Lucky Jim* was so successful it won the Somerset Maugham Award for fiction in 1955. Maugham appreciated the realistic characterisation of Jim Dixon whose idea of celebration was 'to go to a public house and drink six beers'.

Other critics also admired *Lucky Jim* and readers weren't slow to follow suit; collectors have given their firm seal of approval in more recent years. As with all of Kingsley Amis's Gollancz titles up to *The Anti-Death League* in 1966, *Lucky Jim*'s standard yellow dust-jacket was printed on slightly grainy paper, and this is particularly prone to dirt, fraying and fading as the years go by. These dust-jackets (also found on many classic crime and science fiction titles still published by Gollancz today, although they are usually laminated now) are collectable in their own right. I know of one collector whose criterion for collecting is these jackets alone. They are worth the trouble since particularly fine examples look attractive on the shelf. They are Gollancz's own distinctive contribution to the golden age of dust-jacket design.

Amis's literary career has largely maintained the early success of *Lucky Jim*. Apart from a rather slim period in the early 1980s when he seemed to lose his Amis-ness (the trend was hilariously bucked with *The Old Devils* which won the Booker Prize in 1986), all his novels have been of a consistently high standard. In the early years, *Lucky Jim* was followed up with such classics as *That Uncertain Feeling* (Gollancz, 1955), *I Like It Here* (Gollancz, 1958), *Take a Girl Like You* (Gollancz, 1960), *One Fat Englishman* (Gollancz, 1963), and his first collection of short stories, *My Enemy's Enemy* (Gollancz, 1962). All these titles were published in the standard Gollancz style, but none is too hard to find today, although genuinely fine copies remain elusive. It should be possible, however, to pick up acceptable copies in reasonably clean jackets for between £20 and £40. Without their jackets none of these books is worth very much.

Much more scarce from this period are Amis's collections of verse. In the early stages of his career he was a prolific poet, and it is only in more recent years that he has become known mainly as a novelist of the highest order. Although collectors are usually most keen to acquire Amis's novels, they would be foolish to neglect his verse, particularly these early titles. *Bright November* and *A Frame of Mind* are ephemeral items but they have the potential to become very valuable indeed. Some of his poems were collected in No. 22 of the collectable Fantasy Poets series in 1954; and the Fantasy Press issued his *The Evans Country* in 1962, a tiny eight-page pamphlet bound in grey paper wrappers. Despite its skimpy appearance this title can sell for around £30. More significant is his 1956 collection, *A Case of Samples: Poems 1946–1955* issued by Gollancz. Once again, this title's dust-jacket is prone to wear and tear, but very good clean copies can be found — with luck and persistence.

By the mid-1960s Kingsley Amis was acknowledged as a leading poet and novelist. Around this time he changed publishers from Gollancz to Jonathan Cape (he has since settled with Hutchinson). Cape published some of his best-known titles, including *I Want It Now* (1968), *The Green Man* (1969), and *Ending Up* (1974), which many consider to be his best title from this 'middle' period. Cape also published two titles about Ian Fleming's famous spy hero James Bond 007, one of Amis's pet subjects. As well as producing an intelligent study of the books in *The James Bond Dossier* (issued in a clever jacket detailing some of Richard Chopping's Bond designs), Amis also wrote *Colonel Sun: A James Bond Adventure* under his 'Robert Markham' pseudonym. Both titles are as eagerly sought after by Bond enthusiasts as by Amis collectors.

There was something of an interval in Amis's career in the early 1980s when he contented himself with editing anthologies of verse and essays, or writing studies of science fiction. He made an impressive return to his own fiction with *Stanley and the Women* (Hutchinson, 1984) and *The Old Devils* (Hutchinson, 1986), which won the prestigious Booker Prize. Even these titles, and his two most recent novels, *Difficulties with Girls* and *The Folks That Live on the Hill*, sell now for more than their published price. It should be borne in mind though, only fine or even mint copies are acceptable as collectable items. The print-runs for these titles were large enough for lesser copies to be given a wide berth!

Like all collectable writers, some of Amis's books have been issued in special limited editions, and as he was also a political writer there are some pamphlets which should be considered. Fabian Tract No. 304, was Amis's *Socialism and the Intellectuals* (1957), a thirteen-page pamphlet which is quite scarce today; and his *Lucky Jim's Politics*, published by the Conservative Centre in 1968 is also sought after. These two titles show Amis's political development during the 1960s, from Angry Young Men to establishment figure. Much more collectable, though, is his short story *Dear Illusion*, published by the Covent Garden Press in 1972. Only 600 copies were issued in yellow paper wrappers, of which 100 were numbered and signed. And in 1978 the prestigious Tragara Press in Edinburgh published Amis's Sherlock Holmes pastiche *The Darkwater Hall Mystery*, which had originally appeared in *Playboy*. This 35-page book in marbled paper wrappers was limited to just 165 copies.

Title	No dj	In dj
Bright November verse (Fortune Press, 1947)	£50 – £80	£200 – £250
A Frame of Mind verse (Reading School of Art, 1953)	£150 – £200	n/a
Lucky Jim novel (Gollancz, 1953)	£20 – £25	£200 – £300
Fantasy Poets No. 22 verse (Fantasy Press, 1954)	£30 – £40	n/a
That Uncertain Feeling novel (Gollancz, 1955)	£5 – £10	£30 – £40
A Case of Samples verse (Gollancz, 1956)	£20 – £25	£50 – £60
Socialism and the Intellectuals non-fiction (Fabian Tracts, 1957)	£20 – £25	n/a
I Like it Here novel (Gollancz, 1958)	£5 – £10	£20 – £30
Take a Girl Like You novel (Gollancz, 1960)	£5 – £10	£20 – £30
New Maps of Hell non-fiction (Gollancz, 1961)	£5 – £8	£20 – £30
My Enemy's Enemy short stories (Gollancz, 1962)	£5 – £8	£20 – £30
The Evans Country verse (Fantasy Press, 1962)	£30 – £40	n/a
One Fat Englishman novel (Gollancz, 1963)	£5 – £8	£20 – £25

Title	No dj	In dj
The Egyptologists novel (Jonathan Cape, 1965)	–	£10 – £20
The James Bond Dossier non-fiction (Jonathan Cape, 1965)	–	£10 – £20
The Anti-Death League novel (Gollancz, 1966)	–	£10 – £20
A Look Round the Estate: Poems 1957 – 1967 verse (Jonathan Cape, 1967)	–	£10 – £20
Colonel Sun novel by 'Robert Markham' (Jonathan Cape, 1968)	–	£10 – £20
Lucky Jim's Politics non-fiction (Conservative Centre, 1968)	£10 – £20	n/a
I Want It Now novel (Jonathan Cape, 1968)	–	£10 – £20
The Green Man novel (Jonathan Cape, 1969)	–	£10 – £20
What Became of Jane Austen? and Other Questions essays (Jonathan Cape, 1970)	–	£5 – £10
Girl, 20 novel (Jonathan Cape, 1971)	–	£10–20
On Drink non-fiction (Jonathan Cape, 1972)	–	£5 – £10
Dear Illusion short story *limited to 600 copies* (Covent Garden Press, 1972) *100 signed and numbered copies*	£25 – £30 £40 – £50	n/a n/a
The Riverside Villa Murders novel (Jonathan Cape, 1973)	–	£10 – £20
Ending Up novel (Jonathan Cape, 1974)	–	£10 – £20
Rudyard Kipling and His World biography (Thames and Hudson, 1975)	–	£5 – £10
The Alteration novel (Jonathan Cape, 1976)	–	£10 – £15

Title	No dj	In dj
The Darkwater Hall Mystery short story (Tragara Press, 1978) *limited to 165 copies*	£40 – £50	n/a
Jake's Thing novel (Hutchinson, 1978)	–	£10 – £15
Collected Poems verse (Hutchinson, 1979)	–	£10 – £15
An Arts Policy? lecture (Centre for Policy Studies, 1979) *issued in stiff paper wrappers*	£5 – £10	n/a
Russian Hide-and-Seek novel (Hutchinson, 1980)	–	£10 – £15
Collected Short Stories short stories (Hutchinson, 1979)	–	£10 – £15
The Golden Age of Science Fiction non-fiction (Hutchinson, 1981)	–	£5 – £10
Every Day Drinking non-fiction (Hutchinson, 1983)	–	£5 – £10
How's Your Glass? non-fiction (Weidenfeld & Nicolson, 1984)	–	£3 – £5
Stanley and the Women novel (Hutchinson, 1984)	–	£10 – £15
The Old Devils novel (Hutchinson, 1986)	–	£10 – £15
Difficulties with Girls novel (Hutchinson, 1988)	–	£10 – £15
The Folks That Live on the Hill novel (Hutchinson, 1990)	–	£10 – £15
Memoirs autobiography (Hutchinson, 1991)	–	£8 – £10

JOHN BETJEMAN

In a century in which the novel has overtaken poetry as the most popular literary form it is good to see at least one poet avidly collected by book buffs. Other writers like Spender, Auden, Cecil Day Lewis and Dylan Thomas are collectable, of course, but John Betjeman seems to be in a class of his own. Perhaps that's because he was more than just a poet. He was an institution. The personification of suburban England, shabby cardigans and Victorian architecture! Sir John Betjeman loved England. England loved him back. After the phenomenal success of his *Collected Poems* (John Murray, 1958), his little books of verse became regular best-sellers.

John Betjeman's poems are worth collecting and in the past ten years his first editions have soared in value. But it isn't just his books of verse that people seek — all his life he was obsessed by architecture and topography and he actually produced more prose books on these subjects than verse. Whatever medium he used, Betjeman always remains the same: amusing, thought-provoking, charming, and slightly eccentric. John Betjeman was born in Highgate, North London on 26 August 1906, the only son of a businessman who produced high-class cabinets and dressing tables. Many were sold through Asprey's in London, earning Ernest Betjemann (John dropped the second 'n' later in life) a reputation as a modern day and slightly suburban Chippendale. He was also eminently respectable middle-class; a fact which caused his son acute embarrassment as he moved among upper-class circles in the 1920s and 30s. Betjeman took to verse at an early age and there is a story that he once showed a teacher at Highgate Junior School his small, hand-produced collection of poems entitled *The Best Poems of Betjeman*. What the teacher made of them isn't recorded sadly — but his name was T.S. Eliot! In September 1920 Betjeman moved on to Marlborough School which, in the glorious tradition of English public schools, thrived on bullying, cruelty and homosexuality. It was a horrifying experience for the young Betjeman and one which he recorded with poetic and savage poignancy in his autobiographical *Summoned by Bells* in 1960: 'The dread of beatings! Dread of being late!/ And, greatest dread of all, the dread of games!' There was also the dread of 'basketing', one of the more savage rituals carried out by schoolboys on schoolboys who offended the school's code. Apparently it was looked upon by the masters as a fine old tradition. This involved stripping the offending boy, smearing him with ink, treacle or paint and hoisting him to the ceiling in one of two large wastepaper baskets. Whether Betjeman himself suffered this fate is uncertain but as the poet himself never claimed it, it's fairly safe to assume he escaped. During the course of his career Betjeman gained much literary mileage out of his school days.

Despite the dread of Marlborough, he did make some good friends there, including fellow poet Louis MacNeice and Anthony Blunt, the distinguished art historian and Keeper of Her Majesty's paintings (until such times as he was named the fourth man in the Burgess-Maclean-Philby spy ring). Betjeman also became involved in literary work, submitting poems for the official *Malburian* and the decidedly unofficial cock-snooking *The Heretick*, an aesthetic journal. This continued at Oxford, where he developed the bizarre, extravagant, but essentially lovable character which became so popular in his broadcasts later in life.

After leaving Oxford (having failed in Divinity), Betjeman taught for a short while and it wasn't until he landed a job on the *Architectural Review* that he began to contribute stories and poems to magazines, and published his first book of verse. This was *Mount Zion*, an immature volume but one of the most collectable books of verse this century. It is exceedingly scarce. It was published by Betjeman's friend Edward James, who financed the printing at The Westminster Press, and it appeared on 11 November 1931. From a bibliographical point of view it is a highly original volume. The Gothic type, pages of shell-pink and duck's egg blue and the period illustrations by de Cronin Hastings (the editor of the *Architectural Review*) are unique as is the quaint cover showing a woman using an antiquated telephone. A design by Camilla Russell (one of Betjeman's many infatuations from this period) was rejected.

In a letter to Tom Driberg, Betjeman referred to *Mount Zion* as the 'precious little work' — he couldn't have known then how accurate his words would become. It's not known for certain how many copies were printed, but it's unlikely more than 500 were produced. These are in very short supply, and a nice clean copy could cost as much as £400–£500 today. There seem to be a few signed copies around too, because Betjeman was so excited about being a published author he sent out numerous copies to families and friends. According to Edward James, a year of so later he was left with only a few of the copies to sell. In 1975 St James Press issued a facsimile edition.

In the early stages of his career Betjeman was keen to be closely involved in the production of his books. For his first prose work *Ghastly Good Taste* (Chapman & Hall, 1933), he designed the attractive cover featuring a little railway engine from ancient types found in the nineteenth-century premises of a printer. *Continual Dew* (John Murray, 1973) boasted many of the features found in *Mount Zion*; it had an attractive blue dust-jacket designed by E. McKnight Kauffer. John Murray published a facsimile reprint in 1977.

Apart from the signed limited editions which alternately frustrate and excite collectors, these three volumes are by far the hardest Betjeman items to acquire — most other titles may take some finding, but they shouldn't be too expensive. There are a few titles which might be a little confusing though, particularly some small volumes issued by the Architectural Press. These include *Cornwall Illustrated* and *Devon* (1934 and 1936; and both issued without jackets); *A Handbook on Paint* (Silicate Paint Co., 1939); and *Antiquarian Prejudice*, one of the very collectable Hogarth Sixpenny Pamphlets issued in 1939. It's particularly difficult to find these in good condition — their ephemeral nature and flimsy production make them susceptible to wear and tear.

After the Second World War most of Betjeman's verse was issued in uniform post octavo volumes, although one original title was *Poems in the Porch*, a thin paper-bound pamphlet published by the Society for the Promotion of Christian Knowledge in 1954. This featured illustrations by Betjeman's life-long friend

John Piper. Collectors should be careful with this one, though. Although the verso will always read 'First published in 1954 by S.P.C.K.', the title page itself may bear a later date. Check that the date on the title page states 1954 also.

Old Lights for New Chancels (John Murray, 1940) was the first in the series of Murray's paperback-size books of verse which became synonymous with Betjeman and so popular during the 1950s and 60s. This particular title was bound in blue boards with a paper label on the front cover; *New Bats in Old Belfries* (1945) was issued in red boards with a paper label and white dust-jacket; *A Few Late Chrysanthemums* had blue cloth, yellow label and yellow dust-jacket; while *High and Low* (1966) and *A Nip in the Air* (1974) were bound in yellow cloth. These had pink and light green jackets respectively. Despite their popularity (or perhaps because of it) these are all quite easy to find today and shouldn't cost too much. The earliest volumes generally sell for around £30–£50 each, although it should be possible to pick up the two later titles for £20 each. There are numerous copies of these later titles around, so only accept fine copies of *High and Low*. The pink jacket of this book is very prone to sunning.

Two other very popular Betjeman volume of verse are *Summoned by Bells*, published by John Murray in 1960 with green diamond motif boards with a beige and red dust-jacket (which is rather prone to fraying and soiling); and the very attractive *A Ring of Bells* (John Murray, 1962). This selection of autobiographical verse especially for children was charmingly illustrated by another of Betjeman's friends, Edward Ardizzone. For some reason its attractive dust-jacket seems to have stood up to the ravages of time quite well, so it's not too hard to find a nice clean copy for around £10–£15.

Betjeman is most popular for his verse, of course, but his prose works shouldn't be neglected. Some, like the titles issued in the Shell County Guides series and the monograph *John Piper*, issued in the Penguin Modern Painters series, are quite common (but becoming increasingly scarce), and some are genuine rarities. The large format, *An Oxford University Chest* (John Miles, 1938) with illustrations by Osbert Lancaster and photographs by Moholy-Nalgy is a beautiful volume, and *First and Last Loves* (Murray, 1952) is becoming very hard to find in a collectable condition.

A final word on Betjeman's only real book for children (or is it?), *Archie and the Strict Baptists*. This is quintessential late Betjemania, a large format adventure starring Betjeman's teddy bear, Archie (actually Evelyn Waugh's model for Aloysius in *Brideshead Revisited*). No Betjeman collection should be without this book. This wasn't his last volume, though. In fact, several collections of verse appeared in the years up to and immediately after his death in 1984. By the time of his death Betjeman had acquired cult status, and anything he produced was bound to become a best-seller. From a book collector's point of view this meant that titles like *Church Poems* (with its John Piper dust-jacket) and *Uncollected Poems* (1982) were issued in high print-runs and are quite easy to find today. Only accept fine copies. His last collection of verse was *Ah Middlesex*, a slim volume with illustrations by Fougasse published by Warren Editions in an edition of 250 copies. Somewhat surprisingly this doesn't seem too hard to find today. Copies regularly turn up for up to £30 in excellent condition.

Title	No dj	In dj
Mount Zion verse (James Press, 1931)	£400 – £500	n/a
facsimile reprint published by St James Press, 1975	£20 – £30	n/a
Ghastly Good Taste non-fiction (Chapman & Hall, 1933)	£30 – £40	£100 – £150
Cornwall Illustrated non-fiction (Architectural Press, 1934)	£30 – £40	n/a
Devon non-fiction (Architectural Press, 1936)	£30 – £40	n/a
Continual Dew verse (John Murray, 1937)	£50 – £60	£100 – £150
facsimile reprint published by John Murray, 1977	£20 – £30	n/a
An Oxford University Chest non-fiction (John Miles, 1938)	£30 – £40	£60 – £80
Sir John Piers verse (Mullingar, 1938) by 'Epsilon'. *Limited to 150 copies*	£300+	n/a
A Handbook on Paint non-fiction (Silicate Paint Co, 1939)	£60 – £80	n/a
Antiquarian Prejudice non-fiction (Hogarth Press, 1939)	£30 – £40	n/a
Old Lights for New Chancels verse (John Murray, 1940)	£10 – £15	£40 – £50
Vintage London non-fiction (Collins, 1942)	£20 – £30	n/a
English Cities and Small Towns non-fiction (Collins, 1943)	£4 – £6	£10 – £15
John Piper non-fiction (Penguin, 1944)	£5 – £8	n/a
New Bats in Old Belfries verse (John Murray, 1945)	£10 – £12	£30 – £35
Murray's Buckinghamshire Architectural Guide non-fiction (John Murray, 1948)	£5 – £8	£15 – £20
Selected Poems verse (John Murray, 1948)	£5 – £8	£15 – £20

Title	No dj	In dj
Murray's Berkshire Architectural Guide non-fiction (John Murray, 1949)	£5 – £8	£15 – £20
Shropshire non-fiction (Faber, 1951)	£10 – £12	£20 – £25
The English Scene non-fiction (National Book League, 1951)	£3 – £5	n/a
First and Last Loves non-fiction (John Murray, 1952)	£10 – £15	£20 – £30
A Few Late Chrysanthemums verse (John Murray, 1954)	£5 – £8	£20 – £30
Poems in the Porch verse (S.P.C.K., 1954)	£8 – £10	n/a
The English Town in the Last Hundred Years non-fiction (Cambridge University Press, 1956)	£5 – £8	n/a
Collins' Guide to English Parish Churches non-fiction (Collins, 1958)	–	£5 – £10
Collected Poems verse (John Murray, 1958)	£5 – £8	£15 – £20
Summoned by Bells verse (John Murray, 1960) *also a limited edition of 125 signed and numbered copies*	£5 – £8 £100 – £150	£15 – £20 n/a
A Ring of Bells verse (John Murray, 1962)	£5 – £8	£10 – £15
English Churches non-fiction (Studio Vista, 1964) *written with Basil Clarke*	–	£5 – £10
High and Low verse (John Murray, 1966)	£5 – £10	£15 – £20
London's Historic Railway Stations non-fiction (John Murray, 1972)	£5 – £8	£10 – £12
A Pictorial History of English Architecture non-fiction (John Murray, 1972)	£5 – £8	£10 – £12
A Nip in the Air verse (John Murray, 1974)	£5 – £8	£15 – £20

Title	No dj	In dj
Archie and the Strict Baptists children's (John Murray, 1977)	–	£10 – £15
The Best of Betjeman verse (John Murray, 1978)	–	£8 – £10
Church Poems verse (John Murray, 1981)	–	£8 – £10
Uncollected Poems verse (John Murray, 1982)	–	£8 – £10
Ah Middlesex verse (Warren Editions, 1984) *limited to 250 copies*	£20 – £30	n/a

AGATHA CHRISTIE

Agatha Christie is a publishing phenomenon and a publisher's dream. She is by far the best-selling author of all time; only the Bible and the Koran have sold more copies and their authorship is under question. To date over 2,000,000,000 copies of her books have been sold in sixty-four languages worldwide — she has been translated into more languages than Shakespeare. No other author is close to her sales figures; the only one showing any spirit against her supremacy is the American creator of lawyer Perry Mason, Erle Stanley Gardner, who has sold around 400,000,000 copies to date. Unlike Gardner, though, nearly all of Agatha Christie's books are still in print and sell vast quantities every year, particularly since 1990 when her centenary helped boost sales even more. Her play *The Mousetrap* has been running continuously in London's West End for the past forty years, developing into a major tourist attraction.

She is also a collecting phenomenon, although like most collecting phenomena this is a surprisingly recent development. No doubt Christie has been collected for decades but like P.G. Wodehouse and Ian Fleming, it is only since the early 1980s that collectors and dealers have gone wild. People are prepared to kill for her early titles today (although I should point out that there has been no definite proof of this in any law court — not yet anyway), and if not kill, at least get themselves into serious debt! She is certainly the most popular crime novelist and, with Wodehouse and Graham Greene, leads the collectable stakes today. There is really no reason to suggest that this might ever change; too many collectors have invested too much money in these books to allow them to slip back in value now. But don't panic, despite appearances, putting together a respectable Christie collection needn't cost the earth. It is really only the first dozen or so titles that will fetch high prices (although they can be picked up for much less without their dust-jackets); most of the others can be picked up surprisingly cheaply. From an early stage Agatha Christie's novels were popular; this meant that first edition print-runs were relatively large and naturally this means there are more copies in circulation for collectors to snap up. Her later titles are astonishingly cheap. Most of the novels which appeared from the late 1950s onwards can be found in pristine first edition format for little more than the price of a new paperback. Collectors are further helped by the fact that unlike Fleming and Wodehouse, Christie doesn't seem to be *that* popular with American and Japanese collectors. This helps to keep some semblance of sanity on prices.

Agatha Mary Clarissa Miller was born on the 15 September 1890, the third child of an American businessman and his English wife. She was educated at home in Torquay before being sent to a finishing school in Paris where she became an accomplished pianist — for some time she thought of pursuing a career as a concert pianist before taking up writing. Few will argue with the wisdom of this decision. On Christmas Eve 1914 she married Captain Archibald Christie of the Royal Flying Corps. Shortly after, her husband was posted overseas and

Agatha herself went to France to work as a nurse behind the lines. According to her autobiography, while in France she learned much about poisons which later featured in many of her books.

The marriage was not a happy one and after a few years of drifting apart, she mysteriously vanished for ten days after the wreckage of her car was found. Needless to say, the popular newspapers made much of the 'scandal'. Having lost her memory, she was found in a Harrogate hydropathic hotel under an assumed name. During these 'lost' days she had placed an advertisement in *The Times* to try to get in contact with a lost relative. The curious thing was that the name she used was that of her husband's lover! Shortly after this 'lost' period she divorced her husband and in September 1932 she married the archaeologist, Max Mallowan. Thereafter she spent several months each year in Syria and Iraq; hence the setting of novels like *Death on the Nile* (1937), *Murder in Mesopotamia* (1936) and *They Came to Baghdad* (1951), as well as her autobiographical *Come Tell Me How You Live* (1946). By the time of her marriage to Max Mallowan, Agatha Christie was already a highly successful novelist; she had established her position as one of the greatest mystery writers of all time, if not *the* greatest. She had already created her two greatest fictional characters; the small, immaculately dressed Belgian with the schoolboy English, Poirot, and the elderly, spinsterish inhabitant of St Mary's Mead, Jane Marple. Both have been successfully adapted for the large and small screen on many occasions, and both were to some extent inspired by real people. Hercule Poirot was first conceived during Christie's time as a nurse in the First World War. 'We had a colony of Belgian refugees . . .' she wrote of her creation of the detective hero . . . 'how about a refugee police officer? A retired police officer?' When he was finally killed off in *Curtain: Poirot's Last Case* (1975, although it was written during the Blitz), the book was set in the same house as his first adventure half a century earlier. He left a note to his sidekick Captain Hastings: 'We shall not hunt together my friend. Our first hunt was here — and our last.' After his death an obituary with a photograph appeared on the front page of the *New York Times* and, in 1989, a biography of Poirot appeared. Miss Marple, on the other hand, is thought to have been based on the author's grandmother. Christie wrote of Miss Marple: 'She was far more fussy and spinsterish than my grandmother ever was. But she did have one thing in common with her — though a cheerful person, she always expected the worst of everyone and everything, and was, with almost frightening accuracy, usually proved right.'

Poirot first appeared in Christie's very first novel, *The Mysterious Affair at Styles* (he went on to appear in no fewer than thirty-three full-length novels and fifty-five short stories). Like all of Agatha Christie's first six books, *The Mysterious Affair at Styles* was published by John Lane at the Bodley Head (indeed, the success of these early titles did much to halt and reverse the Bodley Head's decline). These titles are attractive books and all have the title and author on the front cover as well as on the spine. *The Mysterious Affair at Styles* (published in America in 1920 before appearing on these shores a year later) was bound in yellow-brown cloth ornately decorated in John Lane's traditional art nouveau design in black. These designs appear in various versions on all the Bodley Head titles. *The Secret Adversary* (1922) was bound in dark green cloth; *Murder on the Links* (1923) repeats the *Styles* design on orange cloth; *The Man in the Brown Suit* (1924) and *Poirot Investigates* (short stories, 1924) have the same pattern stamped on light brown and yellow cloth respectively; and *The Secret of Chimneys* (1925) had an attractive design stamped on grey-blue cloth (although this usually fades with time to look almost white).

All these titles are extremely scarce today — in any condition. *The Mysterious Affair at Styles* was issued in an attractive dark jacket featuring a painting of the main characters and had a light blue spine. Few collectors can hope to find a copy in a jacket, whenever one does turn up it almost always goes to auction. The only jacketed copy to have been sold in recent years went for £4,000. It was probably passed on to a collector for at least £2,000 more. Even copies in nice condition without their jackets can sell for between £600 and £1,000, so it shouldn't be too surprising to learn that early reprints have been known to change hands for three figures. HarperCollins have recently issued facsimile editions (including jackets) of some of Christie's most important titles. I feel sure that the new edition of *The Mysterious Affair at Styles* will become a rare and valuable book in time.

The other early titles also fetch huge sums in their jackets, and they're rising all the time. In recent years nice copies of *The Secret Adversary* and *Poirot Investigates* have sold for £3,000 and £2,000 respectively with clean undamaged jackets. The price falls sharply without these present which is good news because few collectors can hope to see them in their lifetime. Decent unjacketed copies can still set you back a few hundred pounds each.

From *The Murder of Roger Ackroyd* onwards almost all Agatha Christie's books were published by Collins and from *The Murder at the Vicarage* (1930) on, all but one of these Collins titles was issued in their prestigious Collins Crime Club. The pre-Crime Club books were *The Murder of Roger Ackroyd* (1926), *The Big Four* (1927), *The Mystery of the Blue Train* (1928), *The Seven Dials Mystery* (1929), *Partners in Crime* (1929) and *The Mysterious Mr Quin* (1930). All these are exceedingly scarce today, particularly *The Murder of Roger Ackroyd*, generally thought to be her finest book. The book was issued in dark blue cloth lettered in red on the front cover and spine. The first impression is distinguished by two ruled lines at the top and base of the spine; later impressions have just one rule or omit it altogether. Collins were able to produce more copies than John Lane, but this doesn't stop it from being very scarce. Collectors should expect to pay from £2,000 to £2,500 for a decent specimen, and even copies of the first edition without the jacket sell for £100–£150. All Agatha Christie's titles were dated with the exception of *The Mystery of the Blue Train*. The much later *After the Funeral* (1953) is unusually dated at the rear of the book.

Much easier to find than all these titles is the collection of stories *The Hound of Death* (1933). This was the only Christie published by Odhams (although they did issue a early reprint of *Murder in the Mews* which is often mistakenly thought to be the first). *The Hound of Death* was bound in maroon cloth stamped in gold, and issued with a beautiful white jacket featuring a green hound against a ruined convent printed in red, green, black and blue and designed by Demornay. Even copies with this jacket seem to be in fairly plentiful supply and rarely sell for more than £150. Jacket-less copies are good value at around £20. This is by far the commonest of these early Christies.

Philip Macdonald's *The Noose* is generally thought to be the first title in Collins' prestigious Crime Club series founded in May 1930; Agatha Christie's *The Murder at the Vicarage* followed shortly afterwards. The first appearance in her own book of Miss Marple (although she appeared in a short story in a Faber anthology in 1928) is of course very sought after and nice copies in their jackets regularly reach four figures, while copies without jackets sell for £50–£100 depending on condition. Identifying first editions of these Crime Club books is very easy. With the exception of *By the Pricking of My Thumbs*, 1968 (issued in red or green cloth), all the first editions issued by the club were bound in orange or red cloth lettered in black (up to 1964). Any copies found in black or purple cloth are reprints.

All Agatha Christie's books were issued in jackets, and we have already seen how much their presence affects the value. Titles from the 1920s are almost impossible to find with jackets; jackets on titles in the 1930s increase the value ten to twenty times; from the 1940s the factor is more like two to five; and after this date copies without jackets are virtually worthless as collectors' items. This is hardly surprising. Collins used some particularly talented cover artists to create their jackets, and the period feel of these are a very important part of the design. One of the hardest early Crime Clubs to find in a jacket is *The Thirteen Problems* (1932), with a superb opaque-green design; from this auspicious example on they seem to get better and better. One of the very best must be Robin Macartney's gloriously coloured design of the SS *Karnah* sailing past Egyptian monuments against wavering clouds for *Death on the Nile* (perhaps her most famous book) in 1937. Macartney took part in some of the archaeological expeditions of Christie and Max Mallowan, and provided designs for *Murder in Mesopotamia* (1936) and *Appointment With Death* (1938), both of which feature scenes from their travels. Other fine designs include the anonymous *Cards on the Table* (1936) which shows a row of playing cards set against a green baize table and which looks very similar to W. Francis Phillips's designs for the Pan paperback editions of Christie's novels almost thirty years later. Because of her output it is not possible to go through all the designs here. If HarperCollins and their paperback imprint had any sense they would reissue all her titles in facsimile editions of these jackets. Collectors and general readers would snap them up. They are infinitely preferable to the jackets produced in the late 1960s and early 1970s.

Christie collectors need to be aware of some other titles she produced which are not normally seen as part of her output. In 1925 she published a volume of competent but largely uninspired verse entitled *The Road of Dreams* through the now defunct house Bles; several plays came from her pen; and there are also some fairly scarce pseudonymous novels. These are *Giant's Bread* (Collins, 1930), *Unfinished Portrait* (Collins, 1934), *Absent in the Spring* (Collins, 1944), *The Rose and the Yew Tree* (Heinemann, 1948), *A Daughter's a Daughter* (Heinemann, 1952) and *The Burden* (Heinemann, 1956) all by 'Mary Westmacott'; and a collection of stories entitled *Star Over Bethlehem* (Collins, 1965) by 'A.C. Mallowan', her married name. Much cheaper than the regular Agatha Christie novels, even

Giant's Bread can be found in its jacket for under £100. Its possible to pick them up for just a few pounds if you are lucky enough to be dealing with an unknowledgeable book dealer (they do exist, believe it or not).

The most interesting 'irregular' Agatha Christie is *The Underdog*, a short story published together with *Blackman's Wood* by E. Phillips Oppenheim in a single volume entitled *Two New Crime Stories* by the Reader's Library in 1929. This small maroon volume can cost up to £150 today. It's interesting that in 1929 Christie and Oppenheim were considered equal enough to share a single volume; times have changed since then. Sixty years and two billion copies on, E. Phillips Oppenheim is all but forgotten. Only now and again do his bright yellow Hodder & Stoughton jackets appear on the bookshelves and he has no books in print today.

Title	No dj	In dj
The Mysterious Affair at Styles novel (John Lane, 1921)	£600 – £1,000	£4,000 – £6,000
The Secret Adversary novel (John Lane, 1922)	£300 – £400	£2,000 – £3,000
Murder on the Links novel (John Lane, 1923)	£350 – £450	£2,000 – £3,000
The Man in the Brown Suit novel (John Lane, 1924)	£250 – £300	£2,000 – £2,500
Poirot Investigates short stories (John Lane, 1924)	£200 – £300	£2,000 – £2,500
The Secret of Chimneys novel (John Lane, 1925)	£200 – £250	£2,000 – £2,500
The Road of Dreams verse (Bles, 1925)	£50 – £100	£300 – £400
The Murder of Roger Ackroyd novel (Collins, 1926)	£100 – £150	£2,000 – £2,500
The Big Four novel (Collins, 1927)	£50 – £100	£1,000 – £1,500
The Mystery of the Blue Train novel (Collins, 1928)	£50 – £100	£800 – £1,000
The Seven Dials Mystery novel (Collins, 1929)	£50 – £80	£1,000 – £1,200

Title	No dj	In dj
Partners in Crime short stories (Collins, 1929) *reprinted as* The Sunningdale Mystery *in 1933*	£50 – £80	£800 – £1,000
Two New Crime Stories short stories (Reader's Library, 1929) *includes Christie's* The Underdog *and E. Phillips* *Oppenheim's Blackman's Wood*	£10 – £15	£75 – £150
The Mysterious Mr Quin short stories (Collins, 1930)	£50 – £80	£800 – £1,000
The Murder at the Vicarage novel (Collins Crime Club, 1930)	£50 – £100	£800 – £1,000
Giant's Bread novel by 'Mary Westmacott' (Collins, 1930)	£10 – £15	£80 – £100
The Sittaford Mystery novel (Collins Crime Club, 1931)	£50 – £80	£800 – £1000
Peril at End House novel (Collins Crime Club, 1932)	£50 – £80	£800 – £1000
The Thirteen Problems short stories (Collins Crime Club, 1932)	£80 – £100	£800 – £1,000
Lord Edgware Dies novel (Collins Crime Club, 1933)	£50 – £80	£700 – £800
The Hound of Death short stories (Odhams, 1933)	£10 – £15	£100 – £150
Murder on the Orient Express novel (Collins Crime Club, 1934)	£50 – £80	£1,000 – £1,200
The Listerdale Mystery short stories (Collins, 1934)	£40 – £60	£800 – £1000
Why Didn't They Ask Evans? novel (Collins Crime Club, 1934)	£40 – £60	£600 – £700
Parker Pyne Investigates short stories (Collins, 1934)	£50 – £80	£800 – £1000
Unfinished Portrait novel by 'Mary Westmacott' (Collins, 1934)	£10 – £15	£200 – £300
Three Act Tragedy novel (Collins Crime Club, 1935)	£30 – £40	£600 – £700

Title	No dj	In dj
Death in the Clouds novel (Collins Crime Club, 1935)	£30 – £40	£600 – £700
The A.B.C. Murders novel (Collins Crime Club, 1936)	£30 – £40	£500 – £600
Murder in Mesopotamia novel (Collins Crime Club, 1936)	£30 – £40	£500 – £600
Cards on the Table novel (Collins Crime Club, 1936)	£30 – £40	£500 – £600
Murder in the Mews short stories (Collins Crime Club, 1937)	£30 – £40	£500 – £600
Dumb Witness novel (Collins Crime Club, 1937)	£30 – £40	£500 – £600
Death on the Nile novel (Collins Crime Club, 1937)	£30 – £40	£450 – £600
Appointment with Death novel (Collins Crime Club, 1938)	£20 – £30	£450 – £600
Hercule Poirot's Christmas novel (Collins Crime Club, 1939)	£20 – £30	£250 – £300
Murder is Easy novel (Collins Crime Club, 1939)	£20 – £30	£250 – £300
Ten Little Niggers novel (Collins Crime Club, 1939) *title later changed to* Ten Little Indians	£40 – £50	£400 – £600
Sad Cypress novel (Collins Crime Club, 1940)	£30 – £40	£250 – £280
One, Two, Buckle My Shoe novel (Collins Crime Club, 1940)	£20 – £30	£200 – £250
Evil Under the Sun novel (Collins Crime Club, 1941)	£15 – £20	£200 – £250
N or M? novel (Collins Crime Club, 1941)	£10 – £15	£100 – £120
The Body in the Library novel (Collins Crime Club, 1942)	£10 – £15	£100 – £120
Five Little Pigs novel (Collins Crime Club, 1942)	£10 – £15	£100 – £120

Title	No dj	In dj
The Moving Finger novel (Collins Crime Club, 1942)	£10 – £15	£80 – £100
Towards Zero novel (Collins Crime Club, 1944)	£10 – £15	£75 – £100
Absent in the Spring novel by 'Mary Westmacott' (Collins, 1944)	£5 – £10	£40 – £50
Death Comes as the End novel (Collins Crime Club, 1945)	£10 – £15	£50 – £70
Sparkling Cyanide novel (Collins Crime Club, 1945)	£10 – £15	£40 – £60
The Hollow novel (Collins Crime Club, 1946)	£5 – £10	£30 – £50
Come Tell Me How You Live travel (Collins, 1946)	£5 – £10	£20 – £30
The Labours of Hercules short stories (Collins Crime Club, 1947)	£5 – £10	£30 – £50
Taken at the Flood novel (Collins Crime Club, 1948)	£5 – £10	£30 – £50
The Rose and the Yew Tree novel by 'Mary Westmacott' (Heinemann, 1948)	£5 – £10	£20 – £30
Crooked House novel (Collins Crime Club, 1949)	£5 – £10	£30 – £40
A Murder is Announced novel (Collins Crime Club, 1950)	£5 – £10	£20 – £30
They Came to Baghdad novel (Collins Crime Club, 1951)	£5 – £10	£20 – £30
They Do It with Mirrors novel (Collins Crime Club, 1952)	–	£15 – £20
Mrs McGinty's Dead novel (Collins Crime Club, 1952)	–	£15 – £20
A Daughter's a Daughter novel by 'Mary Westmacott' (Heinemann, 1952)	–	£15 – £20

Title	No dj	In dj
After the Funeral novel (Collins Crime Club, 1953) *issued as a Fontana paperback as* Murder at the Gallop *in 1963*	–	£15 – £20
A Pocket Full of Rye novel (Collins Crime Club, 1953)	–	£15 – £20
Destination Unknown novel (Collins Crime Club, 1954)	–	£15 – £20
Hickory, Dickory, Dock novel (Collins Crime Club, 1955)	–	£15 – £20
Dead Man's Folly novel (Collins Crime Club, 1956)	–	£10 – £15
The Burden novel by 'Mary Westmacott' (Heinemann, 1956)	–	£10 – £15
4.50 from Paddington novel (Collins Crime Club, 1957)	–	£10 – £15
Ordeal by Innocence novel (Collins Crime Club, 1958)	–	£10 – £15
Cat Among the Pigeons novel (Collins Crime Club, 1959)	–	£10 – £15
The Adventure of the Christmas Pudding short stories (Collins Crime Club, 1960)	–	£15 – £20
The Pale Horse novel (Collins Crime Club, 1961)	–	£10 – £15
The Mirror Crack'd from Side to Side novel (Collins Crime Club, 1962)	–	£10 – £15
The Clocks novel (Collins Crime Club, 1963)	–	£10 – £15
A Caribbean Mystery novel (Collins Crime Club, 1964)	–	£5 – £10
At Bertram's Hotel novel (Collins Crime Club, 1965)	–	£5 – £10
Star Over Bethlehem short stories by A.C. Mallowan (Collins Crime Club, 1965)	–	£5 – £10

Title	No dj	In dj
Thirteen for Luck short stories (Collins, 1966)	–	£10 – £15
Third Girl novel (Collins Crime Club, 1966)	–	£5 – £10
Endless Night novel (Collins Crime Club, 1967)	–	£5 – £10
By the Pricking of My Thumbs novel (Collins Crime Club, 1968)	–	£5 – £10
Halloween Party novel (Collins Crime Club, 1969)	–	£5 – £10
Passenger to Frankfurt novel (Collins Crime Club, 1970)	–	£5 – £10
Nemesis novel (Collins Crime Club, 1971)	–	£5 – £10
Elephants Can Remember novel (Collins Crime Club, 1972)	–	£5 – £10
Postern of Fate novel (Collins Crime Club, 1973)	–	£5 – £10
Poems (Collins, 1973)	–	£5 – £10
Hercule Poirot's Early Cases short stories (Collins Crime Club, 1974)	–	£5 – £10
Curtain: Poirot's Last Case novel (Collins Crime Club, 1975)	–	£5 – £10
Sleeping Murder novel (Collins Crime Club, 1976)	–	£5 – £10
Miss Marple's Final Cases short stories (Collins Crime Club, 1979)	–	£5 – £10
Autobiography (Collins, 1979)	–	£5 – £10
The Agatha Christie Hour short stories (Collins, 1982)	–	£5 – £10

RICHMAL CROMPTON'S WILLIAM BOOKS

Richmal Crompton must be the most successful failure of all time. However hard she tried to become recognised as a serious novelist her public stubbornly refused to read anything other than her juvenile work, the William books. Like A.A. Milne who tried so hard to play down *Winnie the Pooh* in favour of his plays and other writings, it was a cross she had to bear. She couldn't complain too loudly, though; the young rascal earned her plenty of money and more adoration from children and adults alike than her other titles ever would. Richmal Crompton celebrated her centenary in 1990. It is a mark of the esteem the public still holds for young William Brown that to celebrate the occasion Bethnal Museum of Childhood in London held a special 'Just William' exhibition.

All in, all there were thirty-eight William titles, and each one is eagerly sought after, although it is really only collectors with a huge budget and plenty of time to track down elusive copies who can pursue the early volumes. Some of the early titles fetch just as much as early Wodehouse or Christie titles in their jackets. Thankfully, for the poorer enthusiasts, William stories have appeared in many editions and most are still in print in paperback today. Collectors can choose between the regular first editions, the first cheap reissues of this early edition (which often followed on very quickly), George Newnes's abridged editions of all the titles in 1963, Collins's seven hardback titles published in 1972, Hamlyn's Merlin paperbacks in the late 1960s, the Armada paperbacks from the 1970s, or a host of other reprints. Die-hard enthusiasts will want to acquire a set of William books in first edition, largely because most of these new editions (as opposed to the early reissues) omitted many of the original stories. What use is a complete collection, if it isn't complete after all?

Richmal Crompton Lamburn was born on 15 November 1890 in Bury, Lancashire, the daughter of a schoolmaster, and educated at the Royal Holloway College and London University where she obtained a degree. She followed in her father's footsteps by becoming a schoolteacher herself. In 1915 she took a post as Senior Classics Mistress at one of her old schools and later moved on to Bromley High School for Girls. She stayed there until 1923 when she was forced to give up her career after she contracted polio and became crippled.

Thankfully she had another career to fall back on. In February 1919, a story called 'Rice-Mould' appeared in George Newnes's *Home Magazine*. This was the very first appearance of the mischievous, unruly, scruffy, becapped and totally lovable William Brown. Readers loved him and demanded more. The following month readers were introduced to William's gang 'The Outlaws', including Ginger, Henry and Douglas. William, based initially on Richmal Crompton's own brother, John, but later generally accepted to be based to a large extent on her nephew, Tom Disher, became something of a national institution. A William story appeared in almost every issue of *Home Magazine* up to October 1922 (the story was 'Not Much'), and then he was transferred to Newnes's brighter *Happy Magazine*. On the front page of the Christmas 1922 issue of *Happy Magazine*,

William introduced himself thus: 'I'm always getting into all sorts of scrapes but I don't mind, because I always get out again somehow'. He remained an integral part of the magazine until it was disbanded in May 1940, because of the war. Richmal Crompton then resurrected her hero briefly for ten issues of *Home Notes* from January 1947 to September 1954. William completists often like to acquire copies of these magazines but the good news is you really don't need to if just having the stories themselves is all you want. All but one of these stories was collected into the thirty-eight volumes. The exception was 'William on the Trail', published in *Happy Magazine* in July 1935. But don't worry, the story was rescued from obscurity by W.O.G. Lofts and Derek Adley and published in their impressive *William — a Bibliography*, which was privately printed in soft red covers around 1980. This is becoming something of a collector's item itself.

Following the success of the magazine publication of the William stories, it is hardly surprising that Newnes decided to issue them in volume form. *Just William* was published in May 1922. It was undated, issued in red cloth, priced 2*s.* 6*d.*, and measured 7 inches by 4½ inches. The second title, *More William*, was the same size; all later titles were a uniform crown octavo so it should be easy to identify the first editions. The first edition of *Just William* can be further identified by the unnumbered pages of adverts inserted at the rear of the book announcing other novels issued by Newnes. All the William books were issued in attractive red jackets showing our hero up to some sort of mischief. The jacket for *Just William* has a picture of William with tie askew and cap lop-sided with the half-crown price announced boldly, in a large circle in type bigger than the author's name! As with the other titles it has an attractive pictorial spine showing five different poses of our hero, including William dressed as a cowboy and as a pirate. Copies with this jacket are almost impossible to find today; in fact no copies have been offered for sale in recent years and you might as well abandon all hope here. If one was offered for sale it would fetch at least £2,000, although it could go for much, much more. With titles like this it is absolutely impossible to give an accurate value. Any dealer offering a copy could name any price under the sun and get it. Collectors will attempt to secure either a jacketless copy for around £100 or find a copy of an early reprint in a jacket. The same jackets were used for all the early reprints of the William book; the only difference is that later copies carry the number of the impression in the upper-right corner.

Almost all the William books and dust-jackets were illustrated by Thomas Henry Fisher, an accomplished artist who breathed life into Richmal Crompton's character in the way Shepard gave life to Pooh Bear. Henry's William is *the* William. Thomas Henry Fisher, born in D.H. Lawrence's hometown of Eastwood, Nottinghamshire, in 1879, worked as a lithographer before making a living as an illustrator — one of his first commissions was designing the sailor trademark for Player's cigarettes. In fact, he wasn't the first William artist; 'Rice-Mould' was illustrated by Louise Hocknell but her efforts lacked vigour and Henry was asked to take over. He illustrated every book and story until his death in October 1962. The few remaining William books were illustrated by Henry Ford, although *William and the Witch* (Newnes, 1964) was a joint effort between the two.

By far the biggest headache for William collectors is identifying early first editions up to 1928, a task not aided by the fact that some titles are undated. Up to Lofts and Adley's bibliography, it was generally thought that all the early titles were bound in red cloth and priced half a crown but this was certainly not the case. Certainly the first nine titles up to *William the Good* (May, 1928, undated) are hard to identify. Of these only *More William* (June, 1922), *William Again* (June, 1923) and *William the Fourth* (April, 1924) were dated; they were all issued in red cloth, priced 2s. 6d., making it impossible to distinguish between firsts and the cheap reprints also issued in red cloth unless one has the jacket intact also. The exceptions to this rule are *Just William* and *More William* (featuring our hero being rebuked by an irate adult), both of which were issued in a smaller format. The early reprints would have been published in crown octavo format. Incidentally, as well as the cheap reprints the first three titles were re-issued in special presentation editions priced 6s.

The next few titles are easier to identify without jackets, thanks to some sterling detective work by Lofts and Adley (obviously, with the jackets intact, identification shouldn't cause too many problems). The first editions of *William* (1929), *William the Bad* (March, 1930), *William's Happy Days* (October, 1930 with a marvellous Thomas Henry dust-jacket showing William about to burst in on his sister's *tête-a-tête* with her boyfriend), and *William's Crowded Hours* (July, 1931) were all issued in blue cloth with gold lettering. *William the Pirate* (1932), with an atypical cover showing the hero pushing a pram, was issued in brown cloth. *William the Rebel* (April, 1933) had buff-coloured boards, *William the Gangster* (in a jacket portraying the boy brandishing sharpshooters) reverted to blue cloth with gold lettering, *William the Detective* (July, 1935) sharing the jacket design with a terrier, was issued in brown cloth.

All these first editions were priced at 7s. 6d. (a hefty jump from the earlier half-crown) and all are very scarce. Within six or nine months of the first publication in book form, Newnes re-issued these titles in red cloth at half a crown each. Most readers waited for this edition instead of buying the first impression — hence the difficulty in finding firsts in decent condition, particularly in their jackets. Most collectors make do with a first edition of the book in a later jacket. Copies of these pre-war titles do turn up without jackets fairly frequently though — the prices tend to hover around the £40–£50 mark, depending upon condition. A few of the late 1920s titles (like *William the Outlaw*) seem to have had much higher print-runs and are slightly easier and cheaper to find. The reason for these higher print-runs seems to be the fact that the price of the first edition was still 2s. 6d.: Newnes increased the print-run to recoup their investment. When the price of the first impression was summarily upped to 7s. 6d. the print-run was lowered; the emphasis was placed on selling large numbers of the cheap reprint instead. Hence the scarcity and £50 price tag on first editions of titles like *William the Bad* and *Sweet William*, compared to around half that or *Still William* (1925), *William the Outlaw* (1927) and *William the Good* (1928). Copies of the first editions of these pre-war titles in their original jackets are worth their weight in gold. Even torn, nicked and discoloured jackets could increase values several times over. That is a measure of William enthusiasts' devotion. Some have been known to spend decades completing their collections.

Titles after *William the Detective* are also reasonably easy to identify. First editions were issued in one colour with the first cheap reprint being bound in red cloth. These titles were all originally issued in a variety of green cloths. Up to *William the Bold* they were priced 7*s*. 6*d*; *William and the Tramp* (with a particularly impressive jacket design) and *William and the Moon Rocket* (September, 1954) were priced 8*s*. 6*d*; titles from *William and the Space Animal* (September, 1956) to *William the Superman* (November, 1968) were priced 10*s*. 6*d*.; while the last volume in the series, *William the Lawless* (1970) cost its readers 12*s*. 6*d*.

This last title is one of the scarcest in the entire series, particularly in the fine condition one would demand for such a late title. It was the only late title to be published initially in red cloth (and it was never reprinted) by Paul Hamlyn for Newnes. It was produced on cheap paper susceptible to browning and foxing. It isn't unknown for some dealers to ask up to £350 for a pristine first. £250 is more realistic for a generally decent copy. All the other post-war titles are fairly easy to find in their jackets, although how much you pay for your copy depends to a large degree on its overall condition. Decent copies of most, however, can be found for between £50 and £80, although *William and the Witch* (the last title to feature Henry's drawings) could cost a little more. Spend as much as you can on these later titles. Secure the best possible copy you can find: it really will be worth it because their values are rising much faster than the rate of inflation.

You might find you have one or two titles not listed in the check-list below. This is easily explained. George Newnes changed the name for two titles in the late 1950s. *William and A.R.P.* (1939) was re-issued in June 1956 as *William's Bad Resolution*; and *William and the Evacuees* (1940) became *William the Film Star* at the same time. No doubt these decisions were taken because the war-time flavour of the original titles seemed out of date eleven years into the peace. Because these are really reprints of earlier titles they were issued in red cloth at 7*s*. 6*d*. The other interesting title is *Just William — The Story of the Film*, published by Newnes in August 1939 in green cloth to mark the release of the first *Just William* film starring Dicky Lupino (other Williams have been placed by William Graham and Dennis Waterman). As well as featuring the script of the film it also includes six selected William stories from the *Happy Magazine*. Not a part of the regular series of thirty-eight books, perhaps, but few enthusiasts will want to be without it. It is included in the bibliography for that reason.

Title	No dj	In dj
Just William short stories (Newnes, 1922) *undated*	£100 – £120	£2,000+
More William short stories (Newnes, 1922)	£80 – £100	£500 – £1,000
William Again short stories (Newnes, 1923)	£50 – £60	£400 – £600
William the Fourth short stories (Newnes, 1924)	£30 – £40	£200 – £400
Still William short stories (Newnes, 1925) *undated*	£20 – £30	£200 – £300
William the Conqueror short stories (Newnes, 1926) *undated*	£20 – £30	£200 – £300
William the Outlaw short stories (Newnes, 1927) *undated*	£20 – £25	£200 – £300
William in Trouble short stories (Newnes,1927) *undated*	£20 – £25	£200 – £300
William the Good short stories (Newnes, 1928) *undated*	£20 – £25	£200 – £300
William short stories (Newnes, 1929)	£40 – £50	£200 – £300
William the Bad short stories (Newnes, 1930)	£40 – £50	£200 – £300
William's Happy Days short stories (Newnes, 1930) *undated*	£40 – £50	£200 – £300
William's Crowded Hours short stories (Newnes, 1931) *undated*	£40 – £50	£200 – £300
William the Pirate short stories (Newnes, 1932)	£40 – £50	£200 – £250
William the Rebel short stories (Newnes, 1933) *undated*	£30 – £40	£200 – £250
William the Gangster short stories (Newnes, 1934) *undated*	£30 – £40	£200 – £250
William the Detective short stories (Newnes, 1935)	£30 – £40	£150 – £200

Title	No dj	In dj
Sweet William short stories (Newnes, 1936) *undated*	£30 – £40	£150 – £200
William the Showman short stories (Newnes, 1937) *undated*	£30 – £40	£150 – £200
William the Dictator short stories (Newnes, 1938) *undated*	£30 – £40	£100 – £150
William and A.R.P. short stories (Newnes, 1939) *title changed in 1956 to* William's Bad Resolution	£30 – £40	£100 – £150
Just William — The Story of the Film script and short stories (Newnes, 1939)	£20 – £30	£60 – £80
William and the Evacuees short stories (Newnes, 1940) *title changed in 1956 to* William the Film Star	£20 – £30	£100 – £120
William Does His Bit short stories (Newnes, 1941)	£20 – £30	£100 – £120
William Carries On short stories (Newnes, 1942)	£20 – £30	£80 – £100
William and the Brains Trust short stories (Newnes, 1945)	£20 – £30	£80 – £100
Just William's Luck short stories (Newnes, 1948)	£20 – £30	£80 – £100
William the Bold short stories (Newnes, 1950)	£20 – £30	£60 – £80
William and the Tramp short stories (Newnes, 1952)	£15 – £20	£50 – £60
William and the Moon Rocket short stories (Newnes, 1954)	£15 – £20	£40 – £50
William and the Space Animal short stories (Newnes, 1956)	£15 – £20	£40 – £50
William's Television Show short stories (Newnes, 1958)	£15 – £20	£40 – £50
William the Explorer short stories (Newnes, 1960)	£15 – £20	£40 – £50

Title	No dj	In dj
William's Treasure Trove short stories (Newnes, 1962)	£15 – £20	£40 – £50
William and the Witch short stories (Newnes, 1964)	£20 – £30	£60 – £80
William and the Pop Singers short stories (Newnes, 1965)	£20 – £25	£50 – £60
William and the Masked Ranger short stories (Newnes, 1966)	£20 – £25	£50 – £60
William the Superman short stories (Newnes, 1968)	£20 – £30	£50 – £60
William the Lawless short stories (Hamlyn/Newnes, 1970)	£40 – £50	£200 – £250+

ROALD DAHL

It is a curious and slightly ghoulish fact in book collecting that interest in an author's books seems to really take off when that author dies — perhaps collectors think that with no more books in the pipeline, existing copies can only increase in value. This was certainly the case with Agatha Christie and P.G. Wodehouse; I'm fairly sure it will be the case with Roald Dahl also. Dahl has been a collected author for at least a decade now. His adult fiction and his classic children's titles fetch very good sums.

When Roald Dahl died in December 1990, newspapers were full of tributes from critics but more importantly, from numerous children who seemed to feel that an important part of their lives had gone. Dahl was adored by children, and his books sell hundreds of thousands copies very year in Britain alone. He is popular with children all over the world and according to one unconfirmed source, in 1988 his classic *Charlie and the Chocolate Factory* was published for the first time in China, with a print-run of two million copies — a staggering figure in publishing history. Younger readers of this book might be forgiven for thinking that Dahl wrote nothing but children's books. This is certainly true of the latter part of his career, but early on he wrote almost exclusively for adults, particularly short stories. Indeed, although he is famous now for children's titles like *The Twits*, *The Witches* and *Revolting Rhymes*, during the 1970s almost all his bizarre short stories with their savage twists at the end were successfully filmed by Anglia Television as *Tales of the Unexpected*. Ironically, perhaps, it is his adult work which is most collectable today.

Apart from a slim paperback written for children, the best biographical information on Dahl comes from his own writings, *Boy* and *Going Solo*. Dahl had a truly extraordinary life full of danger, glamour, heartache and success. When his biography comes to be written (what a wonderful commission that would be), it will make riveting reading. As well as covering his wartime exploits it will have to cover his period as a spy, his friendships with Hemingway and John O'Hara, his controversial marriage to the glamorous actress Patricia Neal, his son's horrific accident, and his hugely successful career as a children's author. It will also have to cover his well-publicised arguments with other writers later in life, and his infamous bad humour. It's hard to reconcile the popular image of Dahl the man with Dahl the writer.

Both Dahl's parents were Norwegian, but he was born in South Wales on 13 September 1916. After awful periods at two public schools (at Repton he was flogged by a future Archbishop of Canterbury), Dahl worked in what is now Tanzania for Shell Oil. At the outbreak of the Second World War, he joined the R.A.F. and saw action in Greece, Syria and Palestine. On one excursion behind enemy lines in Libya, his ancient Gloster Gladiator bi-plane crashed leaving him severely injured. Many years later he had his smashed hips replaced and used one of the originals as a paperweight. Then, in 1942, Dahl managed to secure a safer job as Assistant Air Attaché in Washington.

Both Dahl's first two books were inspired by his wartime exploits, but it took another famous writer to encourage him to put pen to paper. Dahl was asked by C. S. Forester to prepare some notes for a series Forester was doing on flying aces. When he delivered them Dahl was told he was a natural writer. He had actually produced a whole story, for which he was paid $900 by the *Saturday Evening Post*. This story, and nine other flying tales, were collected together as *Over to You* by US publishers Reynal & Hitchcock in 1945. The first British edition was published by Hamish Hamilton two years later. It has been out of print for a long time now and very good copies sell for up to £150 complete with their jackets. Dahl's first juvenile title was *The Gremlins*, the story of mischievous little people who tamper with aeroplanes and cause crashes. This was published by Collins in the UK in 1944 and is of legendary scarcity today. The large-format quarto book was published in pictorial boards without a dust-jacket and the spine is prone to tearing today. Very good copies aren't easy to find — they seldom are of children's books. It's not unreasonable to be asked £300 for a copy. Obviously condition affects the price considerably. A shabby copy with torn spine and the previous owner's scribbling inside would be hard pressed to find a taker for £50.

Dahl's next few titles issued during the 1950s were all adult titles. His scarce novel *Sometime Never* is very hard to find in its jacket, and another selection of stories called *Someone Like You* (Secker & Warburg, 1954) might set the collector back up to £60 for a copy in the best condition one might hope for in a book of this age. His adult highlight is undoubtedly *Kiss, Kiss*, a superb collection of eleven new stories published by Michael Joseph in autumn, 1960. This 255-page book was bound in green cloth stamped in gold with a heart design on the spine, and issued in an unusual jacket designed by Charles E. Skaggs featuring blue and red hearts against a net curtain background. It is vital that this jacket is in place and in good condition for it to be collectable today. In fact, only the first one or two Dahl titles are worth acquiring (from a collector's point of view) without jackets. Dahl's later adult titles, including the four erotic stories in *Switch Bitch* and the novel *My Uncle Oswald* failed to live up to these masterly tales. Many of the stories in these early titles reappeared in *Twenty-Nine Kisses* (1969) and *Tales of the Unexpected* (1979), both of which can be picked up for very little. Much scarcer is the 1961 reissue of the hitherto long out of print, *Someone Like You* (with another Skaggs design) from Michael Joseph. This includes two stories not in the original edition.

One other collectable adult title is the slight but masterly 64-page *Two Fables*, published by Viking to celebrate Dahl's seventieth birthday on 13 September 1986. Illustrated with some superb colourwash paintings by Graham Dean, the first trade edition was bound in black cloth and issued in a stark red, white and black jacket by designer Bet Ayer. Viking also issued a signed and numbered edition of 300 copies. This attractive edition included an extra signed page, black endpapers and was quarter bound in red-leather and black, round cloth boards with the title stamped in gold on the front cover. A recent copy was offered for £135, although somewhere around £75 would be a more reasonable sum for a fine or pristine copy. It's unlikely *Two Fables* will reprinted for quite some time, so it might be worth looking out for a copy now.

Roald Dahl will probably be best remembered for his juvenile fiction. He is certainly one of the most popular children's authors of all times because, unlike writers like Enid Blyton, he never wrote down to children. His books were often cruel and risqué, but he knew that that is what real children are like and it's what they like to read. The devotion he inspired in young readers is remarkable. Many adults are wary of his children's books, thinking them too improper for young children, but his greatest service to children was not just entertaining them the way they liked to be entertained, but actually getting them to pick up books at all. In this television and video age this is no mean feat.

Dahl's first few children's titles were issued in laminated boards: *James and the Giant Peach* (1967), *Charlie and the Chocolate Factory* (1967), *The Magic Finger* (1968), *Fantastic Mr Fox* (1970) and *Charlie and the Great Glass Elevator* (1973). Because these seem vulnerable to usage (particularly around the spine) it's quite rare for these to have survived in collectable condition, and the prices quoted in the bibliography will probably only secure nicked or damaged copies. None of these were issued in jackets. Incidentally, Dahl started writing these classic children's tales at a bad time of his life; his son Theo had suffered severe brain-damage in a freak accident, his daughter, Olivia, had died following a bout of measles, and immediately after that, Patricia Neal almost died herself following a rupture of the brain. That such tales should have been written under these traumatic conditions is astonishing.

All these books were illustrated, by artists like William Pène du Bois and Joseph Schindelman, but today Dahl is intimately associated with the gifted Quentin Blake — latter-day Dahl wouldn't be Dahl at all without Quentin Blake's mischievous designs. It is impossible to separate them. Classic titles like *The Enormous Crocodile* (1978), *George's Marvellous Medicine* (1981), *The Witches* (1983) and *Matilda* (1988) won numerous children's book awards as well as the love of millions of children. Collecting fine copies (the only acceptable condition for such late books) can be quite problematical, as many of these books would have been 'loved to bits' by their original owners. It could take some time to put a set together. *The Enormous Crocodile, Revolting Rhymes, Dirty Beasts* (illustrated by Rosemary Fawcett before being re-illustrated by Blake) and *The Giraffe, the Pelly and Me* were issued as large format volumes in pictorial boards — the others were standard octavo or quarto with dust-jackets.

Title	No dj	In dj
The Gremlins children's (Collins, 1944)	£200 – £300	n/a
Over To You short stories (Hamish Hamilton, 1947)	£40 – £50	£100 – £150

Title	No dj	In dj
Sometime Never novel (Collins, 1948)	£20 – £30	£80 – £100
Someone Like You short stories (Secker & Warburg, 1954)	£10 – £15	£50 – £60
Kiss, Kiss short stories (Michael Joseph, 1960)	–	£30 – £40
James and the Giant Peach children's (Allen & Unwin, 1967)	£20 – £25	n/a
Charlie and the Chocolate Factory children's (Allen & Unwin, 1967)	£25 – £30	n/a
The Magic Finger children's (Allen & Unwin, 1968)	£15 – £20	n/a
Twenty-Nine Kisses short stories (Michael Joseph, 1969) *reissue of published stories*	–	£15 – £20
Fantastic Mr Fox children's (Allen & Unwin, 1970)	£10 – £15	n/a
Charlie and the Great Glass Elevator children's (Allen & Unwin, 1973)	£8 – £10	n/a
Switch Bitch short stories (Michael Joseph, 1974)	–	£10 – £15
Danny: The Champion of the World children's (Jonathan Cape, 1975)	–	£8 – £10
The Wonderful Story of Henry Sugar children's (Jonathan Cape, 1977)	–	£8 – £10
The Enormous Crocodile children's (Jonathan Cape, 1978)	£5 – £8	n/a
Tales of the Unexpected short stories (Michael Joseph, 1979)	–	£5 – £10
My Uncle Oswald novel (Michael Joseph, 1979)	–	£8 – £10
More Tales of the Unexpected short stories (Michael Joseph, 1980) *more stories reissued, although it does include four* *new tales*	–	£5 – £10

Title	No dj	In dj
The Twits children's (Jonathan Cape, 1980)	–	£8 – £10
George's Marvellous Medicine children's (Jonathan Cape, 1981)	–	£8 – £10
Revolting Rhymes children's (Jonathan Cape, 1982)	£5 – £8	n/a
The BFG children's (Jonathan Cape, 1982)	–	£5 – £10
Dirty Beasts children's (Jonathan Cape, 1983)	£5 – £8	n/a
The Best of Roald Dahl short stories (Michael Joseph, 1983) *another reissue of old material*	–	£5 – £8
The Witches children's (Jonathan Cape, 1983)	–	£5 – £8
Boy: Tales of Childhood autobiography (Jonathan Cape, 1984)	–	£5 – £10
The Giraffe, the Pelly and Me children's (Jonathan Cape, 1985)	£5 – £8	n/a
Going Solo autobiography (Jonathan Cape, 1986)	–	£5 – £10
Two Fables (Viking, 1986) *signed limited edition of 300 copies*	– £50 – £75	£8 – £10 n/a
Matilda children's (Jonathan Cape, 1988)	–	£5 – £10
Ah Sweet Mystery of Life short stories (Michael Joseph, 1989) *an adult title illustrated by John Lawrence*	–	£5 – £8
Rhyme Stew children's (Jonathan Cape, 1989)	–	£5 – £8
Esio Trot children's (Jonathan Cape, 1990)	–	£5 – £8

Title	No dj	In dj
The Vicar of Nibbleswick children's (Century Hutchinson, 1991) *published posthumously it was written for The Dyslexia Institute.*	–	£5 – £8

COLIN DEXTER AND PETER LOVESEY

Detective fiction has always been enormously popular with book collectors; classics from Agatha Christie, Ngaio Marsh, Dorothy L. Sayers and John Dickson Carr have kept collectors frustrated for years. In more recent times there has been a distinct trend towards collecting *modern* detective novelists. For some reason women seem to be dominating the detective fiction scene today (Ruth Rendell and P.D. James are covered elsewhere in this book) but the men aren't exactly lagging behind. If it's possible to give tips for the future on authors who are already collected extensively, I nominate Colin Dexter and Peter Lovesey. Their careers seem to have run parallel with each other. Both have created memorable characters (Dexter's Inspector Morse and Lovesey's Sergeant Cribb and Constable Thackeray), and both have won several Crime Writers' Association Awards for best crime novel of the year despite having produced no more than a handful of novels each. Colin Dexter's Inspector Morse was recently voted the favourite male detective by the CWA, ahead of Sherlock Holmes, Philip Marlowe, Poirot, Maigret and Father Brown!

Neither author has been in print for much longer than two decades but already it's becoming very difficult to acquire fine copies of their first few books. Because they are so recent it is vital that any copy of their titles you acquire be *pristine*. Copies with inscriptions (other than from the author) should be avoided at all costs, as should bumped or soiled copies. The dust-jacket in particular should be bright, clean and free from any nicks or tears. Any copy without the jacket should be avoided.

Because of the phenomenal success of Central Television's adaptations of the Inspector Morse tales, it is probably Dexter who is the more popular with collectors at the moment, though Lovesey isn't far behind. Colin Dexter was born in 1930 and after reading classics at Cambridge he spent thirteen years teaching Latin and Greek in the Midlands. Increasing deafness forced him to give up teaching and to embark on a second career with the Oxford University Examination Board with whom he worked until 1987. He had other interests, though. Like his Inspector Morse, Dexter is a crossword champion (he has set them for *The Oxford Times* for the past thirteen years) and this is vividly apparent in his books with their strategic quirks of plot. In fact, Morse shares many similarities with his creator. Both men live in Oxford, both love books (particularly the classics), fine music, *The Archers*, and good beer. As a matter of interest Morse got his name from Sir Jeremy Morse, the chairman of Lloyds Bank and one of Dexter's great rivals in the crossword world.

Dexter started writing crime novels when he read a couple of appalling ones on a rainy holiday in North Wales. His first title, *Last Bus to Woodstock*, took eighteen months to complete and six months for Collins to reject. However, Macmillan accepted it by return of post and Inspector Morse and his trusty but rather docile sidekick Sergeant Lewis were born. The book was eventually published by Macmillan in 1975 in brown cloth and with an attractive dust-jacket featuring a young girl with long blonde hair. Fine copies aren't easy to acquire today. Unfortunately, Macmillan used cheap paper for the title and this is particularly prone to browning — so very few copies turn up without some browning. It is rather infuriating that some hardbacks today seem to have a shelf life barely longer than a paperback.

One of the delights of the Dexter titles (other than their content), is their attractive dust-jacket design created by some of the top jacket designers of the day. John Ireland's surreal design for *Last Seen Wearing* (Macmillan, 1976) showing a rather macabre set of schoolgirl's clothing walking down a street — unaided by any schoolgirl inside them — is one of the highlights of 1970s jacket design and essential if the book is to reach its potential top price. Much the same can be said for *The Silent World of Nicholas Quinn* (Macmillan, 1977), bound in a dark green cloth lettered in black, and *The Dead of Jericho*, bound in black cloth lettered in gold and issued in a sinister-looking Mark Wilkinson jacket, showing the houses in Canal Reach. Martin White's design for *The Secret of Annexe 3* (1983) is similar in style to *Last Seen Wearing*.

It is not difficult to see why Inspector Morse is such a favourite with crime readers though it's astonishing he is so popular with collectors already. If his books are fetching such prices now, what of fifty years hence? I don't think it's unrealistic to say that he might one day be on a par with Poirot or Miss Marple. If that does turn out to be the case, get your copies now — you know how hard it is to acquire early Christies in jackets.

Much of Morse's success has been brought about by television, of course — Lovesey has had no such boost. His books have become popular through literary merit alone. Peter Lovesey is the leading exponent of historical detective fiction, seemingly a neglected art today. His main hero or at least the 'star' of his first eight novels is a Victorian policeman, Sergeant Cribb. These novels are set in Victorian London with all its dirt, seediness and vitality; everywhere from the music hall to sport, particularly the world of bare-knuckle prize-fighting. After abandoning Cribb and Constable Thackeray in 1978, all Lovesey's later books have been set in various periods of the late nineteenth or twentieth centuries. Again, condition is absolutely vital and the importance of the presence of a clean, intact dust-jacket *cannot be under-estimated*. Only truly fine copies fetch any price, let alone top prices.

Like Dexter, Peter Lovesey came to crime writing after a career in education. He was born on 10 September 1936, educated at Reading University, and became an English lecturer at Thurrock Technical College in 1961. As with Dexter, his first publications were non-fiction: in 1968 Eyre & Spottiswoode published an account of sporting personalities of the past. This was followed in 1969 by *The Guide to British Track and Field Literature 1275–1968*. He used his knowledge of Victorian sport to write his first crime novel in 1970. *Wobble to Death* won Macmillan's award for the Best First Crime Novel, and from there on his career began to thrive. Bound in red cloth with black lettering and issued in an attractive pictorial jacket, *Wobble to Death* was also issued in Macmillan's cheap paper, unfortunately. Truly fine copies aren't easy to find. A nice copy was on offer for

£80 recently, although this was slightly over-priced. How long that remains the case is anybody's guess.

As with Colin Dexter, one of the major appeals of Lovesey's titles (at least his early titles) is the attractive jackets — what Macmillan saved on paper quality they certainly made up for in dust-jacket design. Peter Brooke's design showing a conjuror impaling a young woman on his sword for *Abracadaver* (1972, red cloth) is one of the highlights although Joseph Wright's superb cartoonesque design of the three characters rowing a boat for *Swing, Swing Together* takes some beating. This title was published in 1976. Incidentally, the one problem with these Macmillan jackets is that the design is on the front cover only and does not extend around the spine. They look rather dull because of that but, to be fair, this is a small defect and the jackets are infinitely preferable to the design Century Hutchinson chose for their Mysterious Press edition of Lovesey's last novel, *On the Edge* (1989). Publishers and some readers consider the photographic, laminated jackets practical, but almost all collectors prefer the old-style, rough-paper jackets popular in the 1930s. Although Lovesey had made his name by 1976, and the print-runs for his novels were reasonably high, these are not too easy to find today, particularly in pristine condition. These books must be in absolutely fine condition — anything else is worthless. Make sure the jacket is bright, clean, and free of any tears, creases or even rubbing.

This is particulary true with Lovesey's later, non-Cribb tales which began with *The False Inspector Dew* (Macmillan, 1982, red cloth with silver lettering). Why Lovesey abandoned Cribb and Thackeray is not known but his books certainly haven't suffered with their demise. Some prefer his later works, particularly the gruesome *Rough Cider*, published by Bodley Head in 1986. The dust-jacket features Tom Scobie's sinister design of a skull/apple. Because it is so recent, it is easy to find pristine copies. Buy these books in fine condition today while you can.

Title	No dj	In dj
COLIN DEXTER		
Last Bus to Woodstock novel (Macmillan, 1975)	–	£200 – £250
Last Seen Wearing novel (Macmillan, 1976)	–	£200 – £250
The Silent World of Nicholas Quinn novel (Macmillan, 1977)	–	£100 – £130
Service of all the Dead novel (Macmillan, 1979)	–	£70 – £90

Title	No dj	In dj
The Dead of Jericho novel (Macmillan, 1981)	–	£40 – £50
Riddle of the Third Mile novel (Macmillan, 1983)	–	£35 – £45
The Secret of Annexe 3 novel (Macmillan, 1986)	–	£25 – £35
The Wench Is Dead novel (Macmillan, 1989)	–	£10 – £15
An Inspector Morse Omnibus anthology (Macmillan, 1991)	–	£10 – £15
The Jewel That Was Ours novel (Macmillan, 1991) *The true first edition was a signed limited edition of 150 copies from Scorpion Press released shortly before official publication. Bound in quarter leather, this edition has an appreciation of Dexter by H.R.F. Keating. It was priced at £40.*	–	–
The Way Through the Woods novel (Macmillan, 1992)	–	–

PETER LOVESEY

Title	No dj	In dj
Wobble to Death novel (Macmillan, 1970)	–	£50 – £60
The Detective Wore Silk Drawers novel (Macmillan, 1971)	–	£30 – £40
Abracadaver novel (Macmillan, 1972)	–	£30 – £40
Mad Hatter's Holiday novel (Macmillan, 1973)	–	£20 – £25
Invitation to a Dynamite Party novel (Macmillan, 1974)	–	£15 – £20
A Case of Spirits novel (Macmillan, 1975)	–	£15 – £20
Swing, Swing Together novel (Macmillan, 1976)	–	£15 – £20

Title	No dj	In dj
Golden Girl novel (Cassell, 1977) thriller written by 'Peter Lear'	–	£10 – £15
Waxwork novel (Macmillan, 1978)	–	£10 – £15
Spider Girl novel (Cassell, 1980) thriller written by 'Peter Lear'	–	£5 – £10
The False Inspector Dew novel (Macmillan, 1982)	–	£10 – £15
Keystone novel (Macmillan, 1983)	–	£10 – £15
Butchers short stories (Macmillan, 1985)	–	£10 – £15
The Secret of Spandau novel (Michael Joseph, 1986) thriller written by 'Peter Lear'	–	£5 – £10
Rough Cider novel (Bodley Head, 1986)	–	£10 – £15
Bertie and the Tinman novel (Bodley Head, 1987)	–	£10 – £15
On the Edge novel (Mysterious Press, 1989)	–	£5 – £10

CONAN DOYLE

Sir Arthur Conan Doyle? Sherlock Holmes and Dr Watson? Modern first editions? Some mistake surely? Many will wonder why Doyle should find his way onto these pages which, after all, are meant to be devoted to modern books but we offer no apologies — Sherlock Holmes deserves a place in any book about collecting books. Doyle remains one of the most popular figures in book collecting and few subjects illustrate the importance of *conditon* better.

Everyone has heard of Sherlock Holmes; perhaps the most famous literary figure ever created. Indeed, it's hard to think of him as a figment of somebody's extraordinary imagination, so real has he become in our national psyche. Over the last hundred years or so since he first appeared in print, the pointed chin and deerstalker of Sherlock Holmes has appeared in numerous books and magazines, and on countless hundreds of tea towels, trinkets, beer mats and other ephemera. Sherlock Holmes is a true cult figure; so vivid in people's minds that since the 1890s literally thousands of letters have arrived at his fictional home 221b Baker Street, London, asking him to solve problems. The site is now occupied by a branch of the Abbey National Building Society, who do their best to pass Mr Holmes's letters on . . . .

Conan Doyle wrote dozens of books but while there are some enthusiasts who collect his entire *oeuvre*, most are pure Sherlockians, eager to acquire first editions of the legendary detective's exploits. It is no exaggeration to claim that Sherlockians exist in all five continents, or to suggest that some spend vast sums of money and all their life in pursuit of scarce precious volumes. And they certainly are precious. It's no exaggeration to suggest either that some Sherlock Holmes titles are worth as much as a country cottage!

Arthur Conan Doyle was born on 22 May 1859 in Edinburgh, the son of a civil servant, and grandson of the famous Victorian caricaturist John Doyle, and nephew of another illustrator, Richard Doyle. After attending a series of Jesuit boarding schools, he gained a medical degree at Edinburgh University in 1880. While much of the 1880s was spent building up a small medical practice in Southsea, he was writing occasional short stories for a wide range of magazines. A longer piece initially entitled 'A Tangled Skein' (but later renamed *A Study in Scarlet*) introduced the immortal Holmes and Watson and earned him fame, if not fortune. After having the detective story turned down by several publishers, he sold the copyright to Ward Lock for a miserly £25. He never received another penny from that story even though it has since been reprinted and reissued hundreds of times in dozens of countries around the world.

A Study in Scarlet was first introduced to an unsuspecting world in Ward Lock & Co's *Beeton's Christmas Annual* for 1887. The story was given star billing in a volume which included 'Two Original Drawing Room Plays' by R. Andre and C.J. Hamilton. It was hardly auspicious company; nor was the annual itself a classic of design. Priced just 1s., it was bound in flimsy, coloured pictorial wrappers, boasting Doyle's story and showing an awe-struck gentlemen saluting the annual's masthead (since D.H. Friston provided three illustrations for *A Study in Scarlet*, it's likely he also designed this cover). Because the annual was meant to be read and discarded, it's hardly surprising so few copies have survived today, or that it fetches phenomenal sums when it (very rarely) comes up for auction. Even then, it's totally out of the reach of the ordinary collector — the only copy to have reached the auction rooms in recent years was nicked with shaky joints but even that didn't stop it being knocked down for $52,000! Whenever a copy is sold at auction it's a sure thing that the room will be packed with dealers operating on behalf of American or Japanese collectors and the price can reach quite dizzying heights. The humble enthusiast rarely gets a look in. You begin to see some of the problems? The only real chance you have of finding a copy is rummaging through your grandmother's attic or the local jumble sale. One collector found a copy just that way.

Ward Lock issued the first 'book' edition of *A Study in Scarlet* in July 1887, a small octavo paperback bound in white wrappers, printed in red with a mosaic design, and featuring illustrations by Doyle's father, like his kinsmen a noted cartoonist in his youth. This is hardly less scarce than *Beeton's Christmas Annual*. A copy without its original wraps but rebound in morocco sold recently in America for $10,000. Prices for either edition are hard to estimate — they really can reach any level. Enthusiasts with the means to do so are prepared to pay any price for them, literally!

A Study in Scarlet attracted virtually no attention. The evidence seems to suggest that Doyle showed little interest in writing more Holmes stories until he was persuaded to by J.M. Stoddart of *Lippincott's Magazine* at a dinner with Oscar Wilde on 30 August 1889. As well as persuading Wilde to put *The Picture of Dorian Gray* onto paper, he also encouraged Doyle to write another Holmes story instead of his favoured historical novels. *The Sign of the Four* was completed in just a few months and appeared in the magazine in February 1890. After appearing in a number of Lippincott's story collections, *The Sign of Four* appeared as separate book from Spencer Blackett in 1890. It is imperative that the volume bound in dark red cloth is firm and bright before paying premium prices for it. Believe it or not, shaky or loose copies with broken spines aren't *that* uncommon. Although collectors prefer first issues of this title, a second issue with the publisher's imprint on the spine and a misprint of '13' for '138' on the contents page is worth around the same.

These items represent the highlights of any Sherlock Holmes collection and they are by far the most difficult to acquire. In fact, they're virtually impossible in acceptable condition. Collectors will be pleased and relieved to learn that other Holmes books are considerably easier to find. From July 1891 to June 1892, twelve Sherlock Holmes short stories appeared in the newly formed *Strand Magazine* and in October 1892, Newnes (*Strand*'s publisher) issued these in book form as *The Adventures of Sherlock Holmes*. The book was bound in light blue decorated cloth, based on the magazine cover. It actually formed the first volume in a projected 'Strand Library'. Newnes retained all Sydney Paget's illustrations which had appeared in the magazine.

Somewhat surprisingly, copies of the *Strand* featuring Holmes can be picked up quite easily (both individual copies in their original wrappers or six-monthly bound volumes), while the first book edition is very scarce. Shaky copies can be found for around £150, but truly sound copies can fetch £500 upwards. A little less will be required to buy a first edition of its sequel, *The Memoirs of Sherlock Holmes*. This was issued in identical covers to *Adventures* (although the cloth was a slightly darker shade of blue), and shares all the same problems of condition. Incidentally, although it was dated 1894 it actually appeared in December 1893.

Perhaps the most famous Sherlock Holmes tale of all is *The Hound of the Baskervilles*, originally serialised in the *Strand* from August 1901 to April 1902. The first book edition appeared from George Newnes at the end of March 1902. An edition of 25,000 copies bound in scarlet cloth stamped in gilt, featured a design of the hound by Alfred Garth Jones. Because of its popularity, truly fine copies without foxing or fraying can sell for at least £400, although lesser copies with stained boards or missing one or two of Paget's sixteen plates would struggle to reach £50. The book was issued with a plain grey dust-jacket but this is rarely seen today. Copies complete with jacket could easily fetch four figures but they are so scarce the bibliography values only books without the jacket.

Sherlock Holmes continued to appear in the *Strand* periodically and almost all these stories were collected in book form. *The Return of Sherlock Holmes* (his 'death' in 'The Final Problem' caused such an outcry that Doyle was obliged to bring him back) was bound in dark blue cloth; while the third novel, *The Valley of Fear*, was issued in red cloth by Smith, Elder in 1915. This too was issued with a dust-jacket but, again, clean examples are notoriously scarce.

His Last Bow; Some Reminiscences had a pictorial jacket featuring Holmes with a cockerel. Don't even think of finding a copy with the jacket today, though. The print-run of this and *The Case-Book of Sherlock Holmes* were very high, so it shouldn't be too difficult to find clean bright copies for between £50–£80. Even *The Case-Book* which was published in June 1927 is almost impossible to find complete with its jacket featuring Holmes holding a revolver. A few years ago a copy in a repaired jacket sold for £1,000 at auction. These jacketed copies don't really have a fixed value — and realised price is totally at the whim of those present at the auction. Private collectors will have to contend with booksellers buying at any price because they know they can pass it on to rich clients at a profit. It's unfortunate for collectors but that's the way of the world. Holmes inspires passions and he inspires enormous sums of money.

Title	No dj	In dj
A Study in Scarlet novel (Beeton's Christmas Annual, 1887)	£15,000+	n/a
1st book edition (Ward Lock, 1887)	£3,000+	n/a
The Sign of Four novel (Blackett, 1890)	£750+	n/a
The Adventures of Sherlock Holmes short stories (Newnes, 1894)	£500	n/a
The Memoirs of Sherlock Holmes short stories (Newnes, 1894)	£350	n/a
The Hound of the Baskervilles novel (Newnes, 1902)	£400	n/a
The Return of Sherlock Holmes short stories (Newnes, 1905)	£350	n/a
The Valley of Fear novel (Smith, Elder, 1915)	£200	n/a
His Last Bow short stories (John Murray, 1917)	£80	n/a
The Case-Book of Sherlock Holmes stories (John Murray, 1927)	£50	n/a

IAN FLEMING

The phenomenal rise in the popularity of modern first editions over the last two decades seems closely linked with the collectability of Ian Fleming's James Bond books. At the start of the 1970s virtually all his first editions could be picked up for a pound or two each, but one would need several thousands of pounds to put together a complete set today. Ian Fleming and James Bond have been the surprise package of the book collecting world in recent years — no one expected Bond books to become so sought after so quickly. This is largely because, until recently, collectors of modern first editions have limited themselves more to 'high-brow' fiction, whether they enjoyed it or not.

Not that the James Bond adventures aren't good books — they most certainly are. But Fleming's work isn't collected for any intrinsic literary merit that it may or may not have. It wasn't until 1963 (nine years after the first James Bond adventure appeared) that the public took much notice of the suave hero and even then they were more interested in the films than the written word (although Pan's paperback versions were phenomenally successful). Today they are among the most collected modern first editions published in the last forty years. Bond is big business! It's easy to see why they are so collectable. The world-wide success of the films makes these originals very desirable and the fourteen books make up a very collectable sequence, particularly those issued with Richard Chopping's superb *trompe l'oeil* dust-jackets. More important than either of these reasons, though, is that all these books are good adventure yarns. They are classics of their genre, and to have the very first issue of books which together have sold well over 100,000,000 copies world-wide is an attractive proposition.

When the first book in the saga *Casino Royale*, appeared on 13 April 1953 there was little to suggest that either Bond or his journalist creator would become so immensely popular. Indeed, for a while it seemed the whole project would be still-born. Fleming was foreign manager of Kelmsley's Newspapers when he sat down in January 1952 to begin his tale; for a while he wasn't particularly interested in what he wrote as long as he wrote something — the whole project was undertaken to alleviate his boredom just before his marriage to Anne Rothermere. Nevertheless, he soon got into the swing of his narrative and became increasingly confident that the book could be a success — he even went so far as to buy a gold-plated typewriter to re-type his finished draft.

Casino Royale is without doubt the hardest of Ian Fleming's trade issues to acquire today (indeed, of his whole *oeuvre* only the signed limited edition of *On Her Majesty's Secret Service* is scarcer — that particular volume was limited to just 250 copies). 4,750 copies of *Casino Royale* were issued by Jonathan Cape. This is a large print-run for a first novel and one might expect fine or very good copies to turn up quite often, but many of these copies were despatched to public libraries and are unsuitable as collectable items. Like all the subsequent Bond novels it was issued in black boards, each with their individual stamped motif — *Casino Royale* features a red heart. The grey-blue dust-jacket bearing the heart motif was designed by Fleming, who also wrote the promotional blurb for the book. First editions of this very important book are notoriously hard to find *and* expensive. Don't expect to acquire a fine copy in fine dust wrapper for under £1,600 although even this price could be a shade conservative. As more and more copies find their way into private collections (from whence they rarely emerge) values will continue to rise rapidly.

Ian Fleming also designed the dust-jackets for his second and third Bond novels, *Live and Let Die* and *Moonraker*, both of which are highly sought after today. *Live and Let Die* was published by Jonathan Cape on 5 April 1954 in an edition of 7,500 copies, bound in black cloth with a medallion motif stamped on the boards. Fleming's rather dull scarlet dust-jacket featured bold yellow lettering but his design for *Moonraker* is a much more vivid affair, a bright yellow and orange flame-like design with the book's title stencilled over the background. This particular title featured silver lettering on its boards and was published by Jonathan Cape on 7 April 1955. Today, both these books are hard to find, despite their relatively large print-runs. Very good copies of *Live and Let Die* with clean, bright jackets could sell for £475; copies of *Moonraker* in a similar condition set the collector back around the same. Needless to say condition is very important. Copies with badly stained or chipped jackets are worth a fraction of these prices, and most dealers find it very hard to sell copies without jackets, regardless of the book's condition. Of course, finding copies in poor condition isn't hard. People bought Fleming's James Bond books as pulp fiction, to be read and discarded. They certainly weren't treated as well as today's collectors would have liked.

From this point on, prices for Fleming's Bond novels tend to fall, but the print-runs were still limited to the extent that they regularly reach three figure sums today. Indeed, both *Diamonds Are Forever* (Jonathan Cape, 26 March 1956) and *From Russia, With Love* (Jonathan Cape, 8 April 1957) regularly fetch around £300 on today's second-hand market, particularly very fine copies. The former features an attractive diamond motif blind-stamped on the boards with an elegant black, pink and white jacket designed by the talented Pat Marriot. *From Russia, With Love*, on the other hand, is interesting as it's the first Bond novel to be issued in one of Richard Chopping's strikingly original and very attractive dust-jacket designs. This first design set against the usual light woodgrain-effect background, features a painting of a Smith & Wesson .38 calibre revolver lying across a sinister-looking blood-red rose. This book is also the first to display its author by just his surname. By this stage in his career, Bond had become a popular character (Pan had just brought out the first paperback edition of *Casino Royale*), and the print-runs of these first editions were quite high. However, these books weren't collected yet. They were bought and read as cheap thrillers so few survive in pristine condition. A further problem for collectors is that Chopping's dust-jackets tend to be 'grainy' and prone to soiling.

Perhaps this explains why Cape chose to revert to a jacket designed by Pat Marriot for the next Bond title, *Dr. No* (31 March 1958). Marriot had served Fleming well up to now — indeed, his cover design for the 1957 reissue of *Casino Royale* was inspired — but *Dr. No* was a disaster, a brown and black mish-mash featuring the silhouette of a girl which was repeated on the boards. The only good thing which can be said about this jacket is that it wears well!

All of Ian Fleming's later Bond novels can be picked up quite easily, although you should avoid copies in less than very good condition like the plague — there are plenty of excellent copies around so why accept less than the best? Accepting an inferior copy to save a few pounds today is a move every book collector comes to regret. All these later novels reflect Fleming's own life at the time of writing — when Fleming was bored with Bond, the novel itself tends to be a little jaded as in *The Man with the Golden Gun*, but when he felt confident, the book was generally exciting and excellent. *Goldfinger* was written when Fleming was on top of the world and it is one of his most exuberant books — Anthony Burgess even went so far as to include it in his *Ninety-Nine Novels: The Best in English Since 1939*, a fitting tribute indeed. The dust-jacket is also one of Chopping's best, featuring a grinning skull clenching a red rose in its mouth. Fine copies of *Goldfinger* could cost the collector around £80–£100 today, although higher prices have been recorded recently.

Although collectors will be keen to acquire all the James Bond books, one title they may have to forgo is the special limited edition of *On Her Majesty's Secret Service*. This beautiful volume printed on special paper, bound in black boards with a white vellum spine and issued in a glassine jacket was limited to 250 copies signed by Fleming and featured a frontispiece portrait of the author by Amherst Villiers. These are notoriously scarce today and can cost £1,500. However, the plus side of this is that when copies do come onto the market, they have invariably been preserved in mint condition, unlike, say *Casino Royale* which was never meant to be a collector's item and which was treated accordingly.

Fleming's last Bond title is far less valuable. *Octopussy and the Living Daylights* was intended to be another set of short stories like *For Your Eyes Only*. Although many dealers catalogue this 1966 title for around £10, it's quite possible to pick up mint copies for much less. It seems that hundreds of copies were bought from the publisher by a London dealer a few years back and for a long time these were being sold in his 50p bargain basement. Whether this is still the case I don't know, but it just goes to show that it's worth looking around — you never know what might turn up. Watch out for *The Man with the Golden Gun*, if there is a gun on the cloth and it is embossed in gold it could be worth £1,800+.

There has been an alarming trend in book collecting in recent years to acquire everything published by a certain author. To me this is quite ridiculous and even masochistic, particularly in the case of Fleming. True, he published the children's classics *Chitty-Chitty-Bang-Bang* (three volumes, 1964–65) and two non-fiction works about diamond smugglers and 'thrilling cities', but why Bond enthusiasts should want these I have no idea. Even books with introductions by Fleming are eagerly purchased and Fleming's very first appearance between hard covers with a chapter in *The Kelmsley Manual of Journalism* is rumoured to change hands for hundreds of pounds. What these have to do with the Bond stories I haven't a clue. What might be worth considering, though, for Bond enthusiasts who want more than just this small collection of titles is the first paperback editions published by Pan Books, together with the numerous film-related books and ephemera, including posters, programmes and publicity material.

Title	No dj	In dj
Casino Royale novel (Jonathan Cape, 1953)	£350	£1,600+
Live and Let Die novel (Jonathan Cape, 1954)	£50	£475+
Moonraker novel (Jonathan Cape, 1955)	£50	£400
Diamonds Are Forever novel (Jonathan Cape, 1956)	£30	£250
From Russia, With Love novel (Jonathan Cape, 1957)	£20	£200
The Diamond Smugglers non-fiction (Jonathan Cape, 1957)	£30	£40 – £50
Dr. No novel (Jonathan Cape, 1958)	£25	£100
Goldfinger novel (Jonathan Cape, 1959)	£15	£80
For Your Eyes Only short stories (Jonathan Cape, 1960)	£20	£70
Thunderball novel (Jonathan Cape, 1961	–	£50
The Spy Who Loved Me novel (Jonathan Cape, 1962)	–	£25
On Her Majesty's Secret Service novel (Jonathan Cape, 1963) *special limited edition of 250 signed copies*	– –	£25 £1,500+
Thrilling Cities non-fiction (Jonathan Cape, 1963)	£10 – £15	£35+
You Only Live Twice novel (Jonathan Cape, 1964)	–	£25
Chitty-Chitty-Bang-Bang children's (Jonathan Cape, 1964–5) *three volumes issued separately*	–	each £30
The Man with the Golden Gun novel (Jonathan Cape, 1964)	–	£20

Title	No dj	In dj
Ian Fleming Introduces Jamaica non-fiction (Deutsch, 1965) *Fleming provided introduction, but it's usually classed as his work*	–	£25 – £35
Octopussy and the Living Daylights short stories (Jonathan Cape, 1966)	–	£12

A Clockwork Orange by Anthony Burgess published by William Heinemann Ltd in 1962. Wrapper design by Barry Trengrove. The first edition first state had black cloth-covered boards and the first edition second state, purple coloured boards. From the Breese collection.

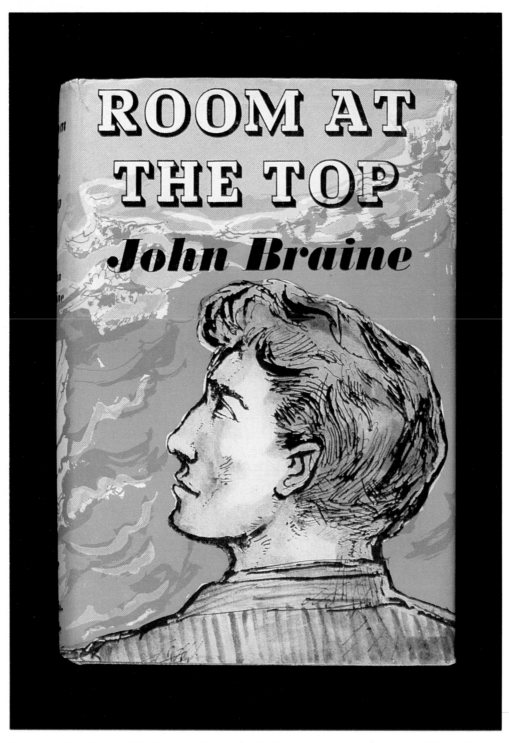

Room at The Top by John Braine. The author's first book and published in 1957 by Eyre & Spottiswoode, London. The jacket was designed by John Minton. This is a highlight for any collection and its value will be increased if found complete with yellow wrapper-band carrying reviews. From the Breese collection.

Stamboul Train by Graham Greene published by William Heinemann Ltd in 1932 with jacket
design by Youngman Carter. The book above is signed by Graham Greene to Osbert Lancaster.
From the Breese collection.

The Hound of Death and Other Stories by Agatha Christie published in 1933 by Odhams Press Ltd. The striking illustration used for the front cover by Demornay represents 1930's jacket design at its very best. From the Breese collection.

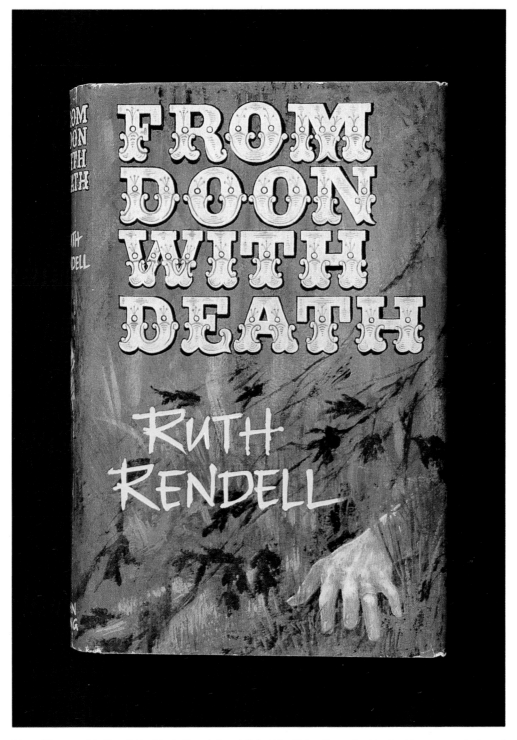

From Doon with Death by Ruth Rendell published by John Long in 1964 with a cover designed by William Randall who designed Rendell's first seven books. This was Ruth Rendell's first book and it featured Inspector Wexford. From the Breese collection.

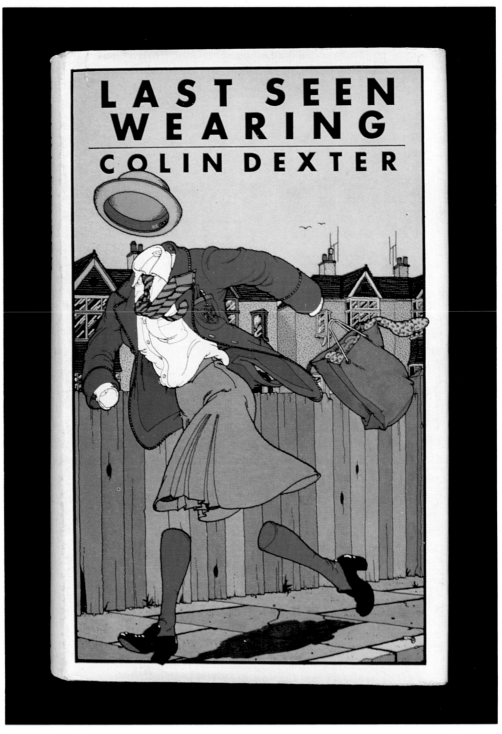

Last Seen Wearing by Colin Dexter, Macmillan 1976, features an unusual and well-designed jacket by John Ireland. This was Colin Dexter's second crime novel. From the Breese collection.

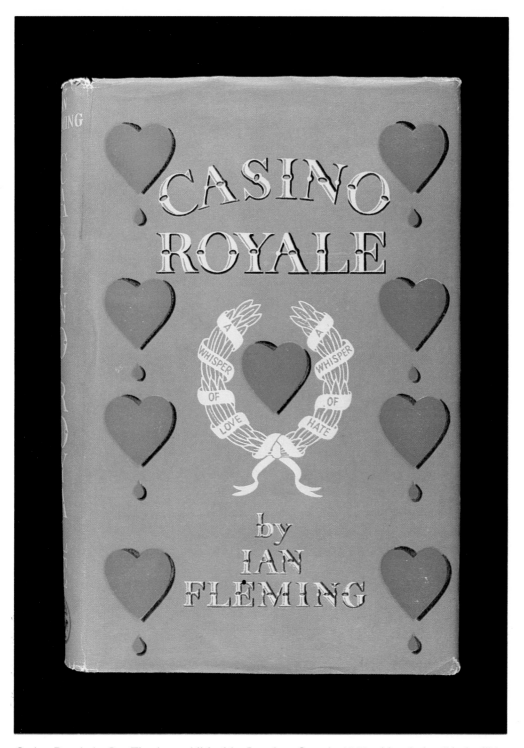

Casino Royale by Ian Fleming published by Jonathan Cape in 1953 with a jacket "devised" by the author. This was the author's first book and the beginning of the James Bond cult. From the Breese collection.

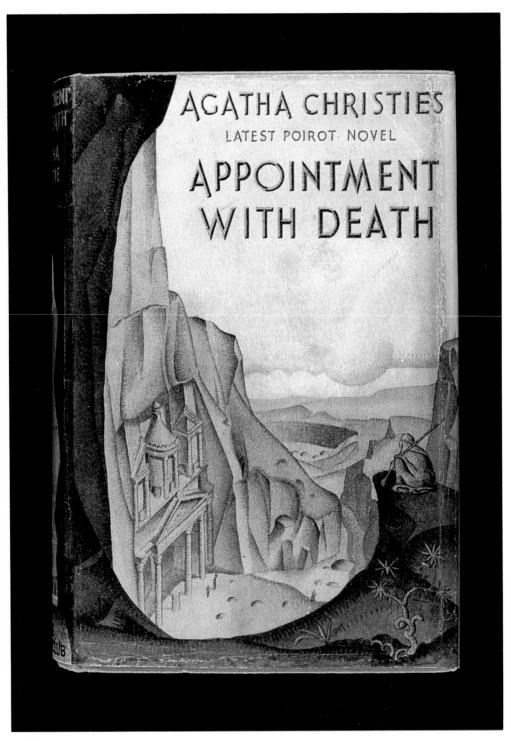

Appointment with Death by Agatha Christie (Collins Crime Club 1938) has a Jacket in soft pastel shades by Robin Macartney who also designed jackets for Death on the Nile and Murder in Mesopotamia. From the Breese collection.

JOHN FOWLES

Few writers command more respect in the literary world than John Fowles, one of the most talented and versatile of our contemporary authors. His reputation is enormous and Fowles deserves special attention because, unlike many modern authors, he is extraordinarily disciplined. Despite being a prolific author his published output is comparatively small. Although he became a published author in the early 1960s, his output to date consists of seven novels and ten other titles, including four photographic books, a history of his home town, two collections of verse published only in America, and an extremely limited edition pamphlet published by the University of Manitoba Press. At the time of writing it is several years since his last book, *The Maggot* appeared. According to his publishers there is nothing imminent in the pipeline. This might be frustrating for his many admirers but it is an excellent indication of his high standards, particularly when it is rumoured that he has at least ten finished manuscripts tucked away unlikely to ever see the light of day. It would take a resourceful publisher indeed who could persuade Fowles to release some of this material.

It would seem an easy task to put together a complete set of Fowles's books but this is not the case. As usual, the first two or three titles are notoriously scarce in nice condition and dealers can virtually ask the first price that comes into their heads — so few copies turn up on the open market. And, as one would expect, the collections of verse published in America are far from common, not to mention the ultra scarce *My Recollections of Kafka*. What is quite surprising, though, is the shortage of fine copies of photographic books like *Shipwreck* and *The Tree*. It seems that all the copies were snapped up on publication — perhaps the print-runs were relatively low. But don't let this deter you from setting out to put a Fowles collection together — there are still bargains to be had. It is worth spending the time and money to own the first printing of novels sure to become classics of twentieth century fiction. One good thing about collecting Fowles is that right from his very first novel it was obvious that he would become a major (and, accordingly, collectable) author, so many copies of his titles have been kept in good condition — more so than books by Agatha Christie or P.G. Wodehouse, whose works were seen at the time as ephemeral.

John Fowles was born in 1926 in Leigh-on-Sea, Essex where, he wrote later, 'the rows of respectable little houses, inhabited by respectable little people . . . caused me intense and continuing dislike of mankind en masse.' After a period at Bedford School (among his duties as head prefect was administering beatings to junior pupils), he served in the Royal Marines before attending Oxford University.

Fowles's novels aren't especially autobiographical but there are parts that seem reflect his experiences. Like his hero in *The Magus*, after college he spent much of his time teaching English at the University of Poitiers in France and at a college on the Greek island of Spetse. He also wrote. He had been writing for a long time — in fact, at least two of his books date from these early days. His volume of personal philosophy called *The Aristos* was actually written whilst he was an undergraduate in the mid-1940s: a full twenty years before it was published; and *The Magus*, published in 1966, was written ten years earlier. Fowles's first attempt to get published wasn't until 1962. He submitted a travel book to literary agent Paul Scott (the author of the famous *Raj Quartet*) but Scott suggested Fowles's real talent might be in the writing of fiction. How right he was. Fowles sat down to work and within a month he produced *The Collector*.

This novel is a strange tale of obsession, the story of a simple-minded butterfly enthusiast who 'collects' a pretty young girl and keeps her captive. Look out for the savage twist at the end. *The Collector* was published by Jonathan Cape early in 1963, complete with a beautiful dust-jacket designed by Tom Adams (although it is highly reminiscent of Richard Chopping's designs for Ian Fleming's James Bond titles) featuring a butterfly, a key and lock of hair against a 'sandy' background. Nice clean copies of this are scarce and becoming more so each year. In the bibliography, a price of at least £300 is given but it should be pointed out that very fine copies have been known to change hands for up to £500 in recent years. Inferior copies (including those inscribed by previous owners) can sell for under £100 — you might have to make do with one like this until a better example comes along. These prices are for book with the jacket. Without Adams's wrapper the book isn't worth more than £10–£15, if that.

It's interesting to note that Cape's proof copy of *The Collector* also had the jacket although in a slightly different form. In the place of the quotation on the rear, this version carried the bold announcement that the film rights to the novel had already been sold, as well as the American rights to Little Brown 'for a very big advance'. For a first novel, *The Collector* certainly made a big splash! The advance proof of *The Collector* is the most collectable item in Fowles's entire *oeuvre*. One copy was recently on offer for a phenomenal £2,000.

The Collector was a considerable success; its follow-up couldn't hope to compare with this. *The Aristos* was never going to be a commercial best-seller though; it was a philosophy title which even his friends advised him not to issue. Nevertheless the book was published by Jonathan Cape in 1965 (after the American first) and a low print-run ensured that fine copies are very scarce today — they could cost up to £200 but prices are prone to fluctuate either way.

If admirers of *The Collector* didn't know what to make of *The Aristos*, Fowles's next two titles were a welcome relief. Both *The Magus* and *The French Lieutenant's Woman* are classics. Tom Adams's beautiful design for *The Magus* is a *tour de force*. The 617-page book was published by Cape in April 1966, and sound, clean copies can sell for as much as £75 today. Fine copies can be hard to track down. *The Magus* was bound in 'fluffy' grey cloth boards with a purple spine, both of which are particularly prone to discolouring. No such problems with *The French Lieutenant's Woman*, published by Cape in May 1969. The 445-page volume bound in black cloth and issued in a burgundy dust-jacket seems to have aged very gracefully, although the flimsy 'feel' of the jacket means that excessive and careless handling can damage it, so beware. *The French Lieutenant's Woman* is many people's choice for the best novel of recent decades, and it's easy to see why. Fowles is a keen historian with an accurate feel for the minutiae of historical detail — his novels are packed with evidence of methodical and painstaking research. Swinburne even pops up as a character in *Lieutenant!* Incidentally, Fowles provided two endings for this particular novel — choose which one you prefer.

Acquiring first editions of John Fowles's novels after *The French Lieutenant's Woman* should prove no problem whatsoever — most dealers and catalogues list one or two later titles. It seems his publishers responded to the huge demand for his work by issuing his first editions in very high print-runs, although they did little to develop the dust-jacket design of his books — with the exception of *A Maggot*, a curious tale presented in contemporary records and enquiry transcripts — all the jackets are uninspiring affairs. *The Ebony Tower*, a collection of novellas, might cause a few headaches, but the others — the massive *Daniel Martin*, the slight *Mantissa* and *A Maggot* — can be picked up for a fiver or two.

Other Fowles rarities include his two collections of verse: *Poems*, published by New York's Ecco Press in 1973, and *Conditional*, issued by the Lord John Press in California six years later. For some reason neither of these have appeared in the UK — particularly galling for British collectors who have to pay up to £60 for each. The scarcest title of all is obviously *My Recollections of Kafka*. Only 25 copies of this slim pamphlet were issued by the University of Manitoba Press in 1970, so they're virtually unobtainable today. If you are lucky to be offered one, buy it — you'll never be offered it again. And pay whatever you're asked, even if it goes up to £200. Any price is a bargain for an item as scarce as this.

It remains to be seen when (or if) John Fowles will produce another novel, but you can be sure it will sell out very soon after publication. Despite his limited output his reputation continues to grow. His first editions are expensive today, but start your collection now if you're going to — they should continue rising in value for many years to come.

Title	No dj	In dj
The Collector novel (Jonathan Cape, 1963)	£10 – £15	£300 – £500
The Aristos philosophy (Jonathan Cape, 1965)	£8 – £10	£150 – £200
The Magus novel (Jonathan Cape, 1966)	£10 – £15	£50 – £75
The French Lieutenant's Woman novel (Jonathan Cape, 1969)	£8 – £10	£50 – £75
My Recollections of Kafka non-fiction (University of Manitoba Press, 1970) *limited to 25 copies in wrappers*	£150 – £200	n/a

Title	No dj	In dj
Poems verse (New York: Ecco Press, 1973)	£50 – £60	n/a
Cinderella translation (Jonathan Cape, 1974)	–	£20 – £30
The Ebony Tower novellas (Jonathan Cape, 1974)	–	£20 – £30
Shipwreck photographs with text by Fowles (Jonathan Cape, 1974)	–	£20 – £30
The Magus revised version of earlier novel (Jonathan Cape, 1977)	–	£10 – £20
Daniel Martin novel (Jonathan Cape, 1977)	–	£15 – £20
Islands photographs with text by Fowles (Jonathan Cape, 1978)	–	£10 – £15
Conditional verse (California: Lord John Press, 1979)	£50 – £60	n/a
The Tree photographs with text by Fowles (Aurum Press, 1979)	£8 – £10	£20 – £30
The Enigma of Stonehenge photographs with text by Fowles (Jonathan Cape, 1980)	–	£10 – £15
Mantissa novel (Jonathan Cape, 1982)	–	£10 – £12
A Short History of Lyme Regis non-fiction (Dovecote Press, 1982)	–	£5 – £8
A Maggot novel (Jonathan Cape, 1985)	–	£5 – £8

DICK FRANCIS

One of the ways thriller and crime enthusiasts know that Christmas is fast approaching is the appearance of the latest Dick Francis novel. Every autumn for the past twenty-five years a new thriller has appeared, invariably heading straight to the top of the best-seller list. For many enthusiasts, it seems, Dick Francis can do no wrong. He is without doubt one of our top thriller writers (if not *the* top), and in recent years he has also become one of the most collectable, with copies of his early titles easily reaching three figures. All his novels are set in the horse racing world and, according to Francis himself, just lately he has had to scrape the bottom of the barrel for new twists and turns in his plots. His readers would barely agree, least of all Kingsley Amis who was once quoted as saying that Francis is the only writer whose work he reads voluntarily. Many millions of copies of his novels have been sold to date, and they have been translated into twenty-three languages, including Swedish, Welsh, Czech and Japanese. He is a publishing phenomenon.

Richard Stanley Francis was born in 1920 in Pembrokeshire on the Welsh coast, and spent his early years exploring his grandfather's farm in the Cleddeau Estuary. It was here he first learned to love horses. After leaving school (he spent little time there so his teachers wouldn't have missed him) he secured a job riding hunting and show ponies including some for the circus impressario Bertram Mills. This promising career was cut short by the Second World War during which he served in Fighter and Bomber Command. Nevertheless, Francis's love for horses never disappeared and in 1948 he achieved his life's ambition by becoming a professional National Hunt jockey.

It was a successful period, and he has since called his years in the saddle 'the best ten years of my life'. By the time he hung up his stirrups in 1957 he had become a household name. He was named Champion Jockey during the 1953–54 season, and he came agonisingly close to winning the famous Grand National in 1956 — his mount, the Queen Mother's horse, Devon Loch, was ten lengths in front when it collapsed just thirty yards from the winning post. 'It was,' says Francis, 'one of the great tragedies and mysteries of racing.' Coupled with the fact that he was taking increasingly longer to get over falls and injuries, this failure prompted his decision to quit racing nine months later to pursue a career as racing correspondent on the *Sunday Express*, a post he held for sixteen years.

Dick Francis's first book was his autobiography. *The Sport of Queens* was published to excellent reviews in December 1957 by Michael Joseph, and collectable copies are not easily found today. Just last year a signed copy was advertised for £125. This is slightly steep (inflated, no doubt by Francis's signature) and I would suggest £40–£50 as a more reasonable price range. Francis was a well-known sporting celebrity when the book appeared — there is nothing to suggest the book had a particularly low print-run.

Francis's first novel, and the highlight of any collection of his works, appeared in 1962 though it was written twelve months earlier. His newspaper work was enjoyable but hardly lucrative and, according to Francis, he had two young boys to educate and the carpet was wearing thin. Writing thrillers based around his beloved horse racing seemed as good a way as any to make a few extra pounds. *Dead Cert* was a huge success and, after *Nerve* and *For Kicks* appeared in autumn 1964 and spring 1965 respectively, he became part of the thriller establishment. Now a new Francis every autumn is as sure as falling leaves. The routine never changes. Francis hopes to get his ideas together in October or November, and he starts writing in longhand in January before transferring it onto his word processor. Each novel takes five months to write. In mid-May his editor at Michael Joseph flies to Florida (where Francis lives with his wife) and picks up the manuscript to get it ready for publication.

From a collecting point of view these early titles represent by far the greatest challenge. First editions of *Dead Cert* complete with its attractive dust-jacket showing a jockey falling from a tumbling horse are notoriously scarce, largely because they weren't originally meant to be kept. Very good examples can cost up to £250. Even copies without their jackets have been known to sell for up to £75, a phenomenal sum for a book lacking what most collectors of modern firsts see as an essential component. This certainly hasn't happened to Francis's second novel, *Nerve*. Even virtually mint copies without Broom Lynne's attractive jacket struggle to break through the £10 barrier, a fraction of its potential price. Broom Lynne designed many of the jackets for Francis's early novels — all of them very attractive. Dick Francis is yet another example of a writer whose early jackets were quite beautiful but, since the use of glossy lamination nowadays, his more recent jackets are being spoilt by this glossy treatment.

None of Dick Francis's novels published during the 1960s are easy to find with clean jackets. *Odds Against* (1965), *Flying Finish* (1966), *Blood Sport* (1967), *Forfeit* (1968), and *Enquiry* (1969) do turn up quite frequently but they can be expensive. Fine copies of *Odds Against* can fetch as much as £60, and it's almost impossible to pick up copies of the other titles for less than £30. As with all recent novels, damaged copies are plentiful but they should be avoided at all costs — only fine copies are worth pursuing.

Apart from a volume of *Great Racing Stories* edited and introduced by Dick Francis and John Welcome (another jockey-author) and published in 1989, none of his novels have been issued in limited or special editions. This is surprising because he is an inveterate and habitual signer of his books — a fact collectors should take into account. As the print-runs of his novels increased during the 1970s and 1980s and seem plentiful in supply, many collectors like to pursue signed first editions of titles like *Slay-Ride* (1973) and *In the Frame* (1976). It is a worthwhile task, and it needn't prove expensive — rarely does it mean more than a £5–£10 increase in the cost. Fine copies of *Whip Hand* (1979), for example, are plentiful for between £10 and £12, and it isn't too hard to find signed copies for around £20. It's quite easy to put together a collection of signed late Francis material for a modest outlay. Because the print-runs of his most recent titles are vast it could be that the clever collector will invest a little extra money in signed material as it is this which will rise most in value in the future.

Francis's titles from the 1980s are even easier to find, and rarely cost more than

£5–£10 in fine condition. How long this remains the case is impossible to tell but it's certainly true that he has a huge following all over the world. It could be worth putting together a collection while you can afford it — who knows how demand will rise in the future?

In 1989 Dick Francis was awarded the prestigious Cartier Diamond Dagger Award by the Crime Writer's Association, a fitting tribute for half a lifetime's work. He has won many more awards in his career, including the Association's Gold Dagger for *Whip Hand* and the Silver Dagger for *For Kicks*, as well as two American Edgars (named after Edgar Allan Poe) for *Forfeit* (1968) and *Whip Hand* (1979). Francis always considered riding a horse easier than walking down the street but writing, he says, is much harder work. Every word is laboured over and he rarely completes more than five pages a day. He has even declared that he doesn't like writing. However, it's hardly likely that he'll give up writing racing novels just yet; his many admirers (including the Queen and the Queen Mother) rely too much on their autumn fix for that to happen.

Dick Francis's novels are more than mere thrillers, despite being action-packed and full of ingenious twists and turns. He likes to term them 'adventure stories'. What makes them lasting is Francis's sensitive and imaginative handling of character. Apart from the Queen and Kingsley Amis, he has many literary admirers, including C.P. Snow who wrote that 'he has a most unusual psychological skill . . . [This] sense of human potential and fatality, of the limits of energy, has almost departed from modern fiction . . . it gives his books their dynamic, the flux of internal energy, and this is what distinguishes him.' Fine praise indeed.

Title	No dj	In dj
The Sport of Queens autobiography (Michael Joseph, 1957)	£10 – £15	£40 – £50
Dead Cert novel (Michael Joseph, 1962)	£50 – £75	£200 – £250
Nerve novel (Michael Joseph, 1964)	£10 – £15	£150 – £200
For Kicks novel (Michael Joseph, 1965)	£10 – £15	£100 – £150
Odds Against novel (Michael Joseph, 1965)	£5 – £10	£50 – £60
Flying Finish novel (Michael Joseph, 1966)	–	£30 – £40

Title	No dj	In dj
Blood Sport novel (Michael Joseph, 1967)	–	£30 – £40
Forfeit novel (Michael Joseph, 1968)	–	£30 – £40
Enquiry novel (Michael Joseph, 1969)	–	£30 – £40
Rat Race novel (Michael Joseph, 1970)	–	£20 – £30
Bonecrack novel (Michael Joseph, 1971)	–	£20 – £30
Smokescreen novel (Michael Joseph, 1972)	–	£10 – £20
Slay-Ride novel (Michael Joseph, 1973)	–	£10 – £20
Knock-Down novel (Michael Joseph, 1974)	–	£10 – £15
High Stakes novel (Michael Joseph, 1975)	–	£10 – £15
In the Frame novel (Michael Joseph, 1976)	–	£10 – £12
Risk novel (Michael Joseph, 1977)	–	£10 – £12
Trial Run novel (Michael Joseph, 1978)	–	£10 – £12
Whip Hand novel (Michael Joseph, 1979)	–	£10 – £12
Reflex novel (Michael Joseph, 1980)	–	£5 – £10
Twice Shy novel (Michael Joseph, 1981)	–	£5 – £10
Banker novel (Michael Joseph, 1982)	–	£5 – £10
The Danger novel (Michael Joseph, 1983)	–	£5 – £10

Title	No dj	In dj
Proof novel (Michael Joseph, 1984)	–	£5 – £10
Break In novel (Michael Joseph, 1985)	–	£5 – £10
Lester biography (Michael Joseph, 1986)	–	£5 – £10
Bolt novel (Michael Joseph, 1986)	–	£5 – £10
Hot Money novel (Michael Joseph, 1987)	–	£5 – £10
The Edge novel (Michael Joseph, 1988)	–	£5 – £10
Straight novel (Michael Joseph, 1989)	–	£5 – £10
Longshot novel (Michael Joseph, 1990)	–	£5 – £10
Comeback novel (Michael Joseph, 1991)	–	£5 – £10

WILLIAM GOLDING

Few contemporary writers have been as consistent throughout their career as William Golding. All his novels from the legendary *Lord of the Flies* to the most recent *Fire Down Below* have been first class literature and he recently received the Nobel Prize for Literature as well as his earlier Booker Prize. Several of his books have found their way into 'Best of . . .' lists, and he ranks in the top three British novelists since the war. *Lord of the Flies* has long been a crucial part of the school examination syllabus and if the number of Golding collectors is anything to go on, it seems that at least some of these children eventually return to the fold. Considering that his first book was published nearly sixty years ago, Golding's output has been relatively low — just nineteen volumes. This is good news for collectors, particularly because most of the books seem to be reasonably accessible. As always there are a few early exceptions, and these can cause collectors all sorts of problems and expense.

William Golding was born in Cornwall on 19 September 1911, the eldest son of a schoolteacher. After an education at Marlborough Grammar School (where he found himself unpopular due to fighting for his own way), Golding embarked on a science degree at Brasenose College, Oxford. He never finished it; halfway through Golding transferred to an English Literature course. After graduating in 1935, Golding worked as a writer, actor and producer in small theatre companies, before working as a teacher for a short while. During the Second World War Golding served in the Royal Navy. He took part in the Normandy landings, the sinking of the *Bismarck* and eventually became a lieutenant. He began his writing career before the war, although his first book is often overlooked by collectors. In 1934 a small, 34-page collection of *Poems* was published in Macmillan's Contemporary Poets series under the 'W.G. Golding' by-line. Golding is thought to have denied its authorship. This title is an example of the almost obligatory slim volume of verse produced by so many writers (like Graham Greene and Kingsley Amis) before they develop into major novelists. Like all such titles it is very scarce today, almost impossible to find. It's not known just how many copies were produced but it was unlikely to be more than 1,000 and probably less. Certainly few copies survive today. Measuring just 13 x 20 cm and issued in printed decorative paper wrappers bearing an art nouveau border design, this booklet is particularly fragile. A *very good* copy (with the usual defects such as rubbed corners or frayed edges and a little spotting or foxing) can fetch at least £2,000 today. It is truly a book that is worth whatever the dealer wants to ask. *Poems* was never reprinted. I'm sure an enterprising publisher could make a fortune by producing facsimile reprints of these scarce 'first volumes'.

After the war Golding returned to teaching and his experiences of the minds of small boys played a great part in the creation of his masterpiece, *Lord of the Flies*. It was in the early 1950s when he asked his wife if she thought it would be a good idea for him to write a story about boys on an island and let them behave the way they really would. She thought it an excellent idea, and he immediately set to work. When the book was published by Faber & Faber in 1954 it received critical and popular acclaim and has never been out of print since. It's unlikely to go out of print for decades to come. While not common, copies without their jackets can be picked up reasonably cheaply; but complete with its wonderfully coloured jacket designed by Anthony Gross, this title is one of the *rarities* of the twentieth century. Despite this, it is only very fine copies in bright unworn jackets that command the premium prices. These can sell for between £1,000–£1,500. Few books' prices are so affected by condition than *Lord of the Flies*. Copies in bright but nicked jackets usually sell for around £500, and lesser copies with inscriptions and/or tears sell for considerably lower sums.

Anthony Gross designed the dust-jackets for all Golding's early novels, *The Inheritors* (Faber, 1955), *Pincher Martin* (Faber, 1956) and *Free Fall* (1959). All these titles confirmed Golding's growing reputation as a major novelist, some are a challenging read — Golding's novels require much concentration and intellectual flexing if the best is to be got out of them. Like *Lord of the Flies* all these titles are hard to find in a truly fine condition and any blemishes affect the values drastically. *The Inheritors* can easily fetch around £200; *Pincher Martin* sells for £150; and *Free Fall* could sell for up to £75. Golding rarely signs his books other than to personal friends. If you can come across signed copies, expect to pay at least double those prices. Last year several signed copies of Golding's early novels sold for huge sums at auction. Another scarce title from this period is his only play, *The Brass Butterfly*. This was published by Faber in 1958, and is rarely offered for sale. The same format as the other Golding titles, fine copies sell for around £150. Lesser copies in just good or very good condition have also been known to sell for around £100, such is their scarcity.

Golding titles from the 1960s become much easier to acquire in collectable condition, although he produced very little then. *The Spire* (1964, jacket designed by John Piper) and *The Pyramid* (1967) invariably sell for around £30–£50 today, much the same as *The Hot Gates* (1965), Golding's volume of essays and occasional pieces in a Michael Ayrton jacket. His only collection of short stories, *The Scorpion God*, appeared in 1971, although one of the stories, 'Envoy Extraordinary', originally appeared in *Sometime Never, Three Tales of the Imagination*. Published by Eyre & Spottiswoode in 1956, this book also contained tales by John Wyndham and Mervyn Peake. Purchased by Peake, Wyndham and Golding enthusiasts, it's not surprising that first editions can sell for as much as £100.

William Golding published virtually nothing during the 1970s and his only book of the decade being *Darkness Visible* in 1979. Because of the high print-run of his more recent titles you will have no problems acquiring them. Be warned, though. Only absolutely mint copies of novels like *The Paper Men* are worth acquiring — anything else is worthless now and can hardly appreciate in value. The only title which will cause problems from the 1980s is the little-known *Nobel Lecture*, the text of Golding's Nobel Prize acceptance speech in 1983. 500 copies were issued in paper wrappers by the Sixth Chamber Press in 1983, and this slim pamphlet could cost £25–£30 today. There were also fifty copies bound in goatskin, signed by Golding and issued with a slipcase. Copies are very hard to come by — most are already in private collections, never to re-emerge and usually sell for at least £200. Another little known title is a slim pamphlet Golding wrote called *The Ladder and the Tree*. A few hundred copies were issued in wrappers by the Marlborough College Press in 1961, and they are notoriously scarce now. Many collectors are quite prepared to do without this, but completists will be alarmed to note that leading dealer Rick Gekoski advertised one copy three years ago for £1,100.

Title	No dj	In dj
Poems verse (Macmillan, 1934) *issued in paper wrappers*	£2,000 – £4,000	n/a
Lord of the Flies novel (Faber, 1954)	£20 – £30	£500 – £1,500
The Inheritors novel (Faber, 1955)	£10 – £20	£150 – £200
Pincher Martin novel (Faber, 1956)	£10 – £15	£100 – £150
The Brass Butterfly play (Faber, 1958)	£10 – £15	£100 – £150
Free Fall novel (Faber, 1959)	£5 – £10	£50 – £75
The Ladder and the Tree pamphlet (Marlborough College Press, 1961)	£1,000 – £1,500	n/a
The Spire novel (Faber, 1964)	–	£40 – £50
The Hot Gates essays/occasional pieces (Faber, 1965)	–	£40 – £50
The Pyramid novel (Faber, 1967)	–	£30 – £50
The Scorpion God short stories (Faber, 1971)	–	£30 – £40
Darkness Visible novel (Faber, 1979)	–	£15 – £20
Rites of Passage novel (Faber, 1980)	–	£10 – £15

Title	No dj	In dj
A Moving Target essays (Faber, 1982)	–	£5 – £10
Nobel Lecture text of acceptance speech (Sixth Chamber Press, 1983)	£25 – £30	n/a
also 50 signed copies bound in goatskin and issued in a slip-case	£200+	n/a
The Paper Men novel (Faber, 1984)	–	£5 – £10
Close Quarters Novel (Faber, 1987)	–	£5 – £10
Fire Down Below novel (Faber, 1989)	–	£5 – £10

GRAHAM GREENE

When Graham Greene died in Vevey, Switzerland on 3 April 1991, aged 86, the curtain was drawn on one of the most distinguished literary careers of the twentieth century. Fellow writers filled pages with tributes and there was a feeling of genuine loss not just within the literary community. There had been a sense that he was indestructible. He made many enemies (the Nobel Prize panel for instance: how can one explain awards to unknown Swiss, Guatemalan, Icelandic and Columbian writers while he was passed over year after year?), but he also won millions of devoted readers all over the world. Furthermore, he was one of the most collectable authors and his books sell for high sums today, particularly early titles in their dust-jackets.

So how will his death affect this state of affairs? During the afternoon of 3 April 1991, we heard that one prominent book dealer who had an impressive Graham Greene list was called by six other dealers within an hour of the news breaking. All were keen to gather as much of the precious commodity as possible. It's a sad but undeniable fact that when an author dies (particularly one as prominent and collectable as Greene) interest shoots up. Without doubt attention to Greene's works will increase even more rapidly in the next few years, probably to the point of supplanting Agatha Christie or Wodehouse as the most collected author of all. Even titles like *The Quiet American* and *Our Man in Havana* which had previously been quite common have become hard to find in genuinely fine condition; now they should rise even more steeply. The prices in the guide reflect a new demand.

Henry Graham Greene was born on 2 October 1904, in Berkhamsted, where his father was headmaster of the local school. Greene was educated at his father's school, but it was far from being a happy experience. Throughout his school life he was tormented because of his father's position. Such misery was an experience he never forgot, and one which haunted him throughout his life. On several occasions he tried to commit suicide (once by sawing into his knee), and when he progressed to Balliol College, Oxford, this tendency took a bizarre twist. Motivated, he says, by acute boredom (and a desire to be on the dangerous edge of things) Greene played Russian roulette with a loaded revolver. With one chance in six of blowing his head off, he did this a couple of times and survived! Later he thought this experience helped him to see life in a fresher and more vivid way. It undoubtedly had a part in shaping his imagination.

As he was a relative of both Robert Louis Stevenson and Christopher Isherwood, it was perhaps inevitable that Greene himself would become a writer. His first appearance in print was with a short story entitled 'The Tick of the Clock' which appeared in the school's magazine, *The Berkhamstedian* in 1921 and which was reprinted in a London evening newspaper, *The Star*, shortly after. At college he was a regular contributor to both *The Weekly Westminster* and *The Oxford Outlook* before his first book appeared. This was the almost obligatory volume of youthful verse favoured by writers as diverse as William Golding and Evelyn Waugh. *Babbling April*, a slim volume bound in grey paper boards and issued in a grey jacket printed in black, was published by Basil Blackwell in April, 1925. Graham Greene may have cringed with embarrassment at the poems' sentimentality in later life, but collectors are prepared to re-mortgage their homes to secure a copy. Only around 300 copies were printed. The good news is that copies turn up at auction or in catalogues quite regularly. The bad news is that decent copies invariably sell for over £2,000 in their jackets.

After a brief spell as a journalist in Nottingham (the scene of many of his early novels or 'entertainments'), Greene worked as a staff journalist on *The Times*. During this period he married and converted to Roman Catholicism, a powerful theme in most of his best books like *The Heart of the Matter*, *The Power and the Glory*, *Brighton Rock* and *Monsignor Quixote*. But Greene didn't like to be called a Catholic novelist; he preferred to be a Catholic who wrote novels. An important distinction as far as he was concerned.

Like many writers, his earliest attempts at fiction were unspectacular (he later disowned them) and if it weren't for collectors they would command little interest, despite the fact that with one exception, they are all in print still. *The Man Within*, a tale of smuggling, was first published in an edition of 2,500 copies by William Heinemann in June, 1929, priced 7s. 6d. A thick volume bound in black cloth, *The Man Within* was issued with a plain dust-jacket decorated on the front cover with a zigzag design surrounding the title. Copies without the jacket are scarce today (£200–£300); the jacket is impossible to find. If a good jacketed copy was offered for sale, expect a price tag similar (or maybe slightly lower) than that for *Babbling April*. Much the same can be said of Greene's next two titles, *The Name of Action* (1930) and *Rumour at Nightfall* (1931), both issued by Heinemann. The former was bound in dark blue cloth and issued in a simple yellow and red dust-jacket. The latter, bound in red cloth, sported a blue/green dust-jacket. Neither is seen with jackets today, so collectors can only realistically hope to acquire copies without. Perhaps hoarding collectors will release their jacketed copies now that the author's death is bound to raise prices. What the asking price for these titles in jackets will be, particularly the former which Greene suppressed, is anybody's guess.

None of these books made Green's fortune; that was *Stamboul Train*'s function. This title is by far the easiest of the early Greene's to acquire today: the book was chosen as the Book Society's Book of the Month, and Heinemann printed around 13,000 copies of the first edition to meet the expected demand (although after a libel threat from J.B. Priestley these were withdrawn and the offending pages altered). It is a small but thick volume and is bound in black cloth. Copies without the attractive, multi-coloured jacket which shows a train heading across Europe, are quite common today. A nice specimen shouldn't cost more than £50–£75. Copies in their jackets are another story altogether, particularly if you want a clean jacket. Expect to pay ten times the price or more for one of these. Ragged copies should be cheaper but it would really be a false economy.

Around this time (between 1936 and 1939) Graham Greene produced two of the best travel books of the century. All his novels have an indubitable sense of place, of course, whether it's Vietnam in *The Quiet American*, West Africa in *The Heart of the Matter*, or Papa Doc's Haiti in *The Comedians*. All these remarkable novels were based on his own visits. Few novelists have travelled so widely, or risked as much danger as Graham Greene. The first of his great travel books was *Journey Without Maps*, based on an expedition Greene made with his cousin to the heart of the Liberian jungle in the 1930s — he was the first white man to visit the previously uncharted area. Published in yellow cloth by Heinemann in May, 1936, this title is extremely scarce today, as is *The Lawless Roads: A Mexican Journey* (1939), Greene's account of his trip to investigate the persecution of the Catholics in Mexico in the late 1930s. Published at 10*s*. 6*d*. and bound in red cloth this title is also very hard to track down. Both titles were issued in dust-jackets, but these are rarely seen.

By far his scarcest jacket, though, is the one issued on *Brighton Rock*, perhaps Greene's most famous book. This was published by Heinemann in July, 1938, in red cloth. Nice copies generally sell for £150–£200. If a copy ever surfaced in its jacket (and most collectors despair of such an event ever taking place) the seller could ask whatever price he chose. In an auction it could literally reach dizzy heights. It certainly wouldn't sell for below £5,000. It's ironic that Greene's other classic title, *The Power and the Glory* (Heinemann, March, 1940) is also the other scarcest volume. Despite having a print-run of around 3,500 copies for the first edition (yellow cloth with a purple dust-jacket bearing the title in a white block on the front cover), copies are unaccountably scarce today. Even copies in nicked or faded jackets sell for over £2,000 at auction, to be passed on to collectors, no doubt, for considerably more. The most likely explanation for the scarcity of *The Power and the Glory* (in any condition) is that much of the first print-run was destroyed during the London Blitz. Many publishers' warehouses were destroyed during the war.

After the war (in which Greene served in Intelligence, most notably in West Africa), Greene resumed his literary career producing a variety of novels, and (in his own words), his less serious 'entertainments'. From this point on the prices for his first editions begin to drop, and most collectors should be able to afford to put together a full collection of later Greenes. But even here, prices have shot up in recent years, and the trend will continue. Just a couple of years ago it was possible to find a nice copy of *Nineteen Stories* (Heinemann, July, 1947, later revised as *Twenty-One Stories*) in its plain grey dust-jacket for under £30. Today a more reasonable asking price would be double that. The same is true of his classic novel dealing with Catholic faith set in West Africa, *The Heart of the Matter*, published in May, 1948, in blue cloth with a red jacket. Again, this title was a Book Society choice, but the resulting high print-run has guaranteed a surfeit of copies today. The book was published on cheap paper so the remaining fine copies can fetch as much as £75 from a specialist dealer, more if the wrap-around promotional band is intact.

Astute critics have always remarked on the impressive cinematographic quality of Greene's writing, so it's hardly surprising that so many of his books have been filmed. It is not surprising either that he was one-time film critic for both *The Spectator* and *Night and Day* in the 1930s. He inadvertently caused the closure of *Night and Day* when his review of a Shirley Temple film prompted a costly libel case. *Brighton Rock* and *Stamboul Train* were early film successes, but perhaps his most important contribution to British cinema came with *The Third Man*, directed by Carol Reed and starring Trevor Howard, Orson Welles and Alida Valli. Originally written as 'raw material' for the film, the 'novelised' version of *The Third Man* was published with *The Fallen Idol* in one volume in July 1950. Again, this is far scarcer today than it was a few years ago. A copy in an undamaged jacket could sell for £50–£75 today. Even copies without their jackets featuring characters from the film manage to attract asking prices of up to £20.

Jackets are vitally important for Greene's post-war titles: few of the books are worth anything without them. Greene was exceptionally fortunate with his jacket artists — his publishers employed some of the best in the business. The unacknowledged design for the 1955 'entertainment' set in Monte Carlo, *Loser Takes All*, is a glorious white, blue and yellow affair, and both Donald Greene's design for *Our Man in Havana* and Lacey Everett's strikingly morbid *A Burnt Out Case* deserve special mention. Less spectacular, but equally effective are Michael Harvey's plain typographic designs for the Bodley Head and Reinhardt Books titles, from *The Honorary Consul* to *Reflections*. Particularly attractive are two designs by Stephen Ross for the collection of short stories, *May We Borrow Your Husband?* and the humorous novel, *Travels With My Aunt*. Both titles were issued in the late 1960s, a period when Greene's essential pessimism melted into warm-hearted irony. Both jackets are colourful and both essential if the price of these books is to reach £15–£20 each.

Graham Greene was an accomplished editor, and perhaps his very finest jacket was on one of his 'sideline' titles, *The Spy's Bedside Book* (Rupert Hart-Davies, 1957), an anthology of spy pieces by John Buchan, William Le Quex and even Thomas Hardy. It was edited by Greene with his brother, Hugh. Despite not being a regular Greene book, *The Spy's Bedside Book* is very collectable today. One of its major attractions is the beautiful jacket with a design by A.S. Douthwaite based on an old game of L'Attaque. On the back cover is a facsimile of the rear of a Victorian yellowback book showing the usual advertisements. The first edition of the book was bound in green cloth. If you are ever offered a copy in blue cloth, beware. It is a second impression, despite the fact that the jacket is identical.

This wasn't the only book he edited. Over the years he either edited or introduced several volumes, including *The Café Royal Story* (1963, Hutchinson Benham Ltd), *Victorian Detective Fiction* (1966, co-produced with Dorothy Glover), *An Impossible Woman: Memories of Dottoressa Moor of Capri* (1975) and *Why Do I Write?*, a 120-page interchange of ideas between Greene, Elizabeth Bowen and V.S. Pritchett published in 1948.

His most collectable edited volume is *The Old School: Essays by Divers Hands*, a collection of reminiscences of schooldays by W.H. Auden, Harold Nicolson, Anthony Powell, Antonia White, Walter Greenwood and L.P. Hartley — all collectable in their own right. This book, rounded off by Greene's account of his own days at Berkhamsted, was published by Jonathan Cape on 23 July 1934, in an edition of 1,517 copies bound in black cloth. Nice copies in their jackets sell for around £100 today.

Greene's later novels are some of his very best: they include classic titles like

Our Man in Havana, The Comedians, The Honorary Consul (perhaps the highlight), *The Human Factor, Monsignor Quixote* and *The Captain and the Enemy*. Although they are much easier to acquire than his earlier titles, don't be fooled into thinking that they are common. The titles from the 1950s and 1960s in particular are becoming increasingly scarce, and could cost up to £30 or more. Fine copies of the 1963 collection of short tales, *A Sense of Reality*, could set you back £40.

While most collectors will tend to concentrate on Greene's novels, entertainments and travel books, genuine enthusiasts will also seek to acquire Greene's other works. Particularly sought after are plays like *The Potting Shed, The Complaisant Lover*, and *Carving a Statue*, and the collection of essays *The Lost Childhood*. This 191-page book was published by Eyre & Spottiswoode in March, 1951, priced 12s. 6d. It was bound in grey cloth stamped in black on the spine and issued in an attractive red, white and brown jacket designed by Stein. But most sought after are Greene's four children's titles. The first was *The Little Train*, published anonymously by Eyre & Spottiswoode in 1946 when Greene was still a director there. It was a slim volume illustrated by Dorothy Craigie and bound in decorated yellow cloth boards with a pictorial dust-jacket. The others were *The Little Fire Engine, The Little Horse Bus* and *The Little Steam Roller*, all published by Max Parrish. All four titles were later reissued with new illustrations by Greene's old friend Edward Ardizzone.

As well as his mainstream books there have been numerous limited edition volumes and pamphlets, the most important of which have been included in the price guide. Many have been left out (like several three or four page volumes published in places like San Francisco, etc).

Greene's first venture into the limited edition field was with the short story, *The Bear Fell Free*, a 40-page book published by Grayson & Grayson in July, 1935. 285 copies were bound in olive green cloth, issued in a buff jacket printed in blue, of which 250 were signed and numbered and offered for sale at 10s. 6d. Three years ago a fine copy was offered for sale at £875! Other important issues have been the limited editions of *May We Borrow Your Husband?* and *A Visit to Morin*, although collectors may prefer to go for the trade editions of both these (the latter appeared in *A Sense of Reality* in 1963). Further collectables include two pamphlets produced by Bodley Head in conjunction with The Stellar Press in the early 1980s and *How the Quixote Became a Monsignor* (Los Angeles, 1980), important because it concerns one of Greene's own favourite novels.

Title	No dj	In dj
Babbling April verse (Basil Blackwell, 1925)	£500 – £800	£2,000+
The Man Within novel (Heinemann, 1929)	£200 – £300	£1,000 – £2,000
The Name of Action novel (Heinemann, 1930) *suppressed by Graham Greene*	£150 – £200	£1,000 – £1,500
Rumour at Nightfall novel (Heinemann, 1931)	£200 – £300	£1,000 – £1,500
Stamboul Train novel (Heinemann, 1932)	£50 – £75	£500 – £750
It's a Battlefield novel (Heinemann, 1934)	£100 – £150	£500 – £750
The Old School anthology (Jonathan Cape, 1934) *edited by Graham Greene*	£20 – £30	£80 – £100
England Made Me novel (Heinemann, 1935)	£100 – £150	£500 – £750
The Bear Fell Free short story (Grayson & Grayson, 1935) *limited to 285 copies, 250 of which were numbered* *and signed. A facsimile edition was published by the* *Folcroft Press in Pennsylvania in the 1970s*	£250 – £300+	£600 – £1,000+
The Basement Room short stories (Cresset Press, 1935)	£50 – £80	£400 – £500
Journey Without Maps travel (Heinemann, 1936)	£50 – £80	£200 – £300
A Gun For Sale novel (Heinemann, 1936)	£100 – £150	£300 – £400
Brighton Rock novel (Heinemann, 1938)	£150 – £200	£5,000+
The Lawless Roads travel (Heinemann, 1939)	£50 – £80	£200 – £300
The Confidential Agent novel (Heinemann, 1939)	£100 – £150	£300 – £400

Title	No dj	In dj
The Power and the Glory novel (Heinemann, 1940)	£150 – £200	£1,000 – £2,000
British Dramatists non-fiction (Collins, 1942) *Britain in Pictures series*	£10 – £15	£20 – £25
The Ministry of Fear novel (Heinemann, 1943) *printed on thin wartime paper, hence very hard to* *find in nice condition*	£30 – £40	£200 – £300
The Little Train juvenile (Eyre & Spottiswoode, 1946) *published anonymously*	£80 – £100	£200 – £250
Nineteen Stories short stories (Heinemann, 1947)	£15 – £20	£50 – £75
The Heart of the Matter novel (Heinemann, 1948)	£10 – £15	£50 – £75
Why Do I Write? essays/non-fiction (Percival Marshall, 1948) *sub-titled 'An Exchange of Views Between Elizabeth* *Bowen, Graham Greene and V.S. Pritchett'*	£10 – £15	£50 – £60
The Third Man and **The Fallen Idol** novellas (Heinemann, 1950)	£15 – £20	£50 – £75
The Little Fire Engine juvenile (Max Parrish, 1950)	£50 – £80	£100 – £150
The Lost Childhood essays (Eyre & Spottiswoode, 1951)	£5 – £10	£30 – £40
The End of the Affair novel (Heinemann, 1951)	£10 – £15	£40 – £55
The Little Horse Bus juvenile (Max Parrish, 1952)	£50 – £80	£100 – £150
The Living Room play (Heinemann, 1953)	£10 – £15	£40 – £50
The Little Steamroller juvenile (Max Parrish, 1953)	£50 – £60	£100 – £120

Title	No dj	In dj
Essaies Catholiques essays (Éditions du Seuil, 1953) *written in French and published in France in printed* *wrappers*	£50 – £75	n/a
Twenty-One Stories short stories (Heinemann, 1954) *includes four stories not published in* Nineteen Stories*:* *'The Hint of an Explanation', 'The Blue Film', 'Special* *Duties' and 'The Destructors'*	£10 – £15	£30 – £40
Loser Takes All novel (Heinemann, 1955)	–	£30 – £40
The Quiet American novel (Heinemann, 1955)	–	£20 – £30
The Spy's Bedside Book (Rupert Hart-Davies, 1957) *edited by Graham and Hugh Greene*	£5 – £8	£50 – £60
The Potting Shed play (Heinemann, 1958)	£5 – £8	£40 – £50
Our Man in Havana novel (Heinemann, 1958)	–	£30 – £45
The Complaisant Lover play (Heinemann, 1959)	£5 – £8	£30 – £40
A Visit to Morin short story (Heinemann, 1959) *250 signed copies issued as Christmas gifts*	£100 – £150+	£250 – £300+
A Burnt-Out Case novel (Heinemann, 1961)	–	£30 – £45
In Search of a Character: Two African Journals travel (Bodley Head, 1961)	–	£35 – £45
Introductions to Three Novels (P.A. Norstedt, Stockholm, 1962) *issued in printed wrappers as Norstedt's annual Christ-* *mas gift. The intros to* The Power and the Glory, The Heart of the Matter, *and* The End of the Affair *were* *later reprinted in the* Collected Edition	£100 – £150	n/a
A Sense of Reality short stories (Bodley Head, 1963)	£5 – £8	£30 – £40

Title	No dj	In dj
The Café Royal Story (Hutchinson Benham, 1963) foreword by Graham Greene	£30 – £35	£85 – £100
The Revenge autobiographical fragment (privately printed, 1963) *issued in wrappers, signed*	£200 – £300+	n/a
Carving A Statue play (Bodley Head, 1964)	£5 – £8	£30 – £40
The Comedians novel (Bodley Head, 1966)	–	£20 – £25
Victorian Detective Fiction anthology (Bodley Head, 1966) *edited by Graham Greene and Dorothy Glover, who also illustrated his children's books as Dorothy Craigie. Limited to 500 signed copies*	£150 – £250+	n/a
May We Borrow Your Husband? short stories (Bodley Head, 1967) *also issued in a signed limited edition of 500 copies*	– £150 – £200+	£15 – £20 n/a
Collected Essays (Bodley Head, 1969)	–	£15 – £20
Travels With My Aunt novel (Bodley Head, 1969)	–	£15 – £20
Mr Visconti . . . An Extract From Travels With My Aunt (privately printed, 1969) *another of Greene's Christmas gift books, limited to 300 copies in wrappers*	£200 – £250+	n/a
A Sort of Life autobiography (Bodley Head, 1971)	–	£15 – £20
Collected Stories (Bodley Head, 1972)	£5 – £8	£20 – £30
The Pleasure-Dome collected film criticism (Secker & Warburg, 1972)	£5 – £8	£10 – £20
The Virtue of Disloyalty (privately printed, 1972) *another Christmas book, limited to 300 copies in wrappers*	£200 – £250+	n/a
The Honorary Consul novel (Bodley Head, 1973)	–	£15 – £20

Title	No dj	In dj
Lord Rochester's Monkey biography (Bodley Head, 1974)	–	£15 – £20
An Impossible Woman: The Memories of Dottoressa Moor of Capri (Bodley Head, 1975) *edited by Graham Greene*	–	£10 – £15
The Return of A.J. Raffles play (Bodley Head, 1975) *issued in wrappers.* *250 copies were also issued in boards with a dj, and* *signed and numbered*	£10 – £15 –	n/a £150 – £200+
A Wedding Among the Owls short story (Bodley Head/Stellar Press, 1977) *Christmas book limited to 250 signed copies in* *wrappers*	£150 – £200+	n/a
The Human Factor novel (Bodley Head, 1978)	–	£15 – £20
Dr. Fischer of Geneva, or, The Bomb Party novel(Bodley Head, 1980)	–	£10 – £15
Ways of Escape autobiography (Bodley Head, 1980)	–	£10 – £15
How Father Quixote Became a Monsignor short story (Sylvester & Orphanos, LA, 1980) *limited to 330 signed and numbered copies*	£100 – £150+	n/a
One November Day in 1980 short story (Bodley Head/Stellar Press, 1980) *Christmas book limited to 250 signed copies in* *wrappers*	£150 – £200+	n/a
The Great Jowett play (Bodley Head, 1981) *only issued as a signed limited issue of 525 copies*	£60 – £100+	n/a
Monsieur Quixote novel (Bodley Head, 1982)	–	£10 – £15
J'accuse: the Darker Side of Nice polemic (Bodley Head, 1982) *printed in French and English, and issued in paper* *wrappers*	£5 – £10	n/a

Title	No dj	In dj
The Other Man: Conversations with Graham Greene non-fiction (Bodley Head, 1983) *Edited by Marie-Françoise Allain*	–	£10 – £15
Yes and No and **For Whom the Bell Chimes** plays (Bodley Head, 1983) *limited to 750 signed copies*	£60 – £100	n/a
Getting to Know the General non-fiction (Bodley Head, 1984)	–	£10 – £15
The Tenth Man novel (Bodley Head/Blond, 1985)	–	£10 – £15
Graham Greene Country art (Pavilion, 1986) *a sumptuous book of full-colour paintings based on Greene's novels by Paul Hogarth who designed the covers for the Penguin editions of Greene's titles. Greene himself provided commentary and foreword.*	£5 – £8	£20 – £25
The Captain and the Enemy novel (Reinhardt Books, 1988)	–	£10 – £15
Dear David, Dear Graham: a Bibliophilic Correspondence (Alembic Press, 1989) *letters between Greene and political cartoonist David Low; limited to 250 numbered copies*	£50 – £60	n/a
Why the Epigraph? (Nonesuch Press, 1989) *a collection of his novels' epigraphs, limited to 950 signed copies*	£60 – £80	–
Yours Etc: Letters to the Press (Reinhardt Books, 1990)	–	£10 – £15
The Last Word short stories (Reinhardt Books, 1990)	–	£10 – £15
Reflections essays (Reinhardt Books, 1990)	–	£10 – £15

CHRISTOPHER ISHERWOOD

Despite being popularly considered the least purely literary of the 'Gang of Three' (which also included Stephen Spender and W.H. Auden), Christopher Isherwood is perhaps the most collected today, and with good cause. Twenty-three books in a sixty-year career is not a huge output but all his titles are eminently readable, accessible and highly entertaining. Much of his career was an attempt to emulate the early success of his famous Berlin stories (and to some extent he failed), but not one of his books deserves to be neglected. In collecting terms, Isherwood combines an intriguing combination of scarcity and accessibility. His early titles fetch very high sums; the titles from the 1960s and 70s can be picked up for just a few pounds each.

Christopher William Bradshaw Isherwood was born in Cheshire in 1904, the son of an army captain who was killed in the First World War. He met Auden at his prep school, and fellow-novelist Edward Upward at Repton; but it wasn't until he embarked on an uncompleted medical degree at Cambridge that he began to write seriously.

Isherwood's first novel (heavily influenced by Virginia Woolf and E.M. Forster) was actually written at Cambridge, although its working title of *Seascape* was changed to *All the Conspirators* when it was published by Jonathan Cape in May, 1928. It's not known how many copies were printed but it's unlikely to have been more than 2,000. Only 300 copies were sold and the book was remaindered (although it found its way back into print in 1939) Copies are very scarce today, particularly in their jackets. Truly fine copies are nowhere to be seen — expect to pay at least £200 for a less-than-perfect copy in a chipped or dirty jacket.

Despite this inauspicious beginning, Isherwood's next few novels were all published by Virginia and Leonard Woolf's prestigious and very collectable Hogarth Press. *The Memorial*, an attempt to describe the horrific effects of the First World War on an ordinary family appeared in 1932 in a dull and badly designed jacket reminiscent of Edward Munch. Despite its unaesthetic appeal, this jacket is very collectable today. Copies of the *The Memorial* without the jacket sell for around £50; with the jacket the price of the book can increase four-fold.

This is much the same with Isherwood's undoubted masterpieces, the three books which resulted from his celebrated sojourn in Berlin in the early 1930s. The dust-jacket for *Mr Norris Changes Trains* is a *tour de force*: a grainy, soft-yellow background with the title and author in snake-like lettering, littered with symbols of Berlin life — kinky, long-legged boots, a whip, money, hammer and sickle, and most alarming of all, the swastika. Good copies of *Mr Norris* aren't easy to find today. Clean copies might cost around £40 without this jacket, and it's almost impossible to find the jacket in pristine condition simply because of the 'rough' nature of the paper used — it picks up dirt very easily. Acceptable copies with light rubbing and a little soiling could cost in the region of £150, possibly a little more.

The two sequels to this book, *Sally Bowles* (1937) and *Goodbye to Berlin*(1939) are rightly considered the classic novels of the period. Nowhere else is the decadence of Berlin in its death throes more accurately portrayed. Both titles were issued by the Hogarth Press. *Sally Bowles* is a small volume, issued in a rather dull typographic jacket designed by Richard Kennedy, later an accomplished book illustrator but then a junior member of the Woolfs' staff. This book is very scarce today, and notoriously difficult to find in an undamaged dust-jacket. *Goodbye to Berlin* on the other hand is somewhat more common — no doubt the success of the earlier titles prompted the Press to increase its initial print-run. Copies without their jackets sell for around £15 – £20. £60 – £80 might be a more reasonable price for a jacketed copy, but is hardly likely to be in fine condition for that price. Again, these prices are for copies with all the usual defects one would expect from a book of that age. These three titles were collected together in purple cloth and issued with a white and red jacket as *The Berlin of Sally Bowles* in 1975.

Another Hogarth volume was the brilliant *Lions and Shadows* (1938), one of his earliest heavily autobiographical titles which can be read as a novel or a straightforward reminiscence. All his friends are there; although they have been re-named. This title seems quite scarce today. Copies in their blue cloth boards with black lettering generally sell for around £20, but complete with their jackets showing a writer at a desk they could set the collector back at least £100 – £150. This represents an almost 100 per cent increase over the last few years, a princely safeguard against inflation.

Three plays and a non-fiction title written in collaboration with Auden are also collected by the poet's enthusiasts, and so fetch good prices on two separate fronts. *The Dog Beneath the Skin* (Faber, 1935), *The Ascent of F6* (Faber, 1936) and *On the Frontier* (Faber, 1938) all fetch good prices today (and seem hard to find in nice collectable condition), but much scarcer is their joint account of a trip to China taken during the Sino-Japanese War in 1938. *Journey to a War* appeared from Faber & Faber that same year, Isherwood's prose complementing Auden's verse perfectly. It is an impressive volume, made even more stirring by the fetching dust-jacket design reprinted as a frontispiece. Unadorned copies rarely fetch more than £10 – £15, but copies with clean, sound jackets rarely sell for less than £50 – £60.

Both Auden and Isherwood suffered the wrath of the British press when they left for America in the early years of the Second World War; they were commonly thought to have 'run away'. Despite that, both writers enjoyed a renaissance in their art, and Isherwood in particular continued writing classics from his new home in California right up until his death in 1986. From around the time of the war almost all his books were first issued in America, but British collectors tend to favour the first British editions of his work.

His early years in America were spent as a screenwriter in Hollywood (rather like Edgar Wallace, P.G. Wodehouse and numerous other Brits before and since), and considering the heavy autobiographical bias in his novels it's hardly surprising his first post-war novel was set around the film industry. *Prater Violet*, one of my favourite Isherwood titles, was published by Methuen in 1946, its cheap purple cloth boards and flimsy paper (it was another war-time volume) unfortunately prone to soiling or tears. The jacket is also rather scarce in fine condition, but nevertheless, the complete book rarely sells for more than £30.

In fact, few of Isherwood's post-war titles are hard to find — he really is a writer of two halves. Some of the post-war novels are disappointing, but *A Single Man* is a classic and a bargain for just £10 – £15. Incidentally, many of the jackets for these later titles were designed by Isherwood's long-term friend Don Bachardy. Much better works of art are his autobiographical titles *Kathleen and Frank* (his account of his parents' lives), *Christopher and His Kind* (a marvellous evocation of the boy's pranks in Berlin in the 1930s); and the two titles inspired by his conversion to eastern philosophy, *Ramakrishna and his Disciples* (Methuen, 1965) and *My Guru and his Disciple* (Eyre Methuen, 1980). First edition copies of these must have pristine jackets to be worth buying. Both will cost little more than £10. Some copies can be picked up for considerably less.

The only post-war title which will give collectors trouble is the American limited edition of *October*, a prose work published by the Twelvetrees Press in California in 1980. This was printed on hand-made paper, bound in leather, signed and priced at a phenomenal $400 on publication. Any collectors who bought this volume at that price will do their damnedest to make sure their copies keep their value, but they could be fighting a losing battle. Fine copies currently fetch around £250 on the open market, so these collectors seem to be keeping their head above water for the time being at least. The first (and only) British edition is also scarce. In 1982 Methuen issued just 1,000 paperback copies. These tend to sell for around £20 today.

Isherwood died in his Santa Monica home in 1986, and since his death there has been a marked increase in interest in his work from collectors. It's almost certain that this will continue in the coming years — good writing rarely goes out of fashion, particularly amongst discerning bibliophiles. It's a strange state of affairs for an author, when you consider that most of his work is now out of print.

Title	No dj	In dj
All the Conspirators novel (Jonathan Cape, 1928)	£50 – £60	£200 – £250
The Memorial novel (Hogarth Press, 1932)	£40 – £50	£150 – £200
Mr Norris Changes Trains novel (Hogarth Press, 1935)	£30 – £40	£120 – £150
The Dog Beneath the Skin play written with W.H. Auden (Faber, 1935)	£10 – £15	£40 – £50
The Ascent of F6 play written with W.H. Auden (Faber, 1936)	£10 – £15	£40 – £50
Sally Bowles novel (Hogarth Press, 1937)	£20 – £30	£80 – £100
On the Frontier play written with W.H. Auden (Faber, 1938)	£10 – £15	£40 – £50
Lions and Shadows non-fiction (Hogarth Press, 1938)	£20 – £30	£100 – £150
Goodbye to Berlin novel (Hogarth Press, 1939)	£15 – £20	£60 – £80
Journey to a War non-fiction written with W.H. Auden (Faber, 1938)	£10 – £15	£50 – £60
Prater Violet novel (Methuen, 1946)	£5 – £10	£20 – £30
The Condor and the Cows novel (Methuen, 1949)	£5 – £10	£20 – £25
The World in the Evening novel (Methuen, 1954)	–	£20 – £25
Down There on a Visit novel (Methuen, 1962)	–	£15 – £20
A Single Man novel (Methuen, 1964)	–	£10 – £15
Ramarkrishna and his Disciples non-fiction (Methuen, 1965)	–	£5 – £10
Exhumations essays, etc (Methuen, 1966)	–	£5 – £10

Title	No dj	In dj
A Meeting by the River novel (Methuen, 1967)	–	£10 – £15
Kathleen and Frank autobiography (Methuen, 1971)	–	£5 – £10
Christopher and His Kind autobiography (Eyre Methuen, 1977)	–	£5 – £10
My Guru and His Disciple non-fiction (Eyre Methuen, 1980)	–	£5 – £10
October prose (Twelvetrees Press, 1980) (Methuen, 1982)	£200 – £250 £15 – £20	n/a n/a
People One Ought to Know children's (Macmillan, 1982)	–	£4 – £6

P.D. JAMES

Since the heyday of Agatha Christie, several authors have been donned with, and probably doomed by, the description 'The New Queen of Crime'. Few have deserved it, as good as they might have been on their own merits. But P.D. James? She really is 'The New Queen of Crime': she has been for the past thirty years since the publication of her first novel and there's no reason to suggest this will change. She has also become as collectable as Agatha Christie although there's little chance that she will ever produce as many titles as her predecessor — eleven novels, two collections and one true crime title have appeared in the last thirty years. But this does mean that when a book appears it is worth waiting for.

Phyllis Dorothy James is a truly literary writer — she has developed the art of crime fiction into literature. Her thrillers are more than just thrillers, they are highly accomplished novels. They all share the attributes of quality literature: taut prose, depth, character development and finely recorded dialogue. Perhaps it is best to call them crime literature since they deserve their place on today's bookshelves, along with all the other big names in twentieth century literature. It was entirely appropriate that she entered the House of Lords early in 1991 as a life baronet for her services to literature and the civil service. It was a crowning point in her career and well deserved.

P.D. James was born on 3 August 1920 and attended Cambridge Girls School. Her most famous character is the poet-detective Adam Dalgliesh who appears in most of her titles and whose exploits have been the subject of a popular television dramatisation in recent years. P.D. James's other major creation is the young private investigator, Cordelia Gray.

P.D. James came to writing slowly. During the war she married a doctor who returned to peacetime life severely ill. She worked to support him and their two daughters. After a period as a hospital administrator, she entered the Home Office in 1968, working for the forensic science service before moving to the criminal policy department during the 1970s. No doubt it is this experience that accounts for the meticulous forensic detail she puts into her work. It was in the mid 1950s when she decided to write and this she did each day before going to work. The result was *Cover Her Face* (1962), a classical whodunnit centred around Sally Jupp and a murder in a large country house. It is impressive in its own right though the book and Dalgliesh show few hints of their amazing breadth in this tale.

Cover Her Face was published by Faber in 1962 and is extremely scarce in fine condition today. Bound in green cloth with traditional gold lettering, it was issued in an attractive cream-yellow dust-jacket designed by the talented and collectable Charles Mozley. The illustration shows the distinctive golden-red hair of Sally Jupp. P.D. James's dust-jackets have changed with fashion over the years, from the opaque softer coloured covers to the harsher laminated designs which are still impressive. All her books are aesthetically pleasing as well as intriguing to read. The price of *Cover Her Face* varies greatly: copies without the dust-jacket are all but worthless while truly fine copies in an excellent jacket could fetch up to

£400. In between are a range of values depending on the extent of nicks, rubbing, soiling and a myriad of other factors.

Charles Mozley is an accomplished artist who has illustrated numerous other books and has been responsible for many memorable dust-jackets. He designed the jacket for James's second novel, *A Mind to Murder* (1963) — another classical whodunnit. A few years ago, the fine pink jacket portraying Enid Bolam dying and clutching a grotesque wood carving would have ensured that the red cloth-bound book would fetch around £100. Today a good copy will sell for anything between £150 and £250, again depending on condition. This is probably the most attractive of all P.D. James's jackets so it is really important that your copy is in as good a state as possible.

Very few of these early titles turn up on bookshop shelves or in dealer's catalogues so you should really buy any copy as soon as you see it. It is so frustrating to 'sleep' on a potential big purchase of a scarce book, decide you want it after all and go back to the shop to find it was sold the minute you walked out. If you are ever offered nice copies of *Cover Her Face*, *A Mind to Murder*, and the next two titles *Unnatural Causes* and *Shroud for a Nightingale*, don't fool yourself. They are really worth snapping up even if the price seems a little steep at the time. A hundred or more spent on an early P.D. James is a good investment. *Unnatural Causes*, the first novel in which Dalgliesh really began to show signs of turning into that well-rounded human individual that James enthusiasts so admire, was bound in red cloth with silver lettering and was issued in a photographically illustrated jacket featuring a map of the Suffolk coast. It was off this coast that the handless corpse, which Dalgliesh was investigating, was found floating when the novel opens. *Shroud for a Nightingale*, a bigger volume and the first to break away from the uniformity of the previous Faber productions, was issued in a rather macabre jacket featuring a skull wearing a nurse's cap. I saw two copies of this on sale in London shops last year. One in a chipped jacket was on offer at £60 and the other better copy had an asking price of £150. I would think that the true value is somewhere between these extremes.

By this stage in her career, James had become a very popular author (although it is only in the past two or three years that the James phenomenon has really taken off) and the print-run of her books was significantly increased. This means, of course, that titles are much easier to find although some still fetch respectable prices. *An Unsuitable Job for a Woman*, the book which introduced Cordelia Gray, the young investigator who inherits Pryde's detective agency after the previous owner committed suicide, was bound in green cloth and issued in a green wrapper showing a noose in the foreground with Kings College Chapel to the rear. A few years ago this was selling for £20–£30 in pristine condition. Double that figure would be a better estimate today. £20–£30 would be a more accurate figure for P.D. James's 1975 title, *The Black Tower*, issued in an attractive jacket designed by Errol Le Cain. It really needs to be in immaculate condition to fetch this price, though, and such copies are by no means common. It is much easier to find less than perfect copies for around £10–£15.

Death of an Expert Witness, was a departure from the traditional detective novel and moved towards the bleak psychological thrillers so impressively written by her great rival, Ruth Rendell. P.D. James was reasonably successful here but not entirely so and many of her thousands of fervent enthusiasts were pleased to see her return to traditional detective fiction with *The Skull Beneath the Skin*, another appearance for Cordelia Gray. This heavy volume was issued in a purple dust-jacket designed by Pentagram and featuring a ghostly hand dripping freshly spilled blood. At the moment, fine copies can be obtained relatively easily.

The same can be said for P.D. James's most recent title, *A Taste for Death* (1986) and *Devices and Desires* (1989). Both these books are imposing volumes both physically and in content. Indeed they were submitted for consideration for the Booker Prize. Another interesting title is James's only non-fiction work, *The Maul and the Pear Tree*, jointly written with police historian T.A. Critchley. Just before Christmas 1811 seven people were brutally murdered in London's East End in what became known as the Ratcliffe Highway Murders. For a few weeks the community came close to hysteria and feelings of revulsion ran so high that the corpse of the alleged murderer was paraded at a busy crossroads with a stake hammered through its heart. However, as the book points out, it is unlikely that this was the real killer. This is one of the author's most interesting titles. It was published by Constable in 1971 and excellent copies sell for around £50 today. True crime books are becoming a very important part of crime literature especially in collectors' circles, so a true crime book by P.D. James is sure to sell for a good price.

Less collectable but worth a mention are two P.D. James omnibus volumes issued by Faber in 1982 and 1990. The first volume has a particularly attractive typographic jacket showing the three books it features: *An Unsuitable Job for a Woman, Shroud for a Nightingale* and *Unnatural Causes*. The latest volume features a photograph of the author on the front of the jacket.

This distinguished writer has been highly successful in many fields so it is hardly surprising that her output has been so small. She writes very slowly, largely because of the meticulous research and attention given to detail. She never lets her readers down and that's why she is so popular. You need to rush to buy first editions of her latest novels as they are published as both *A Taste for Death* and *Devices and Desires* were reprinted on the day of publication making those elusive firsts scarce almost from the first day of sale! It is measure of her collectability — a collectability which seems to grow each year. Apart from the sheer pleasure of reading her work, her books seem to be a sound investment as well.

Title	No dj	In dj
Cover Her Face novel (Faber & Faber, 1962)	£200 – £300	£300 – £400
A Mind to a Murder novel (Faber & Faber, 1963)	£150 – £200	£200 – £250
Unnatural Causes novel (Faber & Faber, 1967)	£100 – £150	£150 – £200
Shroud for a Nightingale novel (Faber & Faber, 1971)	£60 – £80	£100 – £120
The Maul and the Pear Tree non-fiction (Constable, 1971)	£20 – £30	£40 – £50
An Unsuitable Job for a Woman novel (Faber & Faber, 1972)	£30 – £40	£40 – £60
The Black Tower novel (Faber & Faber, 1975)	£10 – £15	£20 – £30
Death of an Expert Witness novel (Faber & Faber, 1977)	£5 – £10	£15 – £20
Innocent Blood novel (Faber & Faber, 1980)	£5 – £8	£10 – £15
P.D. James Omnibus (Faber & Faber, 1982)	£3 – £5	£5 – £10
The Skull Beneath the Skin novel (Faber & Faber, 1982)	£5 – £8	£10 – £15
A Taste for Death novel (Faber & Faber, 1986)	£5 – £8	£10 – £15
Devices and Desires novel (Faber & Faber, 1989)	£5 – £8	£10 – £15
The Second P.D. James Omnibus (Faber & Faber, 1990)	£3 – £5	£5 – £8
The Children of Men novel (Faber & Faber, 1992)	–	–

PHILIP LARKIN

Few poets seem to be among the top collectable authors today. Perhaps it is a sign of the twentieth century to disregard verse in favour of novels as the significant literary form. Modern masters like Eliot and Auden are collected of course, but the bibliographical complexities involved make it a daunting task. And anyway, I'm not entirely convinced that these authors are particularly read these days by anyone other than students and academics and a select band of literati. No such problems with Philip Larkin, though. Like Betjeman, Larkin is collected *and* read. When Larkin's *Collected Poems* was published by Faber in 1989 it went straight to the top of the best-seller lists, an almost unheard of event in the literary world and one achieved by few poets other than Byron and Betjeman.

Larkin produced very little but what he did write deserves the literary and commercial acclaim it has received. His work is accessible, readable, poignant and powerful. Larkin's life conforms to few people's idea of how a poet's life should be conducted — no Byron, Keats or Shelley he. Instead, most of Larkin's working life was spent as a librarian at Hull University. Like T.S. Eliot who worked as a clerk at Lloyd's Bank, Larkin seems to have needed a mundane everyday existence to inspire his poetic imagination. He was a true original, and the choice of many for Poet Laureateship when Sir John Betjeman died in 1984.

In many respects Larkin typifies the new poetry of the 1950s and 60s. His work is a reaction against the confused romanticism of Dylan Thomas and the naive political idealism of Auden, Spender and Cecil Day Lewis. Larkin is more than just a reaction, though. His work is original but as pastorally English as Edward Thomas, and as humorously and self-deprecatingly English as his own favourite, Betjeman.

Philip Larkin was born in Coventry in 1922, into a lower-middle class family. He won a scholarship to Oxford in the 1940s where he first met lifelong friends like Kingsley Amis and Bruce Montgomery; the latter went on to write some collectable detective novels under the name of Edmund Crispin. This wasn't the Oxford of Charles Ryder in *Brideshead Revisited* or Michael Fane in *Sinister Street*; this was a time when both clothes and food were rationed and when undergraduates lived under the shadow of conscription. These college days are vividly recaptured in Larkin's own *Jill*. It was at Oxford too that Larkin developed his long-term passion for jazz music.

Larkin began writing at Oxford. His first published work seems to have appeared in a collection entitled *Poetry from Oxford in Wartime*, and his inclusion attracted the attention of the Fortune Press who invited him to put together a collection of his work. This resulted in *The North Ship*, a slim volume of thirty-one poems which, despite being a first work, seems markedly mature and poignant today. The book was published in 1945 in the Fortune Poets series (which also included Amis's works), printed on hand-made paper bound in black cloth and issued in a maroon dust-jacket. This is exceedingly scarce today, and copies very rarely come up for sale in anything like fine condition. If you are lucky enough to find one, expect to pay up to £750. Beware though. In 1965, 500 pirated copies bearing 'first published in 1945' on the verso of the title page were issued before Larkin found out, and these are also collectable today, selling for up to £100. The main way to differentiate these from the true first is that these books were bound not in black cloth but in maroon cloth. In 1966, Larkin authorised a new Faber edition which contained an introduction by him plus one extra poem. Such is the scarcity of *The North Ship* that even these are collected avidly.

Larkin's next two books were both novels. *Jill* was begun under the creative stimulus of Bruce Montgomery at Oxford in the autumn of 1943 and finished a year later. It is a remarkable achievement for such a young writer, despite Larkin's disclaimer in his introduction to the Faber edition of 1964: 'It will, I hope, still qualify for the indulgence traditionally extended to juvenilia.' It was published by the Fortune Press in 1946 and, again, copies of the first are notoriously scarce in their jackets. They can cost up to £500. Last year a copy without a jacket was offered by one dealer for £100 and the year before, Larkin's signed presentation copy to Bruce Montgomery was offered for a princely £1,000 at a London Book Fair. It's interesting to note that when Kingsley Amis wrote to congratulate Larkin on the book's publication he added that its binding reminded him of *Signal Training: Telegraphy and Telephony*, or possibly *Ciceronis Orationes*. Later Amis reported he had seen a copy in a bookshop perched between *Naked and Unashamed* and *High-Heeled Yvonne*.

A Girl in Winter is equally scarce, despite being published by the more prominent Faber in the usual shabby, wartime economy standards of mottled, blue-green cloth in a jacket with the title in a circle. A copy in collectable condition might cost up to £400. A cheaper alternative is the second impression issued in a completely different (but more attractive) jacket featuring the picture of a girl holding an envelope. Even this can cost up to £50.

Despite receiving the respect of writers like John Wain and Amis, these first books were virtually ignored, and Larkin's immediate post-university years were spent in comparative obscurity as a university librarian in Belfast, Leicester and, finally, Hull. It wasn't until the publication of *The Less Deceived* in 1955, and the inclusion of his best verse in Robert Conquest's 'Movement' anthology *New Lines* a year later, that he really came to the public's attention in a significant way. Before that time, though, two extremely scarce collections of verse were issued. *XX Poems* (many of which reappeared in *The Less Deceived*) was privately printed in 1951. Only 100 copies were issued in wrappers (none for sale), and it's not rare for these to sell for around £800 – £1,000 when they do turn up in average condition. Lesser copies would be hard pressed to reach half that price. Then Larkin's work appeared as No. 21 in The Fantasy Poets series in 1954. Limited to a more accessible 300 copies, this collection could set the Larkin enthusiast back up to £400. Copies were issued without jackets, so at least collectors don't have to worry about that.

Given these high prices, it's rather good news perhaps that Larkin produced so little, although it is a relief to see that prices fall a little from this point on. True, copies of *The Less Deceived* complete with their attractive jackets invariably sell for up to £200, but both *The Whitsun Weddings* (Faber, 1964) and *High Windows*

(Faber, 1974) are easier to acquire, even with their jackets. *The Whitsun Weddings* might cost between £75 and £100, but it should be easy to find *High Windows* for £25 – £30. Both collections are slim volumes issued in Faber's traditional verse jackets.

By far the hardest item to find from this period is *The Explosion*, just one poem printed on a single broadsheet and published by the Poem of the Month club in 1970. This was limited to 1,000 signed copies, and it's not unknown for this to sell for up to £150, a huge sum for just one leaf! Much more affordable are the few volumes of prose Larkin issued towards the end of his life. *All that Jazz* (Faber, 1970), Larkin's record diary and a fascinating account of his passion for music, may be hard to find in fine condition, but *Required Writing* (Faber, 1983) seems in plentiful supply. Interestingly enough, this title was issued as a paperback original with a very large print run.

A last tip. Philip Larkin's *Collected Poems* published by Faber in 1989 could well become one of the most sought after books of the last few years. Not only does it contain much previously unpublished Larkin verse and was thus a literary event of the 1980s, but it seems to have had a reasonably low print-run. It was published at £13.95, but second-hand copies are already changing hands for up to £20. It wouldn't surprise me if the price went up much more than this in future.

Title	No dj	In dj
The North Ship verse (Fortune Press, 1945)	£100 – £150	£500 – £750
pirate edition, 1965	£30 – £40	£80 – £100
new edition with an extra poem, 1966	–	£20 – £30
Jill novel (Fortune Press, 1946)	£50 – £100	£400 – £500
A Girl in Winter novel (Faber, 1947)	£40 – £50	£300 – £400
XX Poems verse (privately printed, 1951) limited to 100 copies in wraps	£800 – £1,000	n/a
The Fantasy Poets No. 21 verse (Fantasy Press, 1954) limited to 300 copies	£300 – £400	n/a
The Less Deceived verse (Marvell Press, 1955)	£40 – £50	£150 – £200
The Whitsun Weddings verse (Faber, 1964)	£10 – £20	£75 – £100

Title	No dj	In dj
All That Jazz: A Record Diary prose (Faber, 1970)	–	£30 – £40
The Explosion (Poem of the Month Club, 1970) *limited to 1,000 signed copies issued as a broadsheet*	£100 – £150	n/a
High Windows verse (Faber, 1974)	–	£25 – £30
Larkin at Sixty (Faber, 1982) *tribute with contributions by Amis, etc*	–	£10 – £15
Required Writing prose (Faber, 1983)	£10 – £15	n/a
Collected Poems verse (Faber, 1989)	–	£10 – £20

LE CARRÉ AND LEN DEIGHTON

Although East and West seem to be coming closer together in these days of *glasnost* and *perestroika*, you can be sure that espionage continues unabated. Espionage and spying are age-old, of course, but only in the twentieth century have they been a major topic for fiction. William le Quex began the trend at the turn of the century and it has been carried on by numerous writers including Edgar Wallace, John Buchan, Sapper and Sydney Horler. In the 1950s the genre was glamourised by Ian Fleming's James Bond sagas. Today the undisputed kings of espionage thrillers are John le Carré and Len Deighton: two writers who have added literary credence to what was previously a rather lowbrow genre. Both these writer's works have become highly collectable, with le Carré's earliest volumes selling for just as much as early Flemings and, in some cases, for significantly more.

Both Len Deighton and John le Carré have only been in print for less than thirty years and they are excellent examples of how publishers have responded to collectors' and readers' demands by issuing huge first print-runs of their later books. While their early titles are very hard to find indeed, collectors will have no problems whatsoever putting together a collection of later works. And, of course, both writers are still working, so acquiring mint copies of new books is as easy as going to your nearest bookshop when a new title is published. Len Deighton usually holds book-signing sessions and inscribed copies of his latest titles aren't particularly rare whereas le Carré avoids the formal public book-signing function which adds value to any of his editions that are signed.

John le Carré is well-suited to write spy thrillers — like Ian Fleming, John Buchan, Somerset Maugham and Graham Greene he once worked in espionage himself: one reason why he used a pseudonym for his early novels and has continued to use one. He was born David John Moore Cornwell in Poole, Dorset in 1931 and educated at Sherborne School and Oxford University. After college he taught languages at Eton College for a short time before joining the Foreign Office. In the early 1960s he was second-secretary at the British Embassy in Bonn (when the Berlin Wall was built) and during this period he spent a lot of time in an intelligence capacity which obviously gave him an invaluable insight into the workings of the Secret Service. This was information which has been put to good effect in his novels, particularly those featuring his most famous creation, George Smiley.

Le Carré was working in Bonn when his first novel was published. *Call for the Dead* has recently become one of the most valuable trade-issued books published in the last few decades. It was published by Victor Gollancz in 1961 in plain red boards and had the standard yellow house-style jacket. It is not known for sure how many copies were printed but it is unlikely to have been higher than 3,000, if that. Copies are notoriously scarce today. I've never seen one myself but the few copies that do turn up at auction invariably reach £1,000 and I would expect them to be passed on to collectors for much more. Of course condition is all important.

Gollancz jackets fray easily and are prone to soiling, so finding truly fine copies is well-nigh impossible. Even so, a soiled copy might easily reach four figures. Copies without their jackets are hardly plentiful. A nice copy without a jacket would sell for £100 – £150 today.

Much of the above applies to *A Murder of Quality*, le Carré's second novel published by Gollancz in 1962. After the relative success of *Call for the Dead*, the print-run of this title was significantly higher but it still sells for many hundreds of pounds in good condition. I recently saw a slightly nicked copy in London on offer for £750. I went back a couple of weeks later and wasn't surprised to see that the book was gone. Le Carré's most famous work is obviously *The Spy Who Came in from the Cold*, in Graham Greene's opinion '. . . the best spy story I have ever read'. Made into a wonderful film starring Richard Burton, this novel really epitomises the cold-war suspense so marked at the time of writing (the Cuban Missile Crisis took place just a year before it was issued). Bibliographically it is an interesting title. Issued in green cloth boards by Gollancz, the small format octavo was issued with a red Gollancz-style jacket with the following promotional blurb printed proudly in a white block: 'This is, in our view, a novel of the first order — a terrible novel, of great actuality and high political import. It is also immensely thrilling.' And like other Gollancz titles, it featured a recommendation from a leading novelist of the day, in this case J.B. Priestly. Gollancz indulged in the practice of stopping the printing presses every thousand copies to announce a 'new impression', giving the effect of greater demand than actually occurred, thus if you have a copy of the 'seventeenth impression' it might not necessarily be just that. It is more likely to be the fourth or fifth. Gollancz did this with many novels including Amis's *Lucky Jim*.

From a collecting point of view, *The Spy Who Came in from the Cold* is an interesting title. Despite having a fairly high print-run, copies aren't that easy to acquire in very good condition. Although Gollancz used cheap paper and binding, copies in fine condition do turn up now and again and often sell for as much as £150. A more realistic price, though, would be £100 – £120 for a copy in a slightly chipped or soiled jacket — the white block on the front cover is invariably stained or marked in some way.

Le Carré collectors seem to spend just a few months acquiring the titles written after 1963 and the rest of their lives searching for these three early titles. The reason for this is quite simple. The phenomenal success of *The Spy Who Came in from the Cold*, when published in the USA, coupled with the fact that it won the Somerset Maugham Literary Award in 1963, firmly established le Carré's name and ensured that the print-runs for his subsequent novels were very high indeed. For this reason they are relatively easy to find at a reasonable price.

Le Carré's two Heinemann titles, *The Looking Glass War* and *A Small Town in Germany* might cost up to £15 but the others shouldn't set you back more than £10 each. Again, you must make sure you acquire only truly fine copies of these later titles; there is no excuse for settling for anything less. With *Call for the Dead*, *A Murder of Quality* and, to some extent, *The Spy Who Came in from the Cold* you will have to accept whatever is offered. A few years ago a first edition of the first title in a second impression dust-jacket was auctioned for a princely £560!

In the past few years, le Carré has been persuaded to issue a limited edition of his new novels simultaneously with the first edition. *A Perfect Spy* (1986), and *The Russia House* (1988) have both 'suffered' this fate. 250 copies of each have been rebound in special boards, signed and issued with a tissue jacket by London Limited Editions. These usually fetch about £40 – £50 when offered to collectors. Buy them if you see fit but personally I wouldn't add them to my own collection. The tissue jackets are nothing compared to Hodder & Stoughton's striking jacket designs for the trade editions although the relatively rare le Carré signature does have some significance.

Len Deighton too has this dichotomy of collectability between his early and later titles. In fact, his career has almost mirrored le Carré's although he has produced many more books on many other subjects, including travel, cookery and the Second World War. These won't interest us here. I maintain that collectors are interested in his thrillers in general, and the original Secret Files in particular.

Len Deighton was born in West London on 18 February 1929, and educated at Marylebone Grammar School, although much of his time there was disrupted by wartime evacuation. After two and a half years of National Service in the Royal Air Force, he studied at St Martin's School of Art and then on a scholarship at the Royal College of Art, where he was art editor and a contributor to *Ark*, the college journal. This training was to prove useful and following these six years of study, he worked for a year as a B.O.A.C. steward which gave him the opportunity to travel world-wide while he continued to draw and paint.

Len Deighton's first novel was *The Ipcress File*, another classic espionage title published by Hodder & Stoughton in 1962. Because only 4,000 copies were printed these are extremely hard to come by today and good copies sell for £100 – £150. This was the Secret File 1. Number 2 was *Horse Under Water*, 15,000 copies of which were published by Cape in 1963. Then 14,000 copies of *Funeral in Berlin* completed the trilogy, also in 1964. Right from the start Deighton was heavily involved in the design of his books. All his early books had jackets designed by his college friend Ray Hawkey and the Secret Files in particular have a pleasing uniformity. They're all based on a white background with heavy black and red lettering. *The Ipcress File* features a hand-gun lying next to an empty coffee cup; *Horse Under Water* features a skull and medal; and *Funeral in Berlin* a cachet of notes, tickets and other ephemera.

Another intriguing facet is the promotional material which was often included with these early titles. *Horse Under Water*, for instance, had a crossword loosely inserted (the clues are on the rear of the jacket), and this needs to be in place if the book is to realise its top price. *Funeral in Berlin* included a facsimile of Deighton's passport in an envelope although this was issued only to the book trade, so finding this might prove quite a problem today.

From this point on, Deighton's initial print-runs increased considerably. *Billion Dollar Brain* (1966, another Hawkey jacket) was issued in an edition of 25,000 copies and *An Expensive Place to Die* (1967) was issued in a coloured Hawkey jacket in an edition of 30,000 copies. This particular title was issued with a very effective 'Top Secret' buff wallet containing letters and documents dealing with

events which lead up to the start of the novel. They are essential to the plot so
they should be in place if you're going to spend up to £30 for a fine first edition.
Needless to say, all Deighton's books must have their jackets in place.

Another interesting title is *Only When I Larf* (1968), a humorous thriller. The
very first edition of this was a privately printed edition of only 150 copies bound
in a plastic binder. Then the first trade edition and first paperback edition were
issued simultaneously by Michael Joseph (9,000 copies) and Sphere (250,000
copies). Their relative scarcity is as might be expected.

Details of all Deighton's books can be found in *Len Deighton: An Annotated
Bibliography 1964–1985* by Edward Milward Oliver. This is a collectable title in its
own right. As well as including a 4,000-word interview with Deighton himself,
375 copies were signed, numbered by Deighton and inserted with a signed proof
page from *London Match* (1985), the last title in the Game, Set and Match trilogy.

Title	No dj	In dj
LE CARRÉ		
Call for the Dead novel (Gollancz, 1961)	£100 – £150	£1,000+
A Murder of Quality novel (Gollancz, 1962)	£75 – £100	£600 – £800
The Spy Who Came in from the Cold novel (Gollancz, 1963)	£10 – £15	£100 – £150
The Looking Glass War novel (Heinemann, 1965)	–	£15 – £20
A Small Town in Germany novel (Heinemann, 1968)	–	£15 – £20
The Naive and Sentimental Lover novel (Hodder & Stoughton, 1971)	–	£10 – £15
Tinker, Tailor, Soldier, Spy novel (Hodder & Stoughton, 1974)	–	£10 – £15
The Honourable Schoolboy novel (Hodder & Stoughton, 1977)	–	£8 – £10
Smiley's People novel (Hodder & Stoughton, 1980)	–	£8 – £10
The Little Drummer Girl novel (Hodder & Stoughton, 1983)	–	£8 – £10

Title	No dj	In dj
A Perfect Spy novel (Hodder & Stoughton, 1986) *London Limited Edition 250 signed copies*	– £40 – £50	£8 – £10 n/a
The Clandestine Muse *limited to 250 signed copies in wrappers*	£75 – £100	n/a
The Russia House novel (Hodder & Stoughton, 1988) *London Limited Edition 250 signed copies*	– £40 – £50	£8 – £10 n/a
A Secret Pilgrim novel (Hodder & Stoughton, 1991)	–	£5 – £10

LEN DEIGHTON

Title	No dj	In dj
The Ipcress File novel (Hodder & Stoughton, 1962)	£10 – £20	£100 – £150
Horse Under Water novel (Jonathan Cape, 1963) *Make sure the crossword is in place.*	–	£25 – £30
Funeral in Berlin novel (Jonathan Cape, 1964)	–	£15 – £20
Billion Dollar Brain novel (Jonathan Cape, 1966)	–	£15 – £20
An Expensive Place to Die novel (Jonathan Cape, 1967) *Again, make sure the special Top Secret wallet is in place.*	–	£25 – £30
Only When I Larf novel (Michael Joseph, 1968, hardback, Sphere, 1968, paperback) *Both issues preceded by limited edition of 150 copies in plastic spiral binding*	– £5 – £8 £100 – £120	£20 – £25 – n/a
Bomber novel (Jonathan Cape, 1970)	–	£10 – £15
Declarations of War short stories (Jonathan Cape, 1971)	–	£10 – £15
Close-Up novel (Jonathan Cape, 1972)	–	£10 – £15

Title	No dj	In dj
Spy Story novel (Jonathan Cape, 1974)	–	£8 – £10
Yesterday's Spy novel (Jonathan Cape, 1975)	–	£8 – £10
Twinkle, Twinkle, Little Spy novel (Jonathan Cape, 1976)	–	£8 – £10
SS–GB novel (Jonathan Cape, 1978)	–	£8 – £10
XPD novel (Hutchinson, 1981)	–	£8 – £10
Goodbye, Mickey Mouse novel (Hutchinson, 1982)	–	£8 – £10
Berlin Game novel (Hutchinson, 1983)	–	£5 – £8
Mexico Set novel (Hutchinson, 1984)	–	£5 – £8
London Match novel (Hutchinson, 1985)	–	£5 – £8
Game, Set and Match (Hutchinson, 1986) *trilogy of the three above*	–	£5 – £8
Spy Hook novel (Hutchinson, 1987)	–	£5 – £8
Spy Line novel (Hutchinson, 1988)	–	£5 – £8
Spy Sinker novel (Hutchinson, 1989)	–	£5 – £8
Hook, Line and Sinker (Hutchinson, 1990) *trilogy of the three above*	–	£5 – £8

A.A. MILNE

A.A. Milne's books featuring the adventures of Christopher Robin, Winnie the Pooh and friends are a delight to read as well as being highly collectable. It is less widely known that Milne wrote well over fifty novels, plays and stories for adults. However, like other authors noted mainly for their output for younger readers, for example, J.M. Barrie and his Peter Pan adventures, Milne's adult works can gather dust in second-hand bookshops, unwanted by collectors. To say this disappointed him would be an understatement, and there were times when he wished he had never invented the little fat bear, but it would have proved a sad loss to children's literature. Winnie the Pooh , and the enormous industry surrounding him, is here to stay.

Alan Alexander Milne was born in London on 18 January 1882. His father, John Vine Milne, was headmaster of his own, private boys' school, Henley House, where A.A. Milne was to be educated as a small boy. At an early age, Alan and his brother Ken wrote articles for *Chums* and *Boy's Own Paper*. Alan sent 'How to Make a Butterfly-net' to *Chums* but it was not accepted. However, it was not to be long before he saw his first poem in print. *The Lay of the Lazy Boy* written in 1892 appeared in the Henley House school magazine.

His writing continued after his scholarship to Westminster School, and he composed light verse and humorous prose for the school magazine. He disappointed his father by deciding to use the little money left over from his education, to make a serious attempt at freelance writing in London. After several unsuccessful attempts his first professional contribution was a parody of Sherlock Holmes, which appeared in *Vanity Fair* in October 1903. Milne's early career was aided by the distinguished author, H.G. Wells, who had taught him briefly at his father's school. Wells was always helpful, encouraging and full of friendly advice and the two corresponded for many years. However, Wells was not a publisher and Milne found it difficult to get his material accepted, until *Punch* started taking his work on his first book, *Lovers in London*. The book, based on writings for the *St James Gazette*, was published by the Alston Rivers Co., the company that also published P.G. Wodehouse's *The Swoop*, four years later. The book, priced at a shilling proved to be a literary embarrassment to its author. Indeed, Milne eventually bought the copyright for £5 to prevent a reprint. Consequently, *Lovers in London* is almost unheard of today.

After the failure of his first book, Milne decided to stop writing for *Punch* and to concentrate on constructing a 'proper novel'. The book, to be called *Philip's Wife* was never completed because early in 1906, A.A. Milne was appointed Assistant Editor of *Punch*. This was to take up the majority of his time and the only books by him to be published in the next ten years were collections of sketches and verse he had written for *Punch*. The remainder of his time was romantically spent and eventually he married the daughter of Hugh de Sélincourt. Daphne, usually known as Daff, also became his collaborator for the rest of his life.

It was not until 1917, when Hodder & Stoughton published his book *Once upon a Time* that Milne attempted anything substantial. The book, his first for children, was written in his home on the Isle of Wight. At Sandown Cottage, A.A. Milne would sit in front of the fire, dictating the story to his wife who sat pen in hand at the table. The book, full of kings and princesses, dragons and other strange animals was moderately successful, but had little acclaim until a new edition was issued in 1925, to 'cash-in' on Milne's success with *When We Were Very Young*. The original edition (1917) very rarely appears on the market and would cost £30 – £40 today. It would certainly have appeared in a dust-jacket although we can find no record of one for sale in recent years. The later edition should be less difficult to find. It was illustrated by the brother of Heath Robinson, Charles, as E.H. Shepard, who was originally approached, was too busy. (Milne had not liked the drawings of H.M. Brock who had illustrated the 1917 first edition.)

The years between this first children's publication and the arrival of *When We Were Very Young* saw an increase in Milne's popularity. After resigning his position at *Punch*, A.A. Milne put all his energy into writing plays, the most successful of which, *Mr Pim Passes By*, opened to rave reviews in London. By 1922, Milne's income ranged from £200 – £500 a week, a fortune at the time. The other notable event in this period, the birth of his only child, was to have a remarkable influence not only on his personal life but on his literary career.

Christopher Robin Milne was born on the morning of 21 August 1920. He was known immediately as 'Billy Moon' ('Moon' was a childish attempt to say 'Milne'), a name he was to keep for many years. When he was about three years old, A.A. Milne wrote the poem 'Vespers', a fairly cynical portrayal of childish egotism, and gave it to his wife as a present. As she was also allowed to keep any money it would earn, it turned out to be a very lavish gift indeed.

A few months later, Rose Fyleman asked Milne to contribute something for a new children's magazine entitled *The Merry Go Round*. He wrote *The Dormouse and the Doctor*, which she liked and soon she asked for further poems. So, during eleven rain-soaked days at a house party in North Wales, Milne wrote *When We Were Very Young*. Some of the verses were published in *Punch* with the illustrations of E.H. Shepard, a man who had little in common with Milne but who delighted him with his unique drawings.

When We Very Young was published on 6 November 1924 by Methuen. The publishers placed an order with the printers, Jarrold of Norwich, for 5,140 regular trade copies and a special edition of 110 copies (only 100 were for sale), on hand-made paper. The first impression sold out on publication day so a few days later they ordered printed endpapers with ten drawings of children by Shepard which were used in the second impression. The cream paper dust-jacket carries four figures on the corners of the front, Little Bo Peep and a bear now recognized as Pooh, and the titles and names in blue. The book, in blue cloth, has three gold figures on the front; one on the back and is dedicated to 'The Little Boy who calls himself Billy Moon'. It sold half a million copies in the first ten years following publication.

Price is greatly reflected by the condition (and to be fair, the dealer who is selling it!). If found in a clean wrapper with minimal wear, it could cost you as much as £1,200, but this figure could be considerably lower if the book is damaged in any way. It must be remembered that children do not treat their books with the reverence you would expect from an adult. The illustrations are often coloured in and the jacket occasionally torn, or thrown away. So premium copies are extremely scarce, hard to find and consequently very expensive. If found without a wrapper then do not despair. The book is still of real value. As the books were all of uniform design — same proportions, top edges gilt etc — with their gold figures on quality cloth, they make a handsome set even without wrappers. So a fine copy if found could still cost anywhere up to £300.

In the mid-twenties, Milne wrote a few fairy stories that appeared in periodicals, and also a series of sketches to accompany the illustrations of H. Willebeek le Mair, for a book entitled *A Gallery of Children*. The trade edition is very scarce and could cost as much as £80 – £120 while one of the limited edition of 500 copies signed by the author, may be three times as much. This volume will hardly be remembered, squashed as it is, between two of the most popular books of modern times.

Most collectors of books concerning Winnie the Pooh will always seek *When We Were Very Young*. Indeed many see this as the first of a quartet of 'Pooh' books, together with *Winnie the Pooh, Now We Are Six*, and *The House At Pooh Corner*. However, a year after his first collection of children's verses, Pooh was still a toy bear and definitely not the bear we know and love today. As a teddy bear he played a small part in *When We Were Very Young*, only making two minor appearances in the illustrations. It was not until Milne was asked to write a children's story for the Christmas edition of the *Evening News*, 1925, that *Winnie the Pooh* was even considered.

Milne was unhappy about what to write for the newspaper until his wife pleaded with him to use one of the two stories he told Christopher Robin at bedtime. So he sat down and started writing

This is Big Bear, coming downstairs . . .

and the rest is publishing history. The stories first appeared in the Evening News, with illustrations not by Shepard, but by J.H. Dowd. Winnie the Pooh, not quite looking himself, was on his way to becoming the most famous and loved bear in literature.

Winnie the Pooh was published on 14 October 1926 by Methuen at a price of 7s. 6d. (all the four books cost the same). Due to the success of *When We Were Very Young* the print-run was much higher. 32,000 copies were bound in dark green cloth, while another 3,000 were bound in red, blue or green leather and issued in a box. There were other limited editions aimed at the more affluent collector. The book had Christopher Robin and Pooh on the front in gold and Shepard's illustrations on the endpapers. The dustwrapper is yellow and shows Christopher Robin and the rabbits pulling Pooh out of a warren with the reverse view, so to speak, on the rear. The price is a good deal less than that of *When We Were Very Young* because of the more generous print-run. Nice clean copies in their wrappers should cost £250–300, while copies without their jackets, £80–100.

There was an annoying misprint in the first edition of *Winnie the Pooh*. At the end of Chapter VII, Milne had left 'his' instead of 'her' for Kanga, interestingly having started off thinking the kangaroo a father, in spite of the pouch.

The setting for Milne's delightful stories was around his own home, Cotchford Farm, and in particular the adjoining Ashdown Forest. It was here around the Five Hundred Acre Wood and Gills Lap that Christopher Robin, Pooh and the other animals had their adventures. Eeyore and Piglet were both toys in Christopher Robin's nursery while Milne invented Owl and Rabbit. The characters of Kanga and Roo were the result of a deliberate mission to Harrods by Milne and his wife, to look for more friends for Pooh. It must be remembered that none of these characters would have stuck in our memories for long without the simple but life-giving drawings of E.H. Shepard. It is his illustrations that decorate the books, pencil cases, rulers, calendars etc. that one sees in the shops today. *Winnie the Pooh* was based upon his own son Graham's bear, 'Growler' and not Christopher Robin's more famous teddy, bought by Milne for this first birthday, and the inspiration for the stories.

It may be interesting to explain that the actual name 'Winnie the Pooh' was derived from two sources: 'Winnie' came from a visit to London Zoo where an American Black Bear with that name was the star attraction. The origin of 'Pooh' is more uncertain. Milne explains, in the Introduction to *Winnie the Pooh*, that Christopher Robin once had a swan called 'Pooh'.

Milne's next book *Now We Are Six* — another collection of poems — was published on 13 October 1927. The poems were originally serialised in America, and written over a two year period. Following the success of his first book of children's poems, *Now We Are Six* was an instant hit. The first print-run of 50,000 trade editions sold immediately and by Christmas, just ten weeks later, 94,000 copies had been sold.

The maroon book with Christopher Robin on the front and Piglet and Pooh on the back had Shepard illustrations on the endpapers. The book in its light green dust-jacket will cost £150–200 today and £60–100 without the dust-jacket.

Although his fame and fortune were almost entirely linked to Pooh, A.A. Milne was coming quickly to the end of that relationship. He was adamant he would do no more poems, and told the world that Pooh would take his bow at the end of *The House At Pooh Corner*. His decision to stop was based around two major concerns. Firstly, Milne felt he should cease while the going was good and Winnie the Pooh's place in literature seemed assured. The second reason, and more distressing, was that Christopher was finding it increasingly difficult to come to terms with the fact that he was the Christopher Robin of his father's books. A.A. Milne was upset that his son was having more publicity than was good for him. He had become famous but not in his own chosen way. Other boys were taunting him at school and mocking him with recordings of 'Vespers', and other poems and stories. In his autobiography, *The Enchanted Places*, Christopher Milne writes of his desire to escape the burden of Christopher Robin, the little boy that never grows old, who follows him about and caused him so much misery. So *The House At Pooh Corner* was to be the last he would write of his son and Winnie the Pooh.

The first edition print-run for *The House At Pooh Corner* was 75,000, so copies of this and *Now We Are Six* should not be too difficult to find. However, the price will still be between £150–200 for the book in its pink cloth with Shepard's illustrations of all the characters on the endpapers. It is the longest of the four books, at over 175 pages, and can be found for £50–80 without the salmon coloured dust-wrapper.

There have been, of course, hundreds of 'spin-off' books published over the years. The most sought after of these is probably *The Christopher Robin Storybook*, which is reasonably cheap without its wrapper but very scarce with. The book, with its flimsy white dust-wrapper decorated with a green border with black crosses and colour illustrations of Pooh and friends, can cost between £150–200. It is, so it says, A.A. Milne's selection (more likely the publishers!) from the four books and is bound in blue cloth.

Two other books that may be of interest to collectors are, *The Christopher Robin Birthday Book*, a yearly volume with illustrations that first appeared in 1930, and a facsimile manuscript of *Winnie the Pooh*, nicely bound and in a slipcase. The latter, published in 1971 by Methuen can cost up to £75 and is quite difficult to find.

After the enormous success of the Pooh books, Milne was unable to reach the same literary heights ever again. It was even more distressing for him that he was to be known only as a writer of children's books. Indeed, his only real success after *The House At Pooh Corner*, was not to be one of his adult books, but an adaptation of Kenneth Grahame's classic *Wind in the Willows*. The play, *Toad of Toad Hall*, was written in 1921, eight years before it was published by Methuen. It was an instant success and soon established itself as a regular Christmas treat for children. Many critics saw it as classic entertainment for youngsters and it is the only play by Milne still regularly produced today. The book itself should not be too difficult to find in the £40–50 price range.

At the time of Milne's death in 1956, the worldwide sales of his children's books had reached seven million, while his books for adults were nearly all out of print. Pooh has been translated into all the major languages and animated by Walt Disney. To say that Milne was disappointed to be known solely for his children's books and in particular his 'Pooh' books would probably be an underestimate of his feelings, but that is what he will be remembered for — and what a memory to leave us!

Title	No dj	In dj

WINNIE THE POOH AND RELATED ITEMS

When We Were Very Young
verse (Methuen, 1924) Illustrated E.H. Shepard
limited edition of 100 numbered copies signed by
author and artist (Methuen, 1924)

	£250 – £300	£800 – £1,200
	–	£1,500 – £2,000

Winnie the Pooh
stories (Methuen, 1926) Illustrated E.H. Shepard
limited edition of 350 copies signed by author and artist
trade edition bound in red, green or blue leather,
with box
de-luxe edition of 20 copies printed on Japanese
vellum

	£80 – £100	£250 – £300
	–	£1,000 – £1,500
	£150 – £200	£400 – £500
	without box	
	–	£3,000 – £4,000

Now We Are Six
verse (Methuen, 1927) Illustrated E.H. Shepard
trade edition bound in red, blue or green leather,
with box
limited edition of 200 copies signed by author and artist
de-luxe edition of 20 copies printed on Japanese
vellum

	£60 – £100	£150 – £200
	£150 – £200	£300 – £400
	without box	
	–	£1,000 – £1,500
	–	£2,000 – £3,000

The House At Pooh Corner
stories (Methuen, 1928) Illustrated E.H. Shepard
trade edition bound in red, green or blue leather,
with box
limited edition of 350 copies signed by author and artist
de-luxe edition of 20 copies printed on Japanese
vellum

	£50 – £80	£150 – £200
	£150 – £200	£300 – £400
	without box	
	–	£1,000 – £1,500
	–	£2,000 – £3,000

The Christopher Robin Storybook
selection of verse/stories (Methuen, 1929)

	£20 – £30	£150 – £200

The Christopher Robin Birthday Book
series first published in 1930 (Methuen)

	–	£20 – £30

**Winnie the Pooh: A Reproduction of the Original
Manuscript** (Methuen, 1971)

	–	£50 – £75

OTHER CHILDREN'S BOOKS BY A.A. MILNE

Once Upon A Time
story (Hodder, 1917) Illustrated H.M. Brock
story (Hodder, 1925) Illustrated C. Robinson

	£30 – £40	n/a
	£10 – £15	£25 – £30

A Gallery of Children
stories (Stanley Paul, 1925) Illustrated H. Willebeek
le Mair
limited edition of 500 copies signed by the author

	£20 – £30	£80 – £120
	–	£350 – £500

Title	No dj	In dj
Toad of Toad Hall play (Methuen, 1929) *limited edition of 200 copies signed by Kenneth Grahame and A.A. Milne*	£15 – £20 –	£40 – £50 £350 – £500
The Ugly Duckling play (French 1941)	£10 – £15	–
Prince Rabbit and the Princess Who Could Not Laugh story (Ward 1966) Illustrated by E.H. Shepard	–	£15 – £20

IRIS MURDOCH

Many readers and critics regard Iris Murdoch as Britain's greatest living novelist, and few would dispute the claim. Others have gone so far as to suggest that when the history of twentieth century literature comes to be written, Iris Murdoch will share the stage with Virginia Woolf as the century's greatest woman novelist. She will also be seen as one of the most collectable. Despite the fact that she has been writing for nearly forty years, it is only in the last ten years that the collectors' interest has been aroused. This is good for those about to start their Iris Murdoch collections. While her first few novels are elusive and expensive, the vast majority of her output can be put together for relatively little outlay.

Irish Murdoch was born in Dublin in 1919. After an education at Somerville College, Oxford, she worked in the Treasury and at the United Nations Relief Administration for a few years. Subsequently, she lectured in Philosophy at Oxford and her first published book was a philosophical treatise: *Sartre, Romantic Rationalist*. This slim volume was published by Bowes & Bowes in 1953, and very good copies can sell for as much as £100 today. This is a phenomenal sum for a recent philosophical work. Iris Murdoch has published several such titles; indeed, in academic circles she is best-known for these works.

Of course collectors pursue these titles but they're keener to acquire first editions of her novels in as pristine a condition as possible. For her early titles this is not as easy as it sounds. Her scarcest title is, predictably, her first novel published by Chatto & Windus in 1954. *Under the Net* was an outstanding debut, an 'Angry Young Man' novel rather similar to Kingsley Amis's *Lucky Jim*. Like all first novels the print-run was small (no more than 2,000 copies), so fine copies complete with their dust-jackets can be very hard to find — many copies were sent to public libraries. When suitable copies do come onto the market they command premium prices, rarely selling for less than £200, and often changing hands for considerably more. As you would expect from a contemporary author, copies of their books without the jackets (regardless of condition) are very hard to sell. I've known one dealer to have a jacket-less copy on his shelves for many months, despite an £8 price tag. In almost all respects, Iris Murdoch is a classic modern first edition author with a sizeable output, much of which is affordable except the first few titles, and all of which are virtually worthless (from a collector's point of view) in anything less than very good condition with jacket.

Iris Murdoch's next two novels (all her titles have been published by Chatto & Windus) appeared in 1956 and 1957, and both confirmed her status as a versatile, promising young author. As its title suggests, *Flight from the Enchanter* contains elements of fantasy, while *The Sandcastle* was her first attempt at a more traditional narrative, although some have found it rather complicated. Whatever their literary merits, both titles are eagerly sought after and the places reserved on collectors' shelves for them can remain unfilled for a long time. Nevertheless, it is still possible to acquire nice copies for between £100 and £150.

From this time on, the initial print-runs of Murdoch's novels increased. This might mean lower prices for collectors but it also means that collectors must be much choosier when they buy their copies. Tatty copies of *The Bell* (1958) and *A Severed Head* (1961) might seem good buys at the time, but they're not — at any price! The message can't be repeated often enough. Even if you can't afford it, buy the very best specimen you are offered — you won't regret it. It's worth spending up to £75 for *The Bell* and up to £50 for *A Severed Head* for truly fine copies (rather than half that sum for tatty copies) because they will keep and even increase their value in due course. Most dealers agree that even at these prices, Iris Murdoch is rather undervalued. A word of warning about *The Bell*, though. Some cheaper copies seen on booksellers' shelves look identical in every respect to the trade edition but they are Book Society Editions, a fact only discovered on the verso of the title page because, even on the spine, the publisher is given as Chatto & Windus. And despite being virtually identical, so many copies were printed that they are all but worthless. Illogical, of course, but what has logic to do with passion?

Despite their obvious literary worth, one of the attractions of collecting Irish Murdoch's novels is their colourful and attractive dust-jackets. Chatto & Windus prided themselves on their jacket designs (with good reason), and their choice of artists for Murdoch's titles is little less than inspired. Artists like Tom Phillips, John Sutcliffe, John Sergeant and particularly Reynolds Stone have managed to produce covers which vividly convey the essence of the novel they adorn. My personal favourite is Reynolds Stone's jacket design for her 1964 novel, *The Italian Girl* (possibly her greatest novel too) but no doubt fellow Murdochians will have other views. Whatever the case, a complete set of these jackets ranged chronologically on the shelf is a wonderful sight, particularly if the jackets are as bright as the day they were printed. Dealers certainly know this. Last year one bookseller offered a complete set of Murdoch's novels, all in at least very good to fine condition, for over £2,000. Each book was signed by the author.

Reynolds Stone, a superb illustrator, was a close friend of Murdoch's and when he died in 1979 Murdoch produced *Reynolds Stone: A Memorial Address*. This is one of her scarcest titles today. Only 750 copies were published (300 of which were signed) by the prestigious Warren Editions in 1981 and fine specimens sell for at least £50 and £100 respectively today. Thankfully for collectors, Iris Murdoch has only one other title in limited edition format, although 100 copies of *The Book and the Brotherhood* were ripped out of their boards, rebound with a tissue jacket in place of the attractive one designed by Tom Phillips and offered at three times the published price by London Editions. I'm sure most collectors will happily settle for the ordinary, humble trade edition. The other scarcity is *A Year of Birds*, Iris Murdoch's only collection of verse published by Compton Press in 1978. This is a beautiful slim volume limited to just 350 copies, each numbered and signed by the author and Reynolds Stone, who provided the illustrations. Once again, very fine copies sell for at least £100, and most seem to have found their way into private collections already.

Many believe Irish Murdoch's very best work came in the 1960s and 1970s, and a run through the titles certainly adds weight to this opinion. These years saw the publication of, among others, *The Time of the Angels* (1966), *Bruno's Dream* (1969), *A Fairly Honourable Defeat* (1970), *An Accidental Man* (1971), *The Sacred and Profane Love Machine* (1974), *A Word Child* (1975), and *The Sea, The Sea* (1978), the novel which won the Booker Prize. It's hard to believe that classic titles like these can be picked up for as little as £10–£25 in almost pristine condition, or to think of an author who represents better value at the moment. But again, anything other than fine copies are really not worth buying — they would be a waste of money.

Mention has already been made of *Satre: Romantic Rationalist*; but that is just one of five philosophical books Murdoch has written. Only completists pursue these books but, because the print-runs of these are considerably lower than for the novels, they usually fetch very good prices indeed. *The Sovereignty of Good* (Cambridge University Press 1967) is a slim pamphlet which is hard to find today but it was reissued in hard covers and dust-jacket with other essays by Routledge in 1971. Also collectable are *The Fire and the Sun* (1977) and *Acastos*, although the latter should be quite easy to find.

Much scarcer are the plays Murdoch has written. In 1964 she wrote a play version of *A Severed Head* with author J.B. Priestley, but more sought after is her dramatic version of *The Italian Girl*, produced in collaboration with James Saunders in 1969. Published by Samuel French, fine copies can sell for as much as £75 today, significantly more than any of her novels from around the same period. Once again, the simple reason is a lower print-run.

Iris Murdoch's later novels can be picked up in pristine condition for little more than their published price, and they are well worth acquiring. With every new title she produces, her reputation as a leading intellectual writer grows, and it is thoroughly deserved. Murdoch is a novelist to read and read again; a truly great talent whose work will outlive that of many of her contemporaries. Gather your collection together now, while her books are still affordable. You will regret it if you don't!

Title	No dj	In dj
Sartre: Romantic Rationalist philosophy (Bowes & Bowes, 1953)	£10 – £15	£100+
Under the Net novel (Chatto & Windus, 1954)	£8 – £10	£200 – £250
The Flight from the Enchanter novel (Chatto & Windus, 1956)	£8 – £10	£100 – £150
The Sandcastle novel (Chatto & Windus, 1957)	£8 – £10	£100 – £150

Title	No dj	In dj
The Bell novel (Chatto & Windus, 1958)	£8 – £10	£50 – £75
A Severed Head novel (Chatto & Windus, 1961)	£5 – £8	£40 – £50
An Unofficial Rose novel (Chatto & Windus, 1962)	£5 – £8	£20 – £30
The Unicorn novel (Chatto & Windus, 1963)	–	£20 – £25
The Italian Girl novel (Chatto & Windus, 1964	–	£20 – £25
A Severed Head play written in collaboration with J.B. Priestley (Chatto & Windus, 1964)	–	£20 – £30
The Red and the Green novel (Chatto & Windus, 1965	–	£15 – £20
The Time of the Angels novel (Chatto & Windus, 1966	–	£15 – £20
The Sovereignty of Good philosophy (Cambridge University Press, 1967)	£20 – £40	n/a
The Nice and the Good novel (Chatto & Windus, 1968)	–	£15 – £20
Bruno's Dream novel (Chatto & Windus, 1969)	–	£15 – £20
The Italian Girl play written in collaboration with James Saunders (Samuel French, 1969)	£40 – £50	n/a
A Fairly Honourable Defeat novel (Chatto & Windus, 1970)	–	£15 – £20
The Sovereignty of Good philosophy (Routledge, 1971)	£5 – £10	£30 – £50
An Accidental Man novel (Chatto & Windus, 1971)	–	£15 – £20
The Black Prince novel (Chatto & Windus, 1973)	–	£15 – £20

Title	No dj	In dj
The Three Arrows and **The Servants and the Snow** novel (Chatto & Windus, 1973)	£10 – £15	£50 – £75
The Sacred and Profane Love Machine novel (Chatto & Windus, 1974)	–	£15 – £20
A Word Child novel (Chatto & Windus, 1975)	–	£15 – £20
Henry and Cato novel (Chatto & Windus, 1976)	–	£15 – £20
The Fire and the Sun — Why Plato Banished the Artists philosophy (Oxford University Press, 1977)	£5 – £10	£30 – £40
The Sea, The Sea novel (Chatto & Windus, 1978)	–	£15 – £20
A Year of Birds verse (Compton Press, 1978) *limited to 350 signed copies*	£50 – £75	£100+
Nuns and Soldiers novel (Chatto & Windus, 1980)	–	£10 – £15
Reynolds Stone memorial address (Warren Editions, 1981) *limited to 750 copies, 300 of which are signed*	£50 – £100+	n/a
The Philosopher's Pupil novel (Chatto & Windus, 1983)	–	£10 – £15
The Good Apprentice novel (Chatto & Windus, 1985)	–	£10 – £15
Acastos philosophy (Chatto & Windus, 1986)	–	£10 – £15
The Book and the Brotherhood novel (Chatto & Windus, 1987)	–	£10 – £15
The Message to the Planet novel (Chatto & Windus, 1989)	–	£10 – £15
The Existentialist Political Myth philosophy (Delos Press, 1989) *limited to 225 copies in paper wrappers, issued in blue* *slip-case: nos 1–45 signed by author* *nos 46–225 unsigned*	£75+ £20 – £30	n/a n/a

GEORGE ORWELL

There is a wonderful story about a George Orwell collector who was so determined to keep his precious first editions with dust-jackets in pristine condition, that instead of putting them on his shelves, he kept them in cardboard boxes. Only the privileged few were allowed a peek at the books, but *nobody* was allowed to touch them. One day a new girlfriend decided that the ugly boxes were cluttering up the place — and gave them to the dustmen. They were all destroyed by the dustcart's grinding mechanism. What became of the girlfriend is not recorded.

It's easy to understand the poor collector's feelings. Nobody likes to lose beloved books; even worthless paperback reprints which haven't been touched for years, but to have boxes of books in some instances literally worth their weight in gold *given* away by a loved one. . . . Your heart must go out to him. George Orwell wasn't a man to inspire much passion and devotion but his books certainly are. First editions with dust-jackets of most of his books (particularly his earliest titles) are of legendary scarcity in the book collecting world; so few early jackets are ever seen today. George Orwell is a big name in the book collecting world, and not just for his two most famous satires, *Animal Farm* and *Nineteen Eighty-Four*. He was first and foremost a journalist who wrote political satires in the manner of Jonathan Swift. Most of his books were social commentary and the novels he wrote were based on his experiences as a social observer. In fact, he had little time for the novelist's aesthetic life lived by many of his contemporaries from Eton. He made little money from his works. For most of his life his writing earned him little more than sixty shillings a week. This is quite remarkable, particularly as sales of *Nineteen Eighty-Four* alone have reached nearly thirty million copies.

He was born Eric Arthur Blair on 28 June 1903, in Motihari, India, where his father was employed selling opium, then quite legally, to China. After leaving Eton College (where his contemporaries included Anthony Powell, Cyril Connolly, Harold Acton and Henry Green), he joined the Indian Imperial Police but on leave in England in 1927, he decided not to return to Burma where he was stationed. Instead he spent five years wandering through England and France, gathering material for what eventually became *Down and Out in Paris and London*. This volume is one of the scarcest titles of the twentieth century and copies in a clean dust-jacket are seen just once or twice in a lifetime. It was published by Victor Gollancz (who chose the Orwell pseudonym) in 1933, a compact volume issued in Gollancz's traditional yellow dust-jacket. As usual with Gollancz volumes, the publisher's blurb was on the front cover. 'This is, in our view, an extremely forceful and socially important document. The picture drawn by the author is completely convincing; and though it is quite terrible (as, of course, it is meant to be) it holds the attention more closely than do 90 per cent of novels.' The book was priced at 8*s*. 6*d*. A first edition in a clean bright dust-jacket will cost closer to £2,000 today. Because the jacket is prone to soiling, even bare copies sell for large sums; around £200–£300 for a tight, bright copy.

Orwell's next three books were all novels, although the theme of *Down and Out in Paris and London* — the ordinary lives of the poor and destitute — is apparent in two of them, *A Clergyman's Daughter* and *Keep the Aspidistra Flying*. The other novel was *Burmese Days*, a no-punches-pulled account of his days in Burma which Gollancz had originally declined to publish, fearing libel action. These titles represent a huge challenge to Orwell collectors and most collectors seem to make do with copies without their jackets, since they so rarely turn up. Even so, each book sells for around £100–£200 and the presence of a clean, complete jacket will increase these values substantially. One begins to appreciate that Orwell enthusiast's grief just a bit more. . . .

George Orwell's next book is probably his easiest to acquire. During the 1930s, Orwell made ends meet by writing articles for various periodicals and on one assignment he visited the North of England which, at the time, was suffering unemployment and depression on a huge scale. The books of his observations, *The Road to Wigan Pier*, was published in Gollancz's famous Left Book Club series in 1937, their successful and influential run of socialist titles which at one time boasted 100,000 subscribers. Because Gollancz wanted to keep the prices of these volumes low, print-runs were high and the books were issued in soft orange wrappers. Genuinely fine copies are hard to come by now, but worn copies with broken spines or frayed covers can be picked up quite cheaply. Later in 1937 Gollancz issued a hardback edition — don't be confused into thinking this is the first.

When the Spanish Civil War broke out in 1936, Orwell went to the area as a freelance journalist, but soon decided to join a small Marxist unit which eventually ended up fighting not only Franco's fascists but also the communists. This experience changed his outlook politically: from then on he wasn't against communism or fascism but against both. To him both were different shades of the same ill: totalitarian authority. Most of his later books dealt with this theme. Orwell's account of his Spanish Civil War experiences (during which he was shot through the throat and narrowly missed being rounded up in the purges) was published in *Homage to Catalonia* (Gollancz, 1938). The dust-jacket for this is particularly attractive, featuring a clenched fist held aloft against a bombed-out building. Few copies survive with this jacket today. Those that do can cost £400–£600, while copies without the jacket seem good value at £50–£100. The reason *Homage to Catalonia* seems to be a little more common in collectable condition is that very few copies were actually sold. After his death many copies lay gathering dust in Gollancz's warehouses.

No collection of modern fiction is complete without copies of Orwell's two famous political satires, *Animal Farm* and *Nineteen Eighty-Four*. *Animal Farm* is the story of the Russian Revolution and its aftermath of political tyranny told allegorically through an animal uprising on a farm. It was rejected by Gollancz, Jonathan Cape and Faber before Secker & Warburg reluctantly published it just two weeks after the Americans bombed Hiroshima in 1945. Despite the problems around publication — Frederick Warburg's pro-Rusian wife threatened to leave him if he handled the title — the 4,500 print-run sold out immediately. Orwell's most pessimistic book to date was also his most successful and so far has been translated into thirty-six languages. It was as if the peace and news of the concentration camps sharpened people's awareness of the excesses of totalitarianism. First editions of *Animal Farm* were printed on thin paper, poor quality boards and issued in a rather plain, two-tone, grey-green dust-jacket. Many surviving copies seem prone to warping, and the few dust-jackets still in circulation are invariably torn. If you come across a genuinely good clean copy with the jacket, expect to pay around £200 for it.

Nineteen Eighty-Four is another interesting title bibliographically. 25,000 copies bound in green cloth were published by Secker & Warburg on 6 June 1949, but there is an interesting variant with dust-jackets. Most copies were issued with a dark green jacket, but a few (probably no more than 1,000) were issued with a salmon pink jacket. It's uncertain which preceded which, but as the salmon variant is by far the scarcer this can sell for up to £1,500. Copies in the green jackets rarely sell for more than £100–£200. An important point to remember with *Nineteen Eighty-Four* is that because strong solid colours were used, they are prone to fading, and any crease tends to break up the colour leaving an unattractive cracked appearance. This can drastically affect the value of the book. Copies of the book without their jackets are in plentiful supply and should be avoided.

In his essays George Orwell covered almost every aspect of modern living, from modern murders to the cartoons of Donald McGill, and from boys' magazines to executions by hanging. Orwell published several collections of essays but by far the hardest to acquire is *Inside the Whale* (Gollancz, 1940). It is not uncommon for copies complete with their jackets to be sold for up to £300, and even bare copies are hardly plentiful. Collectors can take solace from the fact that all Orwell's essays and articles were collected together and published in four volumes in 1968 — these are easily obtainable.

Two intriguing Orwell books are *The English People*, the hundredth title in Collins's rousing *Britain in Pictures* series, and *James Burnham and the Managerial Revolution*. The former was issued in the usual B.I.P. format: inferior paper, large format boards and similarly designed jacket. The latter is an intriguing pamphlet issued in wrappers by the Socialist Book Centre in 1946. Few Orwell enthusiasts have even heard of this title so bargains can be had I'm sure, although I've heard of one copy being sold for £160! It seems dealers are aware of this particular little volume.

By the time *Nineteen Eighty-Four* appeared to critical acclaim, its author was at a sanatorium in Gloucestershire, trying unsuccessfully to defeat the tuberculosis which had ravaged him over the previous few years. Just as his health seemed to be improving and he was planning to go to Switzerland with his new wife, Sonia Brownell (who worked as an editorial secretary at *Horizon*), he suffered a haemorrhage and died. He left behind him a growing reputation as perhaps Britain's greatest political and satirical writer of the twentieth century, and two novels which would sell millions of copies throughout the world. He also left an entire *oeuvre* of extraordinarily collectable books.

Title	No dj	In dj
Down and Out in Paris and London non-fiction (Gollancz, 1933)	£200 – £300	£1,500 – £2,000
Burmese Days novel (Gollancz, 1935)	£100 – £200	£400 – £600
A Clergyman's Daughter novel (Gollancz, 1935)	£100 – £200	£400 – £600
Keep the Aspidistra Flying novel (Gollancz, 1936)	£100 – £200	£400 – £600
The Road to Wigan Pier non-fiction (Gollancz, 1937)	£20 – £30	n/a
Homage to Catalonia non-fiction (Gollancz, 1938)	£50 – £100	£400 – £600
Coming Up For Air novel (Gollancz, 1939)	£50 – £100	£300 – £500
Inside the Whale essays (Gollancz, 1940)	£40 – £60	£200 – £300
The Lion and the Unicorn non-fiction (Secker & Warburg, 1941) *Searchlight Book No. 1*	£15 – £20	£40 – £50
Animal Farm novella (Secker & Warburg, 1945)	£10 – £20	£150 – £200
Critical Essays (Secker & Warburg, 1946)	£10 – £20	£40 – £50
James Burnham and the Managerial Revolution polemical (Socialist Book Centre, 1946)	£100 – £150	n/a
The English People non-fiction (Collins, 1947)	£5 – £10	£20 – £30
British Pamphleteers non-fiction (Allan Wingate, 1948)	£5 – £10	£20 – £30
Nineteen Eighty-Four novel (Secker & Warburg, 1949) *green dust-jacket*	£30 – £40	£100 – £200
salmon pink dust-jacket	£30 – £40	£1,000 – £1,500
Shooting an Elephant essays (Secker & Warburg, 1950)	£10 – £15	£30 – £40

Title	No dj	In dj
England, Your England essays (Secker & Warburg, 1953)	£5 – £10	£20 – £30
Collected Essays (Secker & Warburg, 1961)	–	£15 – £20
Decline of the English Murder essays (Secker & Warburg, 1965)	–	£10 – £20
Collected Essays, Journalism and Letters (Secker & Warburg, 1968) *four volumes*	–	£40 – £50
The War Broadcasts (BBC/Duckworth, 1985)	–	£5 – £10
The War Commentaries (BBC/Duckworth, 1985)	–	£5 – £10

ANTHONY POWELL

Anthony Powell is amongst the best writers Britain has produced this century and his mammoth *Dance to the Music of Time*, a sequence of twelve novels, is generally considered to be an important contribution to English literature, on a par with his old friend Evelyn Waugh's *Sword of Honour* trilogy. And is he collectable! Not only is a complete set of the Powell sequence in their original dust-jackets an extremely desirable set of books to have but copies of his less important but extremely scarce pre-war books fetch huge sums today. See the price guide that follows.

Powell's work is collectable as well as being great literature; not always the case in the world of modern first editions. His books are unlikely to go out of fashion, which means they are unlikely to decrease in value in the future. Don't be put off by the price of the first one or two books in *The Dance to the Music of Time* series — invest in as good a set as possible now, before they go through the roof. Occasionally complete sets in their jackets do come up for auction, but these ready-made sets take the fun out of the pursuit and anyway, you really do have to pay through the nose for them. Complete sets invariably sell for up to £1,000 — much more than a set assembled individually over the years. A couple of years ago a complete set of first editions was offered at a London Book Fair for £1,800. This seems a ludicrous price to me, particularly as they didn't have their jackets intact. In fact, they didn't even have their original boards. They were torn apart and replaced in full morocco. Fine bindings are all very well for eighteenth-century volumes, but for a set of books, the last of which was issued in the mid-1970s? The world has gone mad. I wonder if they were sold?

In many ways Anthony Powell is the Grand Old Man of Engish Letters. He was born Anthony Dymoke Powell in December 1905, and in many ways his life has run along the same lines as many of his literary characters. After the obligatory schooling at Eton (where he was a founder member of the Eton Arts Society run by Harold Acton and Brian Howard and which was later immortalised in Henry Green's *Blindness* in 1926), he went to Balliol College, Oxford. Here he met many of the major literary figures of this century, including Evelyn Waugh, Cyril Connolly, Peter Quennell and Graham Greene. Rarely have so many literary figures been at college at the same time — it was a fascinating period for literary historians.

After college Powell went to work for the publishers Duckworth who also published his first four books, *Afternoon Men* (1931), *Venusberg* (1932), *From a View to a Death* (1933) and *Agents and Patients* (1936). These are all extremely scarce today, and almost impossible to find in their dust-jackets, but keep trying because they do turn up occasionally. Without its jacket, *Afternoon Men* can be found for around £50; this can increase to around £800–£1,000 for a nice copy in its jacket. *Agents and Patients* is probably the most impressive work of this early period. Copies without their jackets sell for £30–£40 today. Because copies in their attractive white jacket (featuring a puppet over a hoard of people) are so rare, it's really difficult to give an accurate valuation. Given the right conditions it might be possible for nice copies to reach four figures. All I can do here is record the fact that in 1988 a copy in a soiled dust-jacket was offered by one dealer for £650.

Another very scarce title from this period is Anthony Powell's only attempt at verse, the privately printed *Caledonia: A Fragment* (1934). A hundred copies of this little book were produced so they are notoriously hard to come by today. No copy has been offered for auction recently. If one were to turn up I wouldn't expect it to reach the levels of Spender's *Nine Experiments*, but it would sell for between £1,000–£2,000. It's possible too that it could be worth many times that.

Powell's literary career was interrupted by the war in 1939, during which he served in the Welsh Regiment until 1941 before becoming a major in the Army Intelligence Corps. He was decorated on many occasions. Back in civilian life he produced two books about the 17th century biographer John Aubrey and then he embarked on the ambitious *Dance to the Music of Time* sequence. It is hard to think of a more important post-war literary work than this veritable *tour de force*. The work views the changes in the lives and fortunes of the English upper-middle-classes over a period of fifty years. The twelve volumes should be read in order if the best is to be got from them. If you don't, the 500 or so characters in the 3,000 pages tend to become blurred and you don't know where you are! In 1977 the literary critic and biographer Hilary Spurling produced an extremely useful *Handbook to Anthony Powell's Music of Time* with an introduction by Powell himself. This is certainly helpful.

The first book in the series was *A Question of Upbringing*, published by Heinemann in 1951: a small octavo volume bound in red cloth with a black label on the spine. This is becoming increasingly scarce today. Nice copies in their dust-jacket featuring the title in large freehand letters and a small motif of typical public school ephemera, can sell for as much as £300 today. All *The Dance to the Music of Time* novels need to be in their jackets if they are to be collectable. Only this first volume is worth anything without its jacket — £10–£20.

These dust-jackets are an integral part of the series. They were all designed by Broome Lynne in a uniform style, and are among the highlights of post-war jacket design. The next two volumes, *A Buyer's Market* (Heinemann, 1952) and *The Acceptance World* (Heinemann, 1955) are both scarce, selling for up to £150 and £100 respectively. A couple of years ago a copy of the first edition of *A Buyer's Market* in a chipped dust-jacket from the third impression was offered for a princely £80. The good news for Powell collectors is that if these titles are just beyond your means later impressions were invariably issued in an identical format with the same jackets as the firsts. Buy these for the time being if you can't afford the originals.

As the saga progresses, from *At Lady Molly's* (1957) onward, first editions become increasingly easy to find although it should be pointed out that the later the title the more important condition becomes. Copies of *Casanova's Chinese Restaurant* (1960) and *The Kindly Ones* (1962) in poor jackets or with soiled boards hardly represent a bargain at any price. Hold out until you can locate genuinely fine copies in good jackets. You'll regret it if you don't. Only the very best copies will appreciate in value. The implication of saying that later copies are progressively easier to find is slightly misleading. A few years ago it seemed that first editions of later volumes like *Books Do Furnish a Room* (1971), *Temporary Kings* (1973) and *Hearing Secret Harmonies* (1975) were all over the place; today acceptable copies seem alarmingly scarce. It seems to be harder each day to find acceptable copies for under £30.

Important as this sequence is, it isn't the only work Anthony Powell has produced since the Second World War. His two most recent novels, *O, How the Wheel Becomes It* (Heinemann, 1983) and *The Fisher King* (Heinemann, 1985) have their admirers and sell for up to £20 in excellent condition, but without doubt his best recent work has been the four volumes of autobiography published between 1976 and 1982. *Infants of the Spring, Messengers of Day, Faces in My Time* and *The Strangers Are All Gone* are an admirable evocation of one of the most exciting periods in English literary history. They represent good reading for anybody interested in the period and they could turn out to be Anthony Powell bargains. At the moment, fine copies of each book can be picked up for modest prices. It's highly likely they will rise significantly in the future.

The same can be said of all Powell's books, in fact. They aren't particularly cheap today (even a collection of two plays published in 1971 fetches up to £30) but then they weren't a couple of years ago and they have shot up in value since then. All the signs are that these books will continue to rise in value so do make sure you acquire the best possible copies.

Title	No dj	In dj
Afternoon Men novel (Duckworth, 1931)	£40 – £50	£800 – £1,000
Venusberg novel (Duckworth, 1932)	£30 – £40	£600 – £800
From a View to a Death novel (Duckworth, 1933)	£30 – £40	£600 – £800
Caledonia: A Fragment verse (privately printed, 1934) *limited to 100 copies*	£1,000 – £2,000	n/a
Agents and Patients novel (Duckworth, 1936)	£30 – £40	£600 – £800
What's Become of Waring novel (Cassell, 1939)	£20 – £30	£300 – £400
John Aubrey and His Friends biography (Heinemann, 1948)	£20 – £30	£60 – £80

Title	No dj	In dj
A Question of Upbringing novel (Heinemann, 1951)	£10 – £20	£250 – £300
A Buyer's Market novel (Heinemann, 1952)	–	£100 – £150
The Acceptance World novel (Heinemann, 1955)	–	£80 – £100
At Lady Molly's novel (Heinemann, 1957)	–	£60 – £80
Casanova's Chinese Restaurant novel (Heinemann, 1960)	–	£50 – £60
The Kindly Ones novel (Heinemann, 1962)	–	£40 – £50
The Valley of Bones novel (Heinemann, 1964)	–	£40 – £50
The Soldier's Art (Heinemann, 1966)	–	£30 – £40
The Military Philosophers novel (Heinemann, 1968)	–	£30 – £40
Books Do Furnish a Room novel (Heinemann, 1971)	–	£30 – £35
The Garden God and The Rest I'll Whistle plays (Heinemann, 1971)	–	£20 – £30
Temporary Kings novel (Heinemann, 1973)	–	£25 – £30
Hearing Secret Harmonies novel (Heinemann, 1975)	–	£25 – £30
Infants of the Spring autobiography (Heinemann, 1976)	–	£10 – £20
Messengers of Day autobiography (Heinemann, 1976)	–	£10 – £20
Faces in My Time autobiography (Heinemann, 1980)	–	£10 – £20
The Strangers Are All Gone autobiography (Heinemann, 1982)	–	£10 – £20

Title	No dj	In dj
O, the Wheel Becomes It novel (Heinemann, 1983)	–	£10 – £20
The Fisher King novel (Heinemann, 1985)	–	£10 – £20

RUTH RENDELL

Why have so many of our greatest crime writers been women? Is there something in the female sex that makes them more susceptible to mystery, suspense and, particularly, murder? Whatever the case there is little doubt that women have been disproportionately represented in the annals of crime literature. Agatha Christie, Margery Allingham, Dorothy L. Sayers, Ellis Peters and Josephine Tey are some of the classic names, of course, and this feminine tradition has continued well into the 1970s, 80s and 90s. P.D. James and Agatha Christie are discussed elsewhere in this book. These few pages are devoted to perhaps the most avidly sought after female crime novelist, Ruth Rendell, a.k.a. Barbara Vine. This is an astonishing achievement, because just a few years ago she was virtually unknown in collecting circles. Almost overnight her books, particularly the early books published by John Long, have become incredibly scarce and collectors are finding it harder and harder to track down nice copies.

Much of this is attributable to TVS's marvellous adaptations of her Inspector Wexford tales, but there is more to it than that. Ruth Rendell is a literary writer who happens to write crime tales. Her unique psychological mysteries are an important contribution not just to crime fiction, but to contemporary English literature. Collectors have come to realise this over the past few years and it is showing in her prices. In 1990 a book collecting magazine suggested that early Rendell titles could fetch from £30 to £40 and £50+ for *From Doon with Death*, her first novel. Obviously these are now considerable undervaluations. A fine copy of *From Doon with Death* would cost around £450 if it has a pristine and bright dust-jacket. Of course, it might be possible to pick up a copy for less from a general shop but it could takes years of looking. I would suggest that any price represents a bargain at the moment. Values for Ruth Rendell's early books in fine condition are sure to rise even higher in the near future.

Although there are rumours that Ruth Rendell is currently planning to write her autobiography, she is very reluctant to discuss her personal life. Little is known of her early years. She was born in Essex in 1930, the only child of two teachers. As her mother was born in Sweden much of her childhood was spent under typical Scandinavian conditions: Christmas was celebrated on 24 December, for example, and even today she can read both Swedish and Danish. After leaving school she worked for a short time on a local newspaper, although her real interest was always in fiction. From an early age she submitted short stories to women's magazines — with little success. She also wrote some novels but initially she didn't try to get them published. When she did submit one, Hutchinson hesitated, eventually made a conditional offer to publish it, then asked if she had written anything else. The result was her first novel, a detective story published as *From Doon with Death* by the Hutchinson crime imprint, John Long. Except for her mainstream novels written under the pseudonym Barbara Vine and published by Viking, she has remained with Hutchinson ever since.

The seven titles published under the John Long imprint are without doubt the hardest Ruth Rendell titles to acquire today. These are four Inspector Wexford novels: *From Doon with Death* (1964), *A New Lease of Death* (1967), *Wolf to the Slaughter* (1967) and *The Best Man to Die* (1969); and three general mystery titles, *To Fear a Painted Devil* (1965), *Vanity Dies Hard* (1965) and *The Secret House of Death* (1968). The main difficulty is finding copies in a good condition; despite being published relatively recently and in fairly sturdy bindings, they are still crime novels and, by their nature, ephemeral.

The early ones are interesting bibliographically, particularly *From Doon with Death* which is bound in green cloth and has the title stamped in white and the author and publisher stamped in yellow — an interesting colour scheme. The first three books are in a slightly smaller format than the others: From *A New Lease of Death* onwards, all Ruth Rendell's books have been issued in the same format. The jackets for the seven John Long titles are all particularly attractive, and were designed by a regular John Long artist, William Randall. Randall's illustration for *From Doon with Death* is largely green with a corpse's hand stretched out from the undergrowth. The sizeable lettering on the front cover for the title is done in a Victorian fairground style. Perhaps the best of these early designs is for *Wolf to the Slaughter* which features a daffodil with a knife and bloodspots.

For the books to reach their higher estimates in the price guide, it is imperative they have their jackets in as near mint condition as possible. Slight nicks to the corners or faint rubbing is O.K., but tears drastically reduce the value and the colouring needs to be bright and fresh. *From Doon with Death, To Fear a Painted Devil* and *Vanity Dies Hard* all attract high prices and it isn't unknown for the other John Long titles to do the same.

Ruth Rendell's novels fall neatly into collectable time-spans: the 1960s titles are obviously the hardest to find, those published in the 1970s are merely hard to find in a collectable condition, and the 1980s and 1990s books can be picked up for a song in genuinely mint condition. Rendell produced some of her best work during the 1970s, including *A Guilty Thing Surprised* (1970), *Some Lie and Some Die* (1973) and *A Judgement in Stone* (1977). It's a shame that that can't be said of Hutchinson's jacket designs. With very few exceptions they are based on fairly mundane, photographic images. When will publishers realise that (as in the good old days) one of the delights of book collecting is enjoyment of the book as a physical object, as an aesthetic item just as much as a piece of fiction? It is surely worth spending a little extra on a jacket designed by a talented artist rather than relying on photography alone without the essential graphic design element.

When Hutchinson did invest in cover artists for Rendell books the result has usually been impressive, although, again, the laminated jacket generally ruins the effect. Terry Pastor's designs for *Put on by Cunning* (1981), *Master of the Moor* (1982) and *The Fever Tree* (1982) are effective, although his best work was undoubtedly on *The Lake of Darkness* (1980). This jacket features a tarot card with a skeleton holding a scythe. Equally impressive is Tim Gill's design featuring a country house and a bright orange Chinese dragon for *The Speaker of Mandarin* (1983), and Trevor Scobie's simple but effectively macabre design for *The Tree of Hands* (1984).

Ruth Rendell's books from the 1970s are hard to find in genuinely pristine condition but not impossible, and they shouldn't cost much more than £75 each. Many will be much cheaper, and it certainly won't be necessary to rely on specialist dealers to provide them — most second-hand dealers will have one or two titles available. And this applies even more to the later titles, none of which will set you back more than £20 apiece. It should be possible to pick some of them up for even less if you look around. One recent title which might prove elusive is the proof copy of her latest novel, *Going Wrong*. The trade edition is still in print at the time of writing of course, but Hutchinson issued a limited edition of 500 copies in soft wrappers. Some collectors want this sort of thing; others don't. I include it only because it exists and because I've seen one dealer offer a copy for £30. Personally, I wouldn't touch proof copies at all, particularly proof copies which have rather cynically been published as a collectable item like this.

Title	No dj	In dj
From Doon with Death novel (John Long, 1964)	£80	£400 – £600
To Fear a Painted Devil novel (John Long, 1965)	£80	£300 – £475
Vanity Dies Hard novel (John Long, 1965)	£30	£250
A New Lease of Death novel (John Long, 1967)	£30	£150
Wolf to the Slaughter novel (John Long, 1967)	£30	£150
The Secret House of Death novel (John Long, 1968)	£20	£125
The Best Man to Die novel (John Long, 1969)	£20	£100
A Guilty Thing Surprised novel (Hutchinson, 1970)	£15	£80
One Across, Two Down novel (Hutchinson, 1971)	£15	£80
No More Dying Then novel (Hutchinson, 1971)	£15	£65
Murder Being Once Done novel (Hutchinson, 1972)	£10	£55

Title	No dj	In dj
Some Lie and Some Die novel (Hutchinson, 1973)	£10	£50
The Face of Trespass novel (Hutchinson, 1974)	£10	£45
Shake Hands for Ever novel (Hutchinson, 1975)	£10	£25
A Demon in My View novel (Hutchinson, 1976)	£10	£25
The Fallen Curtain short stories (Hutchinson, 1976)	£10	£20
A Judgement in Stone novel (Hutchinson, 1977)	£10	£20
A Sleeping Life novel (Hutchinson, 1978)	£10	£20
Make Death Love Me novel (Hutchinson, 1979)	£5 – £8	£10 – £15
Means of Evil short stories (Hutchinson, 1979)	£5 – £8	£10 – £15
The Lake of Darkness novel (Hutchinson, 1980)	–	£15
Put on by Cunning novel (Hutchinson, 1981)	–	£15
Master of the Moor novel (Hutchinson, 1982)	–	£10
The Fever Tree short stories (Hutchinson, 1982)	–	£10
The Speaker of Mandarin novel (Hutchinson, 1983)	–	£10
The Killing Doll novel (Hutchinson, 1984)	–	£10
The Tree of Hands novel (Hutchinson, 1984)	–	£10
The New Girlfriend short stories (Hutchinson, 1985)	–	£10

Title	No dj	In dj
An Unkindness of Ravens novel (Hutchinson, 1985)	–	£10
Live Flesh novel (Hutchinson, 1986)	–	£10
A Dark-Adapted Eye novel by Barbara Vine (Viking, 1986)	–	£10
Talking to Strange Men novel (Hutchinson, 1987)	–	£10
Matters of Suspense short stories (Eurographica, Helsinki, 1986) *edition of 350 signed copies*	–	£95
Heartstones novella (Hutchinson, 1987) *embellished with some fine illustrations by George Underwood*	–	£8
A Fatal Inversion novel by Barbara Vine (Viking, 1987)	–	£10
Collected Short Stories (Hutchinson, 1987)	–	£10
The Veiled One novel (Hutchinson, 1988)	–	£10
The House of Stairs novel by Barbara Vine (Viking, 1988)	–	£10
Wexford: An Omnibus collection (Hutchinson, 1988)	–	£8
The Second Wexford Omnibus collection (Hutchinson, 1988)	–	£8
The Third Wexford Omnibus collection (Hutchinson, 1989)	–	£8
Ruth Rendell's Suffolk non-fiction (Frederick Muller, 1989) *with photographs by Paul Bowden*	–	£10
The Bridesmaid novel (Hutchinson, 1989)	–	£8

Title	No dj	In dj
Three Cases for Chief Inspector Wexford short stories (Eurographica, Helsinki, 1990) *Signed edition limited to 350 copies*	–	£90
Gallowglass novel by Barbara Vine (Viking, 1990)	–	£8
Going Wrong novel (Hutchinson, 1990) *The publishers also issued 500 wrappered proof copies*	– £30	£8 n/a
The Strawberry Tree novella (Pandora, 1990) *published in one volume with Helen Simpson's* Flesh and Grass	–	£8
The Copper Peacock short stories (Hutchinson, 1991) *includes one Wexford story*	–	£8
King Solomon's Carpet novel by Barbara Vine (Viking, 1991)	–	–
Kissing the Gunner's Daughter novel (Hutchinson, 1992)	–	–

FRANK RICHARDS

It was George Orwell who wrote that 'it may well be found that Frank Richards during the first quarter of the twentieth century had more influence on the mind and outlook of young working-class England than any other single person, not excluding Baden-Powell'. He wasn't exaggerating. Every week for more than thirty years he wrote both *The Magnet* and *The Gem* magazines virtually unaided, a prodigious task in any circumstances. He created literally hundreds of characters, but he will almost certainly be best remembered for his Greyfriars School stories, featuring the detestable Mr Quelch, Form Master of the Remove; the 'famous five' (Harry Wharton, Bob Cherry, Johnny Bull, Hurree Jamset Ram Singh, Frank Nugent) and the immortal William George (Billy) Bunter.

Bunter made his first fictional appearance on 15 February 1908 in Harmsworth's *Magnet*. The story was 'The Making of Harry Wharton'. Bunter appeared on the scene and promptly fell over Wharton's recumbent body. It was an inauspicious beginning for the chap who eventually became literature's most famous schoolboy. To begin with he was a minor character, and a kind of anti-hero (greedy, sneaky and unreliable) to the upright Harry Wharton. Despite his reputation today, though, Billy Bunter was a minor part of Richards's output, which also included westerns, romances, detective stories and marine adventures. Frank Richards was without doubt the most prolific author of all time. In a career spanning more than seventy years Richards is estimated to have written at least 72,000,000 words (the equivalent of a thousand full-length novels — eat your heart out Miss Cartland!), and new work by The Old Man is being discovered all the time. It's not as easy to find as one might imagine. Frank Richards was just one of twenty-eight pseudonyms he used (others included Martin Clifford, Harry Clifton, Clifford Owen, Hilda Richards and Talbot Wynward), most of which have been traced by those indefatigable researchers of popular fiction W.O.G. Lofts and the late Derek Adley. Considering his astonishing output it is quite remarkable that Richards's work didn't appear in book form until 1947, over fifty years after his first story was printed.

Frank Richards's life has been admirably documented in Mary Cadogan's 1988 biography. He was born Charles Harold St John Hamilton in Ealing, West London on 8 August 1876, the son of a journalist and occasional bookseller. Richards attended various day schools, but it is not known whether he went to the type of public school portrayed in his stories. According to John Arlott who quizzed him on the question, 'he was very evasive on this point . . . perhaps in his heart and mind, after all those years of writing, he really believed that he had'.

Undecided about what career to follow Richards began contributing stories to boys' magazines like *Big Budget* from the age of seventeen, and two years later began writing for various Harmsworth publications. Before long he had created St Jim's school and its main pupil Tom Merry. In 1907 Percy Griffith, the editor of *Gem*, asked Richards to write the stories which would fill a new weekly called *Magnet*. It was in these pages that he first called himself Frank Richards. He later explained that the reason for adopting so many pseudonyms was partly to make him feel like a different person each time, and so enable him to write from a different angle. 'I have been told,' he wrote in his autobiography, ' — by men who do not write — that this is all fanciful. . . . This only means that they don't understand.' (The Autobiography of Frank Richards, Skilton, 1952)

For decades Frank Richards wrote most the text for both *Gem* and *Magnet*, as well as *Boy's Friend* after 1915. It was a breathtaking feat, equivalent to writing a lengthy novel every single week (although when he was ill Harmsworth often printed substitute writers' stories under Richards's by-lines, something which infuriated him intensely). Despite his numerous pseudonyms few of his readers ever realised Frank Richards, Martin Clifford or Owen Conquest were actually the same man and he guarded his privacy jealously. The Harmsworth papers occasionally printed stories in which these authors met each other. He wrote straight onto a trusty Remington typewriter which had a purple ribbon, and rarely made any alterations or corrections. In his spare time he loved to travel and often spent his considerable £2,500 salary losing at the gambling tables of Nice or Monte Carlo.

Copies of *Gem, Magnet* and other weeklies are all very popular today — Frank Richards has attracted a cult status and everything about him is sought-after. In fact, the Wimbledon-based publisher Howard Baker has made a living out of publishing facsimile issues of these papers and they are collectable in their own right.

It wasn't all good news and hard work, though. During the Second World War Richards's life changed drastically when both *Magnet* and *Gem* were forced to close down as a result of paper shortages. In one fell swoop Richards's livelihood was taken away from him; he had no savings and his only income was £5 a week, which he received from the *Knockout* comic for their Billy Bunter comic strip. Worse still, his early contract with Amalgamated Press prohibited him from writing Greyfriars stories for other periodicals. His war-time writing about Carcroft (a new school series) and his new Jack of All Trades series were of typical Richards quality, of course, but he found it hard to sell them. The public wanted Billy Bunter.

In 1947, Frank Richards and Billy Bunter were offered a new lease of life when the small but ambitious publisher, Charles Skilton, saw an article on the author in *Picture Post* magazine he thought it might be a good idea to publish new Greyfriars stories in book form. The Amalgamated Press raised no objection as long as none appeared in any rival magazines and, for the first time, Richards found himself between hard covers. He wanted to be paid as a magazine writer though, and asked Skilton for the same thirty shillings per thousand words he had received before the war but wisely accepted his new publisher's advice to accept a royalty. Instead of the £150 he might have expected from the first book, *Billy Bunter of Greyfriars School* quickly earned the author over £1,000 as it progressed smoothly to its fourth edition.

The Billy Bunter books were just what his fans wanted, proving much more durable than the original *Magnets* and significantly easier to acquire for a younger audience. Young readers wanted them as did their parents who had first come across Greyfriars when they too were children. The *Evening News* summed it up when they wrote that 'Bunter is a national institution'.

Billy Bunter of Greyfriars School was published in September 1947 and priced at 5s. 6d. It sold all its first impression of 25,000 copies and Skilton reprinted it three times making a total of 40,000 copies. All these editions are collectable today and many Bunter enthusiasts will accept any copy but it is really the first impressions that fetch the best prices. All the Bunter books were issued in a standard octavo format with yellow dust-jackets featuring a scene from the story. Because of the post-war paper restrictions, this particular title was issued on very thin paper and the book is no more than half-an-inch thick. Copies in their 'yellow-jackets' (as they were called) are becoming increasingly scarce and their value has more than doubled in the past couple of years. An acceptable copy could set you back at least £60–£80 — and don't expect any bargains. Dealers are aware of the tremendous upsurge of interest in Greyfriars and they know they can get premium prices.

Most children's books end up the worse for wear but in the case of Billy Bunter the original owners seemed to cherish these volumes and look after them. Having all the volumes issued in the same attractive format obviously contributes to this. It's also possible that many of the original buyers might well have been adults, glorying in the reappearance of their heroes (although Billy Bunter's name was used in the title to sell copies, all the old favourites were featured). It is certainly true that even as early as the 1940s, collecting circles were starting to spring up around Richards. These included the Old Boys' Book Clubs and two boys' paper collecting magazines, *Story Paper Collector* and *Collectors' Digest* (still going strong today). Despite this don't expect to find genuinely fine copies of these early titles. You will probably have to make do with chipped or soiled jackets. I find that putting these jackets in protective plastic covers helps their appearance no end and stops defective jackets from deteriorating further.

The next two Bunter volumes appeared simultaneously in October 1948. Both *Billy Bunter's Banknote* and *Billy Bunter's Barring Out* were priced at 7s. 6d. and both sold out immediately. They were followed in March 1949 by *Billy Bunter in Brazil* and, in October 1949, by *Bunter's Christmas Party*. Then the only failure of the series appeared. Under the 'female' pseudonym, Hilda Richards, the only Bessie Bunter book was produced, *Bessie Bunter of Cliff House School*. Some collectors ignore this book; they shouldn't. In the same format as the Billy Bunter books, it was obviously intended by Richards to be part of the series (or a new companion series at least). It was a huge flop. Evidently thousands of copies were unsold and had to be pulped by Cassell many years later, it was certainly never reprinted. This makes it very scarce today and fine copies often sell for over £50. Incidentally, all these volumes are prone to having chipped dust-jackets: try to avoid these if at all possible. A genuinely fine reprint is just as sought after and as valuable as a shabby first, particularly because the same jacket design and format were used for later impressions.

After *Billy Bunter and the Blue Mauritius* (1952) the series had grown so much that Skilton was forced to sell the rights to Cassells who could more easily handle the demand for Billy Bunter books. Collectors were (and still are) delighted when Cassell decided to issue their Bunter titles in the same attractive format as those from Skilton. In fact, they were even more attractive. The two titles that appeared each year had the same yellow-jackets, but they were all issued in different colour cloths, making them an attractive set even without their jackets.

One of the delights of these books is that they were illustrated by former *Gem* or *Magnet* artists. The first seventeen books in the series up to *Billy Bunter's Double* (from both Skilton and Cassell) were illustrated by R.J. Macdonald, a prolific artist who started illustrating boys' magazines in the 1890s and was a regular contributor to the *Gem* from 1909 to 1940. He concentrated on illustrating Richards's 'St Jim' stories. When he died in 1955 the task of illustrating these new books was taken over by Charles Henry Chapman, a friend of Richards since 1912. Bunter fans were delighted. Chapman was the Bunter artist without equal and his superb graphic designs admirably summed up the spirit of Richards's stories. It was Chapman who first put the Fat Owl in his famous checked trousers. Yarooh!

From this point on, the Bunter books continued to appear at regular intervals and later volumes seem easy to pick up in first edition format. In fact, it is only possible to pick up first editions of titles after *Bunter the Bad Lad*. All titles published after this date were given print runs of 50,000 copies and were never reprinted or reissued in the same format — although they later reappeared as paperbacks. There is one title, however, which causes some confusion. In June 1961 Cassell published *Billy Bunter at Butlin's* in the normal yellow-jacket format priced at 9*s*. 6*d*., as well as a special edition for Butlin's Beaver Club, on inferior paper and boards. This special edition sported a grotesque dust-jacket. The normal edition commands around £20–£25 from a specialist dealer, whereas the Butlin's Beaver Club edition can be obtained for less than a tenner.

By the time Frank Richards died on Christmas Eve 1961, these second generation Bunter books had sold around half a million copies. This secured a new generation of readers in the second half of the century to add to the hundreds of thousands from the first. But even this wasn't all. Cassell still had eight titles to issue (up to *Bunter's Last Fling* in 1965) and the paperbacks during the 1970s and 1980s multiplied sales even further. Nostalgia is a curious thing, hard to define, even harder to justify but it is real and it is a safe bet that these Bunter books will increase their value for many years to come. Buy them now, and enjoy the stories all over again, whatever your age!

Title	No dj	In dj
Billy Bunter of Greyfriars School novel (Skilton, 1947)	£20 – £30	£60 – £80
Billy Bunter's Banknote novel (Skilton, 1948)	£10 – £20	£40 – £50

Title	No dj	In dj
Billy Bunter's Barring Out novel (Skilton, 1948)	£10 – £20	£40 – £50
Billy Bunter in Brazil novel (Skilton, 1949)	£10 – £15	£30 – £40
Billy Bunter's Christmas Party novel (Skilton, 1949)	£10 – £15	£30 – £40
Bessie Bunter of Cliff House School novel (Skilton, 1949)	£10 – £15	£50 – £60
Billy Bunter's Benefit novel (Skilton, 1950)	£5 – £10	£25 – £30
Billy Bunter Among the Cannibals novel (Skilton, 1950)	£5 – £10	£25 – £30
Billy Bunter's Postal Order novel (Skilton, 1951)	£5 – £10	£25 – £30
Billy Bunter Butts In novel (Skilton, 1951)	£5 – £10	£25 – £30
Billy Bunter and the Blue Mauritius novel (Skilton, 1952) *only one impression of this title was issued*	£10 – £20	£50 – £60
Billy Bunter's Beanfeast novel (Cassell, 1952)	£5 – £10	£25 – £30
Billy Bunter's Brainwave novel (Cassell, 1953)	£5 – £10	£25 – £30
Billy Bunter's First Case novel (Cassell, 1953)	£5 – £10	£25 – £30
Billy Bunter the Bold novel (Cassell, 1954)	£5 – £10	£25 – £30
Bunter Does His Best novel (Cassell, 1954)	£5 – £10	£25 – £30
Billy Bunter's Double novel (Cassell, 1955)	£5 – £10	£25 – £30
Backing Up Billy Bunter novel (Cassell, 1955)	£5 – £10	£25 – £30
Lord Billy Bunter novel (Cassell, 1956)	£5 – £10	£25 – £30

Title	No dj	In dj
The Banishing of Billy Bunter novel (Cassell, 1956)	£5 – £10	£25 – £30
Billy Bunter Afloat novel (Cassell, 1957)	£5 – £8	£20 – £25
Billy Bunter's Bargain novel (Cassell, 1958)	£5 – £8	£20 – £25
Billy Bunter the Hiker novel (Cassell, 1958)	£5 – £8	£20 – £25
Bunter Out of Bounds novel (Cassell, 1959)	£5 – £8	£20-£25
Bunter Comes for Christmas novel (Cassell, 1959)	£5 – £8	£20–25
Bunter the Bad Lad novel (Cassell, 1960)	£5 – £8	£20 – £25
Bunter Keeps It Dark novel (Cassell, 1960)	£5 – £8	£20 – £25
Billy Bunter's Treasure Hunt novel (Cassell, 1961)	£5 – £8	£20 – £25
Billy Bunter at Butlins novel (Cassell, 1961) *parallel issue for the Butlin Beaver Club*	£5 – £8 £5 – £10	£20 – £25 £20 – £25
Bunter the Ventriloquist novel (Cassell, 1961)	£5 – £8	£20 – £25
Bunter the Caravanner novel (Cassell, 1962)	£5 – £8	£20 – £25
Billy Bunter's Bodyguard novel (Cassell, 1962)	£5 – £8	£20 – £25
Big Chief Bunter novel (Cassell, 1962)	£5 – £8	£20 – £25
Just like Bunter novel (Cassell, 1963)	£5 – £8	£20 – £25
Bunter the Stowaway novel (Cassell, 1964)	£5 – £8	£20 – £25
Thanks to Bunter novel (Cassell, 1964)	£5 – £8	£20 – £25

Title	No dj	In dj
Bunter the Sportsman novel (Cassell, 1965)	£5 – £8	£20 – £25
Bunter's Last Fling novel (Cassell, 1965)	£5 – £8	£20 – £25

GEORGES SIMENON

Georges Simenon, born at Liège in Belgium on 13 February 1903, was one of the most prolific writers of the twentieth century. His output, spread across sixty years, included novels, short stories, volumes of autobiography, many articles for newspapers and magazines, prefaces to other writers' work, texts of lectures and theatrical adaptations. It is a body of work that can be divided into two distinct periods.

The first concerns his work to the age of twenty-seven. He was employed as a junior reporter on the *Gazette de Liège*, a daily newspaper, just before his sixteenth birthday, staying with the paper for four years, during which time he wrote his first novel. His move to Paris in December 1922 gave him the opportunity to establish his writing career from which he supported himself from the age of twenty-one until the end of his life.

Although his output during the years 1924 to 1930 was prodigious — 190 novels and well over a thousand short stories all published under some thirty pseudonyms — the interest is for French readers and collectors as none of this work has yet been translated into English.

Years later Simenon called this period 'his years of apprenticeship', the learning of his craft. He was writing for a wide public, his subject matter spreading across adventure stories, romance and crime. He had developed the ability to write quickly, starting very early in the morning, keeping to a schedule, so that a novel would be completed in five days.

Other traits had manifested themselves from childhood and adolescence that were to play a major role in his later writing. He had an innate curiosity about people and places around him, taking in the visual aspects, sounds, smells, gestures and people's reaction to everyday living. His memory of situations, seen and felt, was a storehouse from which he was able to draw and transform.

Two examples of novels drawing on some of his youthful experiences are *The Crime of Inspector Maigret* (Hurst and Blackett, 1933) and *The Night Club* (Hamish Hamilton, 1979). Simenon recalls his Liège days when he was associated with a group called La Caque, so named by the participants, mainly students of the Arts, who met at a bar named L'Ane Rouge and in an old building near the church of Saint Pholien. Maigret in the novel written in 1931 is in Liège investigating the background of former student, one Emile Klein who in reality Simenon knew as Joseph Kleine, a member of La Caque. In *The Night Club* written in 1932, the French title is *L'Ane Rouge*, Simenon changing it from a bar to a rather seedy night club, but incorporating aspects of his social and family life during his journalist days.

Simenon's decision to move towards the serious novel was taken around the year 1929. From 1928 until 1930 he was living on board his boat in which he explored the canals and rivers of France, Belgium, the Netherlands and North Germany, visiting Norway and Lapland by passenger ship. Returning through the canals he wrote *Pietr-le-Letton* (*The Case of Peter the Lett*, Hurst and Blackett,

1933), a novel that established the second period of his work.

To many, Simenon is synonymous with Jules Maigret, the Chief Inspector of the French Police Judiciary, based in the building along the Quai des Orfèvres on the Ile de Cité in Paris. *Pietr-le-Letton*, written in the spring of 1930 is the first true Maigret novel. True in the sense that it was the first in which the character of Maigret was at all developed. During the previous year or so, Simenon had written seven novels under pseudonyms, four of which included a prototype character called Maigret. Also in these novels other figures who are to be Maigret's colleagues in the series appear: Torrence, Lucas, Coméliau (the examining magistrate with whom Maigret has many differences of opinion) and Maigret's wife, although in another guise.

With *Pietr-le-Letton* Simenon was now published under his own name and had established Maigret; middle aged, tall and well built, agile, gruff, not a sufferer of fools, but with much patience and sensitivity. He smokes a pipe, enjoys good food and alcohol. He is compassionate with people down on their luck, often preferring petty criminals and gangsters to the established affluent strata of society with their rigid code and predicability. When asked about his methods, Maigret simply replied that he has none, and although all the police resources are there, he preferred to act by intuition and instinct, visiting people and places, immersing himself in the atmosphere of the protagonists, getting the feel of their environment, their existence, trying to get beneath their skin, to know them as human beings, not passing judgement, but leaving that to the legal profession.

An outstanding quality of all Simenon's novels manifest in his work from now on is his use of atmosphere to pervade everything, from the location to the demeanour of a character, treated often with a poetic feeling. He has the gift of plunging the reader into the atmosphere from the first paragraph. There are no lengthy passages of description, but a directness in the use of words, an economy of means that carries the reader along.

Simenon wrote 74 novels, 2 novellas and 27 short stories involving Maigret. From the spring of 1930 until January 1934 he produced nineteen Maigret and eleven other novels and these first French editions were published on average at one per month.

The early Maigret novels were translated into English and published by Hurst and Blackett, and Routledge, between 1933 and 1941 in double volumes, each being given an overall title.

The first three volumes from Hurst and Blackett are very scarce, especially in dust-wrappers and if located would fetch £150 or more. For collectors wishing to read the six titles contained in the Hurst and Blackett volumes, these have been reissued, but with new translations and retitled by Penguin Books in 1966 and 1967. In these circumstances, the paperbacks constitute a set of six first editions the titles being: *Maigret and the Hundred Gibbets (The Crime of Inspector Maigret)*, *Maigret Stonewalled (The Death of Monsieur Gallet)*, *Maigret at the Crossroads (The Crossroad Murders)*, *Maigret and the Enigmatic Lett (The Case of Peter the Lett)*, *Maigret Meets a Milord (The Crime at Lock 14)* and *Maigret Mystified (The Shadow in the Courtyard)*.

The seven Routledge volumes, though not as scarce as the Hurst and Blackett editions, are still difficult to find in dust-wrappers and collectors must expect to pay the prices indicated in the bibliography.

The first four Routledge volumes have dust-wrappers designed by Edward McKnight-Kauffer (1890–1954), an American born painter, illustrator and designer who produced outstanding posters and other work during the 1930s and 1940s.

Selecting from this first set, *The Case of Peter the Lett*, although it established Maigret, is a transitional novel with certain parts of the narrative glanced over. The setting ranges from the luxury Majestic Hotel in Paris to the seedier parts of the rainswept Channel port of Fécamp. *The Crime at Lock 14*, the second novel to be written, finds Maigret amid canal life several miles east of Paris, and is one of several novels set along canals, in ports and at sea, using Simenon's expert knowledge of these settings. *At the Gai-Moulin* is set in Simenon's Liège and has echoes of his youth. Paris is the venue of both *A Battle of Nerves* and *The Shadow in the Courtyard* but they are very different in content. The first has Maigret gambling his reputation and pitting his wits against an associate of the Montparnasse crowd, and it introduces a new member of Maigret's team, the then young Inspector Janvier, who features in many later works. The second takes place in one of the apartment blocks of the quiet elegant seventeenth century Place des Vosges where Simenon lived for part of the 1920s.

Simenon wanted to focus on the straight novel, so he has Maigret taking his retirement in *The Lock at Charenton*. To reinforce this situation in the last novel of this set, Maigret has retired to his house in the French countryside, when he is called upon to help in a private capacity. The translation is called rather curiously *Maigret Returns*.

Simenon then concentrated on writing other novels but the public wanted more of Maigret. He acquiesced by producing two sets of short stories and, during the Second World War, wrote six more Maigret novels, *To Any Lengths, Maigret in Exile, Maigret and the Spinster, Maigret and the Hotel Majestic, Maigret and the Toy Village* and *Maigret's Rival*, the first published by Routledge, the rest by Hamish Hamilton.

From 1946 Simenon began to write a steady flow of Maigret novels averaging two a year until 1972 when he gave up writing novels altogether.

Those published by Hamish Hamilton were issued in reasonable quantities, the first a double volume, the rest as single titles and with judicious searching it is possible to acquire them all in very good condition at between £10 for the earlier ones and £5 for the later.

For most of his Maigret novels Simenon chose a contemporary setting, but in two he made a diversion. *Maigret's First Case* (Hamish Hamilton, 1958) occurs in April 1913 with Maigret as a young Police Secretary at a neighbourhood station in Paris. This is one novel recalling the early career, but in *Maigret's Memoirs* (Hamish Hamilton, 1963) there is an ingenious idea, a circle within a circle. Simenon writes about Maigret writing of his background, his vocation and attitude to life, who early on is introduced to a journalist turned author by the name of Georges Sim (one of Simenon's early pseudonyms), who wishes to observe Maigret in his daily routine around the Quai des Orfévres.

In *Madame Maigret's Friend* (Hamish Hamilton, 1960), Maigret's wife is brought more into the limelight and the young Inspector Lapointe joins his team. Simenon does not fully explore the character of Maigret's colleagues except as a series of well-drawn sketches as they come and go.

Two novellas and all but three short stories have been translated and collected together in two volumes from Hamish Hamilton under the titles *Maigret's Christmas* (1976) and *Maigret's Pipe* (1977), with the sub-title of 'The Complete Maigret Short Stories'. This is somewhat of a misnomer as 'L'Improbable Monsieur Owen', 'Ceaux du Grand Café' and 'Menaces de Mort' have not been translated.

With Maigret, Simenon had created a central figure around which he could develop themes and other characters — characters that are seen and understood through Maigret's eyes and mind.

From July 1931 until October 1971 he wrote 117 straight novels and two volumes of autobiography. The short stories number 142 including those written before 1930 but published under his own name. Of these 117 novels all but 12 have been translated into English. Whilst writing the first fifteen Maigret novels he wrote only two others: *The Mystery of the Polarlys* and *The Man from Everywhere* but later the pattern changed. These titles are effectively detective novels; the first set at sea with the captain of the ship acting as detective, and the second has Inspector Labbé from Paris searching out an international swindler in the heights of Alsace. Although having elements that were to be developed in later novels, both echo some of Simenon's early work written under pseudonyms.

At various times between 1932 and 1935, Simenon travelled, to Africa, Turkey and Russia and undertook a world tour lasting five months. He was largely financed by freelance journalism, but his travels provided him with material for several novels.

Tropic Moon, Talatala and *Aboard the Aquitaine* (Hamish Hamilton, 1979) are set in and around Africa, *The Window over the Way* (Routledge and Kegan Paul, 1951) is located in Russian dominated Batum, near the Black Sea, and 'Banana Tourist' (in *The Lost Moorings*, George Routledge & Sons, 1946) takes place mainly in Tahiti. A couple on the run from Dieppe to Colombia and Tahiti is the theme of *Long Exile* (Hamish Hamilton, 1983), one of Simenon's few long novels.

A selection of titles illustrates the range of themes explored in his novels. The theme of 'flight' occurs in a number of the works. This is interpreted in a number of ways, physically running away to a different or better existence, remaining in the same place but breaking the pattern, hiding away from people or blotting out the world through alcohol or by some mental process.

For example Jean-Paul Guillaume is a schoolmaster in La Rochelle in *The Disintegration of J.P.G.* (Routledge, 1937) who for years has followed the same routine until he catches sight of someone from his past. This is enough for him to seek escape. This title was the first straight novel of Simenon to be translated and published by Routledge. Like the first three Maigret volumes it is very scarce and likely to cost over £150. It is made more elusive as there are no reprints or paperback editions of this title.

The Man Who Watched the Trains Go By (George Routledge & Sons, 1942) is a study of Kees Popinga whose world is changed by the emptiness of his family life and the loss of his employment. He commits a crime in Amsterdam and as a fugitive takes the train to Paris. In *Uncle Charles* (Hamish Hamilton, 1988) Charles Dupeux flees the world by shutting himself up in a room in his house. The novel explores humiliation and revenge.

Childhood is depicted in three Simenon novels. Living in the south west of France during the Second World War, Simenon was diagnosed to have heart disease, later to be proved false. Under the shadow of the illness he wrote about his family's background for the later benefit of his son, then three years old. On reading the manuscript the writer André Gide urged Simenon to turn the work into a novel. The result was *Pedigree* (Hamish Hamilton, 1962), his longest novel. It is about the life of Roger Mamelin from birth until the age of sixteen, his parents and family, and the events that affect them. A novel that mirrors Simenon's early life with him in the guise of Roger.

Two other novels about childhood are *Black Rain* (Routledge and Kegan Paul, 1949) and *The Little Saint* (Hamish Hamilton, 1966). In the first, seven-year-old Jerome Lecoeur watches the world outside through the window of his Normandy home, piecing together what is happening in the street and the house opposite, against his own background of family life dominated by his uncaring aunt. It is written with understanding and tenderness. The Little Saint is the name given to Louis Cuchas by his schoolmates as he serenely refuses to tell anyone when they take advantage, chide and taunt him. He lives with his mother, brothers and sisters in poor circumstances in the Rue Mouffetard on the Left Bank of Paris. His mother supports her family by selling vegetables from a cart near their home, everyday visiting Les Halles, the market, to which Louis is taken, adding to his joy. Simenon traces Louis's life from the age of four, dwelling largely on his childhood with a remarkable evocation of the world seen through a child's eyes. This was Simenon's own favourite from amongst his work.

The Stain on the Snow (Routledge and Kegan Paul, 1953) is a powerful novel set in an unidentified city under German occupation. Nineteen-year-old Frank Friedmaier, utterly callous, lives off his mother and seemingly heedless of the result, pushes himself to the edge. It is a novel of contrasts with the all pervading snow creating an atmosphere of purity and evil.

An outstanding lawyer, Hector Loursat in *The Strangers in the House*, (Routledge and Kegan Paul, 1951), has for eighteen years been a recluse in his large house at Moulins, drinking his wine and reading his books, until a crime involving his daughter stirs him out of his sloth. A group of young people are involved, reminiscent of La Caque in Simenon's Liège days.

The two part *Account Unsettled* (Hamish Hamilton, 1962) is a novel of opposites. Elie Waskou, a poor but brilliant student, lives in a boarding house in Liège. Elie is happy with his world in the kitchen corner until a new student arrives. Conflict simmers.

Resulting from the ten years that Simenon lived in the United States, he wrote thirteen novels with American settings. *Belle* (Hamish Hamilton, 1954) is located in Connecticut, a novel of alienation, brought about by the community's gradual hostility towards one of their number.

The earliest novels published by Routledge are the most difficult to locate in dust-wrappers. Several of these titles were brought out in the 1940s, during the war and during the period of paper restriction. The values vary as indicated in the bibliography.

The non-Maigret short stories number 142, but only 38 have been translated, thirteen of which appear in the volume entitled *The Little Doctor* (Hamish Hamilton, 1978), a series of detective stories with the doctor investigating. The other short stories are scattered throughout various magazines and anthologies.

Between 1960 and 1968 many of the dust-wrappers were illustrated by Philip Youngman Carter whose wife was Margery Allingham, the crime fiction writer.

The novel *The Old Man Dies* (Hamish Hamilton, 1968) was issued with an alternative dust-wrapper. The first was designed by Peter Bate which was substituted for one by Philip Youngman Carter with Bate's name pasted over on the front flap.

Simenon wrote his last novel in 1972, *Maigret and Monsieur Charles* (Hamish Hamilton, 1973), but continued until 1979 with his autobiography using a tape recorder. The tapes were transcribed by his secretary, edited and then published in 21 volumes, but none have been translated into English. There are other works of autobiography available. *When I Was Old* (Hamish Hamilton, 1972) was written between 1960 and 1963, *Letter to My Mother* (Hamish Hamilton, 1976) written in 1974 and *Intimate Memoirs, including Marie-Jo's Book* (Hamish Hamilton, 1984) written in 1980. Relations with his mother had always been difficult and his letter to her, outlining his feelings, was written three years after she died. *Intimate Memoirs*, the last work Simenon produced, was written to the memory of his daughter, Marie-Georges (Marie-Jo) who committed suicide at the age of 25 in May 1978.

Georges Simenon died on 4 September 1989 at the age of 86. There are four biographies available and these are listed at the end of the bibliography. In the bibliography that follows, prices stated are for books and dust-jackets in very good condition.

Title	No dj	In dj

MAIGRET TITLES

	No dj	In dj
Introducing Inspector Maigret 1. The Crime of Inspector Maigret 2. The Death of Monsieur Gallet novels (Hurst and Blackett, 1933)	£50	£150+
Inspector Maigret Investigates 1. The Crossroad Murders 2. The Case of Peter the Lett novels (Hurst and Blackett, 1933)	£50	£150+
The Triumph of Inspector Maigret 1. The Crime at Lock 14 2. The Shadow in the Courtyard novels (Hurst and Blackett, 1934)	£50	£150+
The Patience of Maigret 1. A Battle of Nerves 2. A Face for a Clue novels (George Routledge & Sons, 1939)	£20	£60
Maigret Travels South 1. Liberty Bar 2. The Madman of Bergerac novels (George Routledge & Sons, 1940)	£15	£50
Maigret Abroad 1. A Crime in Holland 2. At the Gai-Moulin novels (George Routledge & Sons, 1940)	£15	£50
Maigret to the Rescue 1. The Flemish Ship 2. The Guinguette by the Seine novels (George Routledge & Sons, 1940)	£15	£50
Maigret Keeps a Rendez-Vous 1. The Sailors' Rendez-Vous 2. The Saint-Fiacre Affair novels (George Routledge & Sons, 1940)	£12	£40
Maigret Sits It Out 1. The Lock at Charenton 2. Maigret Returns novels (George Routledge & Sons, 1941)	£12	£40
Maigret and M. Labbé 1. Death of a Harbour Master 2. The Man from Everywhere (*non-Maigret title*) novels (George Routledge & Sons, 1941)	£10	£35

Title	No dj	In dj
Maigret on Holiday 1. A Summer Holiday 2. To Any Lengths novels (Routledge and Kegan Paul, 1950)	£5	£12
Maigret Right and Wrong 1. Maigret in Montmartre 2. Maigret's Mistake novels (Hamish Hamilton, 1954)	£5	£10
Maigret and the Young Girl novel (Hamish Hamilton, 1955)	£5	£10
Maigret and the Burglar's Wife novel (Hamish Hamilton, 1955)	£4	£9
Maigret's Revolver novel (Hamish Hamilton, 1956)	£4	£9
My Friend Maigret novel (Hamish Hamilton, 1956)	£4	£9
Maigret Goes to School novel (Hamish Hamilton, 1957)	£4	£9
Maigret's Little Joke novel (Hamish Hamilton, 1957)	£4	£9
Maigret and the Old Lady novel (Hamish Hamilton, 1958)	£4	£9
Maigret's First Case novel (Hamish Hamilton, 1958)	£4	£9
Maigret has Scruples novel (Hamish Hamilton, 1959)	£4	£9
Maigret and the Reluctant Witnesses novel (Hamish Hamilton, 1959)	£4	£9
Madame Maigret's Friend novel (Hamish Hamilton, 1960)	£4	£9
Maigret Takes a Room novel (Hamish Hamilton, 1960)	£4	£8
Maigret in Court novel (Hamish Hamilton, 1961)	£4	£8
Maigret Afraid novel (Hamish Hamilton, 1961)	£4	£8

Title	No dj	In dj
Maigret in Society novel (Hamish Hamilton, 1962)	£4	£8
Maigret's Failure novel (Hamish Hamilton, 1962)	£4	£8
Maigret's Memoirs novel (Hamish Hamilton, 1963)	£4	£8
Maigret and the Lazy Burglar novel (Hamish Hamilton, 1963)	£4	£8
Maigret's Special Murder novel (Hamish Hamilton, 1964)	£4	£8
Maigret and the Saturday Caller novel (Hamish Hamilton, 1964)	£4	£8
Maigret Loses His Temper novel (Hamish Hamilton, 1965)	£4	£8
Maigret Sets a Trap novel (Hamish Hamilton, 1965)	£4	£8
Maigret on the Defensive novel (Hamish Hamilton, 1966)	£4	£8
The Patience of Maigret novel (Hamish Hamilton, 1966)	£4	£8
Maigret and the Headless Corpse novel (Hamish Hamilton, 1967)	£4	£8
Maigret and the Nahour Case novel (Hamish Hamilton, 1967)	£4	£8
Maigret's Pickpocket novel (Hamish Hamilton, 1968)	£4	£8
Maigret Has Doubts novel (Hamish Hamilton, 1968)	£4	£8
Maigret Takes the Waters novel (Hamish Hamilton, 1969)	£4	£8
Maigret and the Minister novel (Hamish Hamilton, 1969)	£4	£8
Maigret Hesitates novel (Hamish Hamilton, 1970)	£3	£7

Title	No dj	In dj
Maigret's Boyhood Friend novel (Hamish Hamilton, 1970)	£3	£7
Maigret and the Wine Merchant novel (Hamish Hamilton, 1971)	£3	£7
Maigret and the Killer novel (Hamish Hamilton, 1971)	£3	£7
Maigret and the Madwoman novel (Hamish Hamilton, 1972)	£3	£7
Maigret and the Flea novel (Hamish Hamilton, 1972)	£3	£7
Maigret and Monsieur Charles novel (Hamish Hamilton, 1973)	£3	£7
Maigret and the Dosser novel (Hamish Hamilton, 1973)	£3	£7
Maigret and the Millionaires novel (Hamish Hamilton, 1974)	£3	£7
Maigret and the Gangsters novel (Hamish Hamilton, 1974)	£3	£7
Maigret and the Loner novel (Hamish Hamilton, 1975)	£3	£7
Maigret and the Man on the Boulevard novel (Hamish Hamilton, 1975)	£3	£7
Maigret and the Black Sheep novel (Hamish Hamilton, 1976)	£3	£7
Maigret's Christmas complete Maigret short stories volume I 1. Maigret's Christmas 2. Seven Little Crosses in a Notebook (*non-Maigret title*) 3. Maigret and the Surly Inspector 4. The Evidence of the Altar Boy 5. The Most Obstinate Customer in the World 6. Death of a Nobody 7. Sale by Auction 8. The Man in the Street 9. Maigret in Retirement (*novella*) (Hamish Hamilton, 1976)	£4	£7

Title	No dj	In dj
Maigret and the Ghost novel (Hamish Hamilton, 1976)	£2.50	£5
Maigret and the Spinster novel (Hamish Hamilton, 1977)	£2.50	£5
Maigret and the Hotel Majestic novel (Hamish Hamilton, 1977)	£2.50	£5
Maigret's Pipe complete Maigret short stories volume II 1. **Maigret's Pipe** (*novella*) 2. **Death Penalty** 3. **Mr Monday** 4. **The Open Window** 5. **Madame Maigret's Admirer** 6. **The Mysterious Affair in the Boulevard Beaumarchais** 7. **Two Bodies on a Barge** 8. **Death of a Woodlander** 9. **In the Rue Pigalle** 10.**Maigret's Mistake** 11.**The Old Lady of Bayeux** 12.**Stan the Killer** 13.**The Drowned Men's Inn** 14.**At the Etoile du Nord** 15.**Jeumont, 51 Minutes Stop!** 16.**Mademoiselle Berthe and her Lover** 17.**The Three Daughters of the Lawyer** 18.**Storm in the Channel** (Hamish Hamilton, 1977)	£4	£7
Maigret in Exile novel (Hamish Hamilton, 1978)	£2.50	£5
Maigret and the Toy Village novel (Hamish Hamilton, 1978)	£2.50	£5
Maigret's Rival novel (Hamish Hamilton, 1979)	£2.50	£5
Maigret in New York novel (Hamish Hamilton, 1979)	£2.50	£5
Maigret and the Coroner novels (Hamish Hamilton, 1980)	£2.50	£5

Title	No dj	In dj

OTHER TITLES

Title	No dj	In dj
The Disintegration of J.P.G. novel (George Routledge & Sons, 1937)	£50	£150+
Maigret and M. L'Abbé 1. **Death of a Harbourmaster** (*Maigret title*) 2. **The Man from Everywhere** novels (George Routledge & Sons, 1941)	£10	£35
In Two Latitudes 1. **The Mystery of the Polarlys** 2. **Tropic Moon** novels (George Routledge & Sons, 1942)	£10	£35
Affairs of Destiny 1. **Newhaven–Dieppe** 2. **The Woman of the Grey House** novels (George Routledge & Sons, 1942)	£8	£30
The Man who Watched the Trains Go By novel (George Routledge & Sons, 1942)	£8	£30
Havoc by Accident 1. **Talatala** 2. **The Breton Sisters** novels (George Routledge & Sons, 1943)	£7	£25
Escape in Vain 1. **The Lodger** 2. **One Way Out** novels (George Routledge & Sons, 1943)	£7	£25
On the Danger Line 1. **Home Town** 2. **The Green Thermos** novels (George Routledge & Sons, 1944)	£7	£20
The Shadow Falls novel (George Routledge & Sons, 1945)	£6	£15
The Lost Moorings 1. **Banana Tourist** 2. **Blind Path** novels (George Routledge & Sons, 1946)	£3	£12
Magnet of Doom novel (George Routledge & Sons, 1948)	£5	£10

Title	No dj	In dj
Black Rain 1. The Survivors 2. Black Rain novels (Routledge and Kegan Paul, 1949)	£5	£10
Chit of a Girl 1. Chit of a Girl 2. Justice novels (Routledge and Kegan Paul, 1949)	£5	£10
A Wife at Sea 1. A Wife at Sea 2. The Murderer novels (Routledge and Kegan Paul, 1949)	£5	£10
Strange Inheritance novel (Routledge and Kegan Paul, 1950)	£5	£10
Poisoned Relations 1. Monsieur la Souris 2. Poisoned Relations novels (Routledge and Kegan Paul, 1950)	£5	£10
The Strangers in the House novel (Routledge and Kegan Paul, 1951)	£5	£10
The Window over the Way 1. The Window over the Way 2. The Gendarme's Report novels (Routledge and Kegan Paul, 1951)	£5	£10
The House by the Canal 1. The House by the Canal 2. The Ostenders novels (Routledge and Kegan Paul, 1952)	£5	£10
The Burgomaster of Furnes novel (Routledge and Kegan Paul, 1952)	£5	£10
The Trial of Bébé Donge novel (Routledge and Kegan Paul, 1952)	£5	£10
The Stain on the Snow novel (Routledge and Kegan Paul, 1953)	£5	£10
Aunt Jeanne novel (Routledge and Kegan Paul, 1953)	£5	£10
Act of Passion novel (Routledge and Kegan Paul, 1953)	£5	£10

Title	No dj	In dj
Across the Street novel (Routledge and Kegan Paul, 1954)	£5	£10
Ticket of Leave novel (Routledge and Kegan Paul, 1954)	£5	£10
Violent Ends 1. Belle 2. The Brothers Rico novels (Hamish Hamilton, 1954)	£5	£10
Danger Ahead 1. Red Lights 2. The Watchmaker of Everton novels (Hamish Hamilton, 1955)	£5	£10
A Sense of Guilt 1. Chez Krull 2. The Heart of a Man novels (Hamish Hamilton, 1955)	£5	£10
The Judge and the Hatter 1. The Witnesses 2. The Hatter's Ghosts novels (Hamish Hamilton, 1956)	£5	£10
The Sacrifice 1. Mr Hire's Engagement 2. Young Cardinaud novels (Hamish Hamilton, 1956)	£4	£8
The Little Man from Archangel novel (Hamish Hamilton, 1957)	£4	£8
The Stowaway novel (Hamish Hamilton, 1957)	£4	£8
The Son novel (Hamish Hamilton, 1958)	£4	£8
Inquest on Bouvet novel (Hamish Hamilton, 1958)	£4	£8
The Negro novel (Hamish Hamilton, 1959)	£4	£8
Striptease novel (Hamish Hamilton, 1959)	£4	£8
In Case of Emergency novel (Hamish Hamilton, 1960)	£4	£8

Title	No dj	In dj
Sunday novel (Hamish Hamilton, 1960)	£4	£8
The Premier novel (Hamish Hamilton, 1961)	£4	£8
The Widower novel (Hamish Hamilton, 1961)	£4	£8
The Fate of the Malous novel (Hamish Hamilton, 1962)	£4	£8
Pedigree novel (Hamish Hamilton, 1962)	£6	£10
Account Unsettled novel (Hamish Hamilton, 1962)	£4	£8
A New Lease of Life novel (Hamish Hamilton, 1963)	£4	£8
The Iron Staircase novel (Hamish Hamilton, 1963)	£4	£8
The Patient novel (Hamish Hamilton, 1963)	£4	£8
The Train novel (Hamish Hamilton, 1964)	£4	£8
The Door novel (Hamish Hamilton, 1964)	£4	£8
The Blue Room novel (Hamish Hamilton, 1965)	£4	£7
The Man with the Little Dog novel (Hamish Hamilton, 1965)	£4	£7
The Accomplices novel (Hamish Hamilton, 1966)	£4	£7
The Little Saint novel (Hamish Hamilton, 1966)	£4	£7
The Confessional novel (Hamish Hamilton, 1967)	£4	£7
Monsieur Monde Vanishes novel (Hamish Hamilton, 1967)	£4	£7

Title	No dj	In dj
The Old Man Dies novel (Hamish Hamilton, 1968)	£4	£7
The Neighbours novel (Hamish Hamilton, 1968)	£4	£7
The Prison novel (Hamish Hamilton, 1969)	£4	£7
Big Bob novel (Hamish Hamilton, 1969)	£4	£7
The Man on the Bench in the Barn novel (Hamish Hamilton, 1970)	£4	£7
November novel (Hamish Hamilton, 1970)	£4	£7
The Rich Man novel (Hamish Hamilton, 1971)	£4	£7
Teddy Bear novel (Hamish Hamilton, 1971)	£4	£7
When I was Old autobiography (Hamish Hamilton, 1972)	£4	£7
The Disappearance of Odile novel (Hamish Hamilton, 1972)	£4	£7
The Cat novel (Hamish Hamilton, 1972)	£4	£7
The Glass Cage novel (Hamish Hamilton, 1973)	£4	£7
The Innocents novel (Hamish Hamilton, 1973)	£3	£6
The Venice Train novel (Hamish Hamilton, 1974)	£3	£5
The Magician novel (Hamish Hamilton, 1974)	£3	£5
Betty novel (Hamish Hamilton, 1975)	£3	£5
The Others novel (Hamish Hamilton, 1975)	£2.50	£5

Title	No dj	In dj
Letter to my Mother autobiography (Hamish Hamilton, 1976)	£2.50	£5
Three Beds in Manhattan novel (Hamish Hamilton, 1976)	£2.50	£5
The Girl in his Past novel (Hamish Hamilton, 1976)	£2.50	£5
Four Days in a Lifetime novel (Hamish Hamilton, 1977)	£2.50	£5
The Bottom of the Bottle novel (Hamish Hamilton, 1977)	£2.50	£5
The Girl with a Squint novel (Hamish Hamilton, 1978)	£2.50	£5
The Family Lie novel (Hamish Hamilton, 1978)	£2.50	£5
The Little Doctor 1. The Doctor's Hunch 2. The Girl in Pale Blue 3. A Woman Screamed 4. The Haunting of Monsieur Marbe 5. The Midwinter Marriage 6. The Corpse in the Kitchen Garden 7. The Dutchman's Luck 8. Popaul and his Negro 9. The Trail of the Red-Haired Man 10.The Disappearance of the Admiral 11.The Communication Cord 12.Arsenic Hall 13.Death in the Department Store short stories (Hamish Hamilton, 1978)	£3	£5
The Night Club novel (Hamish Hamilton, 1979)	£2.50	£5
African Trio 1. Talatala (reissue) 2. Tropic Moon (reissue) 3. Aboard the Aquitaine novels (Hamish Hamilton, 1979)	£2.50	£5
The White Horse Inn 1. The White Horse Inn 2. The Grandmother 3. The Country Doctor novels (Hamish Hamilton, 1980)	£2.50	£5

Title	No dj	In dj
The Long Exile novel (Hamish Hamilton, 1983)	£2.50	£5
The Reckoning novel (Hamish Hamilton, 1984)	£2.50	£5
Intimate Memoirs **including Marie-Jo's Book** autobiography (Hamish Hamilton, 1984)	£5	£7
The Couple from Poitiers novel (Hamish Hamilton, 1985)	£2.50	£5
The Outlaw novel (Hamish Hamilton, 1986)	£2.50	£5
Uncle Charles novel (Hamish Hamilton, 1988)	£2.50	£5
The Rules of the Game novel (Hamish Hamilton, 1989)	£2.50	£5

BIOGRAPHY AND BIBLIOGRAPHY

Title	No dj	In dj
Fenton Bresler **The Mystery of Georges Simenon. A biography.** (London, Heinemann/Quixote Press, 1983)	£5	£8
Stanley G. Eskin **Simenon. A critical biography** (Jefferson, N. Carolina, USA, McFarland & Co., 1987) *published without dust-wrapper*	£10	n/a
Patrick Marnham **The Man Who Wasn't Maigret. A portrait of** **Georges Simenon** (Bloomsbury, 1992)	n/a	£17.99
Pierre Assouline **Simenon: biographie** (Julliard, 1992) *large paperback in French*	n/a	£13.50
Peter Foord **Georges Simenon. A bibliography of the British first** **editions in hardback and paperback and the princi-** **pal French and American editions.** (Dragonby Press, 1988) *A5 format, soft covers*	n/a	£10

JOHN STEINBECK

It is hard to agree with Joseph Connolly that there is little interest amongst British collectors for John Steinbeck. True, he may not be so popular here as he is in his native America, but offer dealers fine copies of Steinbeck's early novels in particular and watch them snap them up. Steinbeck was one of the greatest writers of this century and *Of Mice and Men, The Winter of Our Discontent* and *The Grapes of Wrath* have all become required reading. In recent years there has been a significant increase in the popularity of twentieth-century American writers like Hemingway and Raymond Chandler.

British collectors of American writers are always faced with the same big dilemma — should they collect the first American edition, or the first appearance of the book in this country? In an ideal world, perhaps, many would prefer the US first (and they are certainly enormously expensive), but many collectors actually prefer to fly the flag and prefer the inaugural publication of their favourite book on these shores. In most cases, the British edition of American authors follows very shortly after the initial publication so there's very little to get worked up about. We will assume that British collectors are after British editions — for all intents and purposes they are more accessible, cheaper, and easier to acquire. Once you've assembled your collection of British firsts and you feel you want to extend your set, go ahead, go after the American editions. However, you might have to re-mortgage your house to do so. . .

Steinbeck's deceptively simple prose is moving: serious, but gently humorous. His books are quintessentially American, and perhaps that is their appeal to British collectors. They seem the perfect antidote to the excesses of modern living, whether they concern the poverty of grape pickers in Californian vineyards, or the adventures of a group of kind-hearted down-and-outs in Monterey. The appeal of his work is huge.

John Steinbeck was born in Salinas, California (the setting for most of his novels) on 27 February 1902, the son of a flour mill owner. Despite this middle-class background, Steinbeck grew up amongst poverty. The 1910s and 20s were a time of great change and trouble in California — farming was developing into an industry, jobs were being lost and labour unrest was endemic. It was here that the Wobblies, an early American left-wing trade union organisation, gained most ground. After school, Steinbeck worked in a Salinas sugar factory before enrolling in the University of Stanford where he studied marine biology. He was occasionally forced to break off studies to work on ranches or in factories to pay for his course. He never graduated, but he did contribute a few stories to the college paper.

Steinbeck left California to become a writer in New York in 1925 but the lean years weren't over yet. After working as a labourer on the construction of Madison Square Gardens, he managed to land a job on a newspaper, *The New York American*, for whom he did some 'lousy reporting'. He started more sustained writing though, and in 1929 his first novel was published by McBride.

Cup of Gold (subtitled 'A Life of Henry Morgan, Buccaneer, with Occasional Reference to History') is a swashbuckling historical novel set at sea, and nothing like the Steinbeck of later years. Despite being his first novel it didn't appear in Britain until January, 1937, after four other titles. The UK edition of *Cup of Gold* was issued by Heinemann in blue cloth stamped in gold (with the ubiquitous Heinemann windmill blind-stamped on the lower right-hand corner of the back cover), and in a printed dust-jacket. Naturally copies in the jacket are extremely hard to come by — most collectors settle for paying £50–£60 for a copy without a jacket.

The first British Steinbeck was actually his second book, *The Pastures of Heaven*, a series of short stories about a few families living in the Salina Valley. This was published by Philip Allan in May, 1933. Bound in green cloth lettered in black, copies seem hard to come by today. The book was virtually ignored by critics, and sales were low: it's unlikely the print-run was more than 2,000 copies. However, copies without their jackets seem reasonably common as long as you are prepared to accept slightly battered boards. A clean unmarked copy would cost up to £100, and a jacket would increase this considerably. This is roughly the same as *To a God Unknown*, published by Heinemann in April, 1935. This 268-page volume bound in blue cloth was originally priced 7s. 6d. (it's interesting to note that most new novels were issued at 7s. 6d. from around 1920 to 1950 — it just shows how little inflation affected the book trade then!). It will cost considerably more now.

Steinbeck's literary career really took off with *Tortilla Flat*, his first recognisably Steinbeckian book. This was issued by Heinemann in November, 1935, bound in blue cloth and issued in an attractive dust-jacket. Like all the early titles the print-run was low (it was an unexpected success) and finding copies in collectable condition is not easy. Easier to acquire are copies of *Of Mice and Men* (Heinemann, September, 1937): blue cloth with a blue dust-jacket printed in black with a design by Michael Rothstein, although variant issues have a white pictorial jacket or Rothstein's design printed in black and pink. This seems to be quite common without a jacket (£5–£10). *The Grapes of Wrath*, Steinbeck's masterpiece, was published by Heinemann in September, 1939, in aqua-blue cloth and issued in a rose jacket with reversed lettering. Copies with clean boards and sound joints sell for £10–£15. Copies in jackets could fetch up to £100.

Finding reasonable copies of Steinbeck's post-war novels is much easier — the print-runs seemed to increase dramatically after the war. This is particularly the case of Steinbeck's best-loved short novel, *Cannery Row* (Heinemann, 1945), although fine copies are impossible to locate. *Cannery Row* was Steinbeck's only title to be issued in accordance with wartime economy standards: it is a flimsy 136-page volume bound in orange-yellow cloth lettered in black on the front cover and spine. The dust-jacket is dark blue with the title in yellow script and the author's name set in Gill. The boards, in particular are prone to warping and the pages to browning. Steinbeck's sequel to *Cannery Row* was *Sweet Thursday*, published by Heinemann on 21 October 1954, in green cloth and issued in a colourful jacket designed by Paul Galdone (the same jacket was used for the first US edition published on 10 June the same year). Copies without this jacket are virtually worthless. Incidentally, if you can't afford the first UK hardback, spend a pound or two on the first UK paperback edition issued by Pan Books in April 1958. Cy Webb's exquisite cover painting is worth a fortune in itself.

Before *Sweet Thursday* appeared, two other classic titles strengthened Steinbeck's claims to literary greatness. The first was *The Wayward Bus*, published by Heinemann in October 1947, in coarse red cloth with a plain green dust-jacket. Interestingly enough, the first US edition suffered a little mishap early on. 5,000 copies were destroyed when the lorry carrying them from the bindery crashed into an oncoming vehicle — a wayward bus! The other classic title is *East of Eden*, immortalised for ever by the film starring James Dean. William Heinemann published the book on 24 November 1952, bound in green cloth and issued in an attractive blue and yellow jacket used on the first US edition. Because the book is bulky (525 pages) finding copies without warped or broken spines is not as easy as one might imagine, despite the high print-run. Finding copies in a clean sound jacket is even harder. One was on offer in a specialist dealer's in London for £100. With all books this size, finding absolutely fine, unblemished copies is impossible — don't even bother looking.

The last important Steinbeck is the classic *The Winter of Our Discontent*, Steinbeck's definitive tale of small-town American life featuring shopkeeper Ethan Hawley and his plan to rob a bank. This was published on 26 June 1961, a compact 365-page volume bound in purple cloth stamped in gold and issued in an attractive rose yellow and white jacket designed by Lacey Everett, a popular Heinemann artist in the early 1960s. This volume seems to have aged well, and most copies are in at least very good condition today. The dust-jacket, however, rarely turns up in pristine condition.

Steinbeck wrote little of worth after this novel, although he did reach the peak of his career when he was awarded the Nobel Prize for Literature in 1962. John Steinbeck's last few years were spent in his New York apartment where he died in 1968 of a heart attack. Since then his reputation has increased significantly and more and more collectors on this side of the Atlantic are following their American colleagues. There are distinct signs that his books are rising in value considerably. The bibliography here lists only the British editions of his work: it should be pointed out that in many cases these are actually the *fourth* appearance of the particular book, following the limited edition or proof copy, the first American trade issue, and the first Canadian edition (from Macmillan in Toronto). Collectors interested in these (and in several limited editions such as 1,500 signed copies of *East of Eden*), or in a number of pamphlets such as *A Letter From John Steinbeck Explaining Why He Could Not Write an Introduction for This Book* (1964), his tongue-in-cheek 'refusal' to introduce Ted Patrick's *The Thinking Dog's Man*, are advised to consult Robert B. Harmon's admirable bibliography, *The Collectible* [sic] *John Steinbeck, A Practical Guide*. Published by McFarland in North Carolina in 1986, I'm sure this will become a collectable volume in its own right.

Title	No dj	In dj
The Pastures of Heaven short stories (Philip Allan, 1933)	£60 - £100	£300 - £400
To a God Unknown novel (Heinemann, 1935)	£40 - £50	£200 - £300
Tortilla Flat novel (Heinemann, 1935)	£5 - £10	£100 - £150
In Dubious Battle novel (Heinemann, 1936)	£10 - £20	£75 - £100
Cup of Gold novel (Heinemann, 1937)	£50 - £60	£200 - £300
Of Mice and Men novel (Heinemann, 1937)	£5 - £10	£150 - £200
The Long Valley novel (Heinemann, 1939)	£10 - £20	£100 - £150
The Grapes of Wrath novel (Heinemann, 1939)	£10 - £15	£80 - £100
The Moon Is Down novel (Heinemann, 1942)	−	£10 - £15
Cannery Row novel (Heinemann, 1945)	−	£20 - £25
The Wayward Bus novel (Heinemann, 1947)	−	£10 - £15
The Pearl novel (Heinemann, 1948)	−	£10 - £15
A Russian Journal non-fiction (Heinemann, 1949) *features photographs by Robert Capa*	£10 - £20	£30 - £40
Burning Bright novel (Heinemann, 1951)	£5 - £10	£15 - £20
East of Eden novel (Heinemann, 1952)	£10 - £15	£50 - £100
Sweet Thursday novel (Heinemann, 1954)	−	£5 - £10
The Short Reign of Pippin IV novel (Heinemann, 1957)	−	£5 - £10

Title	No dj	In dj
The Log from the Sea of Cortez novel (Heinemann, 1958)	–	£10 - £15
Once There Was a War wartime dispatches (Heinemann, 1959)	–	£10 - £15
The Winter of Our Discontent novel (Heinemann, 1961)	–	£10 - £20
Travels with Charley documentary (Heinemann, 1962)	–	£10 - £15
America and the Americans documentary (Heinemann, 1966)	–	£10 - £15
The Acts of King Arthur and His Noble Knights novel (Heinemann, 1977)	–	£5 - £10

TOLKIEN AND MERVYN PEAKE

One of the most interesting developments in collecting modern first editions in the last twenty years is the rise in popularity of fantastic literature. English literature has a long and rich tradition of this particular genre from Jonathan Swift and John Bunyan in the seventeenth century, to writers like Arthur Machen at the end of the nineteenth. In the world of modern first editions, however, the two undoubted masters are J.R.R. Tolkien and Mervyn Peake.

Tolkien achieved what few writers have ever done: he created a whole world for his characters, a world which has been read about, studied and analysed by readers and critics for decades, and which continues to charm, amuse and occasionally infuriate readers all over the world. Mervyn Peake's *Gormenghast* trilogy is classic and will be read for many, many years to come. He published a wide range of work in his lifetime and all of this is collectable. He also provided illustrations for books by all kinds of authors including classics like Lewis Carroll and Honoré de Balzac, contemporaries like C.E.M. Joad and E.C. Palmer, and writers who refuse to be classified like Quentin Crisp. Everything Peakian is sought after today.

John Ronald Reuel Tolkien was born in the Orange Free State of South Africa on 3 January 1892, where his father was a bank manager in Bloemfontein. During a holiday in Birmingham with his mother, Tolkien's father died and the family decided to stay in Britain. For four very important years, Tolkien lived deep in the English countryside — his love of this landscape was to prove useful in later years when he came to describe Middle Earth.

In 1900 Tolkien was sent to King Edward's School in Birmingham where he proved an excellent pupil with an exceptional gift for languages, particularly medieval languages like Old Norse and Middle English although he also learned to speak Finnish and Welsh, for instance. He also became interested in medieval myths and legends — much later he published *A Middle English Vocabulary* (1922), edited new versions of *Sir Gawain and the Green Knight* and produced a lecture on *Beowulf* (1936). There are many of these myths in *The Hobbit* and *The Lord of the Rings*. He was always fascinated by languages, and invented languages of his own as well as myths to surround these languages. Around this time he also became a Roman Catholic.

In 1910, Tolkien entered Exeter College, Oxford, where he eventually gained a first class degree in English but before he could continue his studies, he became a signaller in the Lancashire Fusiliers, serving a few months at the front before contracting trench fever and being invalided home. After the war he worked as a lexicographer on the *Oxford English Dictionary*, before being appointed to an academic post at the University of Leeds. It was while he was at Leeds that his early philological works were published. Both *A Middle English vocabulary* and *Sir Gawain and the Green Knight* (co-edited with E.V. Gordon) are eagerly sought after today. The former was issued in printed wrappers and can sell for £50–£80 today; the latter fetches up to £150 in its rather plain jacket, £50 without.

When Tolkien moved on to become Professor of Anglo-Saxon at Oxford in 1925 he immersed himself in his beloved languages and secret worlds. Before long, the well-chronicled Inklings were formed and, over the years, Tolkien, C.S. Lewis and Charles Williams drank beer and discussed their respective works. You can read about them in Humphrey Carpenter's eponymous book as well as his biography of Tolkien. It was an important period in Tolkien's creative life; in the early 1930s, the wonderful saga of Middle Earth and the hobbits like Bilbo Baggins and Frodo was beginning to take shape in his mind.

The first readers knew of these developments was the publication of *The Hobbit* on 21 September 1937, by Allen & Unwin. Although it was originally intended for children it is one of the most read books of the twentieth century, and certainly one of the most collectable. A few years ago it was possible to find copies in their jackets for around £500–£600; a couple of years ago one copy was sold at auction for a princely £2,800 and in October 1992 a dealer was asking £6,500. Even copies without their jackets can sell for around £300. The first edition of *The Hobbit* carried several fine line illustrations by Tolkien himself; the second impression issued in 1938 also included four colour plates by the author which makes this impression almost as collectable as the first. A fine copy in its jacket could well sell for £500–£600 on the current market. This isn't the only collectable title from the 1930s. In 1936 Tolkien and others produced a collection of verse entitled *Songs for the Philologists*. Issued in paper wrappers and printed at the authors' expense, this is extremely rare today. Any copy that does turn up could sell for £500.

Tolkien's *The Lord of the Rings* was issued in three volumes by Allen & Unwin in 1954 and 1955, although Tolkien had been working on it for nearly twenty years. 3,500 copies of *The Fellowship of the Ring* were issued in the summer of 1954 followed three months later by *The Two Towers*. The final part, *The Return of the King*, was issued in October 1955. The three volumes make up a truly remarkable work, although few are agreed over its meaning. Some dismiss it as merely being an imaginative children's work while others view it as one of the most impressive moral tales ever told. Arguments still rage over its merits but it must be said that it makes impressive reading and has acquired something of a cult status, particularly amongst the young. It is still in print today, in many editions from the humblest one-volume paperback to the Folio Society's sumptuous three volume set in a slip-case.

Most collectors would love to own the first impressions, particularly in their dust-jackets. The first title is by far the hardest to find now, and it's not unknown for copies in good condition to sell for £500. Copies without jackets invariably reach £50–£80, although they would have to be in almost tip-top condition to fetch these prices. *The Two Towers* is slightly easier to find (but not much) whilst, as you would expect, *The Return of the King* is the most common. However, although plenty of copies seem to be in circulation, dealers are aware of the demand (particularly from the other side of the Atlantic) and the prices are by no means negligible. Good copies with no sunning to the spine or nicks at the edges can sell for around £250–£300, and even those without their jackets have been known to sell for £30–£40. Complete sets of all three volumes in their jackets are occasionally offered but the asking price is invariably significantly higher than the sum of the individual volumes. If the jackets are clean and reasonably unsullied, a set could fetch as much as £2,000, perhaps slightly more.

Mervyn Peake's *Gormenghast* trilogy won't fetch those sort of prices, but they are still very hard to come by today. Mervyn Lawrence Peake was born on 9 July 1911, in Kuling, Central China but, because his father was a missionary doctor during revolutionary times, the family soon moved to Tientsin. When he was twelve the family returned to England. He was educated at Eltham College before attending Croydon School of Art and the Royal Academy Schools. After college he went to the Isle of Sark to paint (it was there that the Sark Group was set up), exhibiting in London before teaching life drawing at the Westminster School of Art from 1935 to 1938.

Peake's first book was published by Country Life in 1939. Intended originally for children, *Captain Slaughterboard Drops Anchor* is very scarce today and very good copies sell for at least £300 today in their dust-jackets. It's hard to find these today, though. Most collectors make do with a jacketless copy, but even this could cost around £100. It is a beautiful book and contains some of Peake's best drawings.

During the Second World War, Peake served in an anti-aircraft regiment before being invalided out in 1943. This allowed him to concentrate on his writing and drawing, although he did visit Germany in 1946 to record the devastation for *Leader* magazine — his time spent making drawings at Belsen affected his later art greatly. In 1947 he returned to Sark with his wife, Maeve Gilmore, where he wrote *Gormenghast*, before returning to London to teach at the Central School of Arts and Crafts from 1950 to 1960. However in 1955 his health started to fail. He eventually contracted Parkinson's Disease and spent the last four years of his life in hospital. Mervyn Peake, one of the greatest illustrators of the twentieth century, died in 1968.

Peake's highlight is of course the three volumes *Titus Groan* (Eyre & Spottiswoode, 1946), *Gormenghast* (Eyre & Spottiswoode, 1950) and *Titus Alone* (Eyre & Spottiswoode, 1959). All three volumes feature jackets designed by Peake himself and none is hard to find in collectable condition. It seems that the print-run of the first book was particularly low which may account for the current asking price of £150+. *Gormenghast* might fetch up to £80 if the jacket is clean, and *Titus Alone* isn't too hard to find in the region of £50. Copies of these books without their jackets aren't really worth acquiring. A copy of *Titus Groan* might fetch £10–£15, but certainly not any more.

Considering Peake's genius as an illustrator, it's very surprising that the first editions of his masterpiece had none of his drawings, especially as the original manuscripts were accompanied by numerous sketches. Some of these found their way into the later editions which appeared in the late 1960s by which time the trilogy was rivalling Tolkien's as the bible of the hippy movement.

The trilogy is by no means Peake's only collectable work. He was also an accomplished poet and produced no fewer than eight volumes of verse. The first was *Shapes and Sounds*, published by Chatto & Windus in 1941. This is particularly scarce today, and very good copies sell for at least £150, often much more. Some of Peake's verse collections were issued in attractive limited editions. *Poems and Drawings* was issued in wrappers in an edition of 150 copies by the Keepsake Press in 1965; *A Reverie of Bone* was published in soft wrappers with a dust-jacket in an edition of 320 copies by Bertram Rota in 1967; and the posthumous *Twelve Poems* (with a dust-jacket) from the Bran's Head Press in 1975 was limited to 350 copies. None of these collections was reprinted in their own right, although poems from the first two appeared in Faber's *Selected Poems* in 1972, and from all three in *Peake's Progress: Selected Writings and Drawings* (Allen Lane, 1979). This last title is a wonderful introduction to his work in its entirety, but it is far from scarce. In fact, unsold copies of the first edition (edited by Peake's widow) were remaindered at just a few pounds each. Copies still turn up in those 'Book Bargain' stores many collectors avoid.

Title	No dj	In dj
TOLKIEN		
A Middle English Vocabulary non-fiction (Oxford University Press, 1922)	£50 – £80	n/a
Sir Gawain and the Green Knight (Oxford University Press, 1925) *edited with E.V. Gordon*	£40 – £50	£100 – £150
Songs for the Philologists verse (privately printed, 1936)	£400 – £500	n/a
Beowulf: The Monsters and the Critics lecture (Oxford University Press, 1936)	£50 – £60	n/a
The Hobbit novel (Allen & Unwin, 1937)	£250 – £300	£4,500+
Farmer Giles of Ham novel (Allen & Unwin, 1949) *illustrated by Pauline Barnes*	£10 – £20	£60 – £80
The Fellowship of the Ring novel (Allen & Unwin, 1954)	£50 – £80	£400 – £500
The Two Towers novel (Allen & Unwin, 1954)	£40 – £50	£300 – £400
The Return of the King novel (Allen & Unwin, 1955)	£30 – £40	£250 – £300
Ancrene Wisse non-fiction (Oxford University Press, 1962)	£4 – £6	£10 – £15

Title	No dj	In dj
The Adventures of Tom Bombadil verse (Allen & Unwin, 1962)	£5 – £10	£30 – £40
Tree and Leaf essay (Allen & Unwin, 1964)	£5 – £10	£25 – £30
Smith of Wootton Major novella (Allen & Unwin, 1967)	£10 – £15	£20 – £25
The Road Goes Ever On verse (Allen & Unwin, 1968)	–	£15 – £20
Bilbo's Last Song poster poem (Allen & Unwin, 1974)	£15 – £20	n/a
Sir Gawain and the Green Knight, Pearl and Sir Orfeo translation (Allen & Unwin, 1975)	–	£10 – £15
The Homecoming of Beorhtnoth poem (Allen & Unwin, 1975)	–	£10 – £15
The Father Christmas Letters children's (Allen & Unwin, 1976) *issued in pictorial boards*	£8 – £10	n/a
The Silmarillion novel (Allen & Unwin, 1977)	–	£10 – £15
Pictures by J.R.R. Tolkien paintings (Allen & Unwin, 1979)	£4 – £6	£10 – £12
Poems and Stories (Allen & Unwin, 1980) *issued in a slip-case*	£10 – £15	£20 – £25
Unfinished Tales of Numenor and Middle Earth Novel (Allen & Unwin, 1980)	–	£10 – £15
Letters (Allen & Unwin, 1981)	–	£5 – £10
Mr Bliss children's (Allen & Unwin, 1982)	–	£5 – £8
Finn and Hengest (Allen & Unwin, 1983)	–	£5 – £8
The Book of Lost Tales 1 (Allen & Unwin, 1983)	–	£5 – £8

Title	No dj	In dj
The Book of Lost Tales 2 (Allen & Unwin, 1984)	–	£5 – £8
The Book of Lost Tales 3: The Lays of Beleriand (Allen & Unwin, 1985)	–	£5 – £8
The Book of Lost Tales 4: The Shaping of Middle Earth (Allen & Unwin, 1986)	–	£5 – £8

MERVYN PEAKE

Title	No dj	In dj
Captain Slaughterboard Drops Anchor children's (Country Life, 1939)	£80 – £100	£300 – £400
Shapes and Sounds verse (Chatto & Windus, 1941)	£30 – £50	£150 – £200
Rhymes Without Reasons verse (Eyre & Spottiswoode, 1944)	£30 – £40	£80 – £100
The Craft of the Lead Pencil non-fiction (Wingate, 1946) *issued in pictorial boards*	£40 – £60	n/a
Titus Groan novel (Eyre & Spottiswoode, 1946)	£10 – £15	£150 – £200
Letters from a Lost Uncle from Polar Regions children's stories (Eyre & Spottiswoode, 1948)	£30 – £40	£100 – £150
The Drawings of Mervyn Peake (Grey Walls Press, 1949)	£20 – £30	£50 – £80
The Glassblowers verse (Eyre & Spottiswoode, 1950)	£10 – £20	£50 – £80
Gormenghast novel (Eyre & Spottiswoode, 1950)	–	£50 – £80
Mr Pye novel (Heinemann, 1953)	–	£40 – £50
Titus Alone novel (Eyre & Spottiswoode, 1959)	–	£40 – £50
The Rhyme of the Flying Bomb verse (Dent, 1962)	£5 – £10	£30 – £40

Title	No dj	In dj
Poems and Drawings (Keepsake Press, 1965) *150 copies issued in soft wrappers*	£150 – £200	n/a
A Reverie of Bone verse (Bertram Rota, 1967) *320 copies in soft wrappers with dust-jacket*	£40 – £50	£80 – £100
Selected Poems (Faber, 1972)	–	£10 – £15
A Book of Nonsense (Owen, 1972)	–	£10 – £15
The Drawings of Mervyn Peake (Davis-Poynter, 1974)	£5 – £10	£15 – £20
Twelve Poems 1939–1960 (Bran's Head, 1975)	£20 – £30	£40 – £50
Peake's Progress: Selected Writings and Drawings (Allen Lane, 1979)	–	£5 – £8

EVELYN WAUGH

Evelyn Waugh is without doubt one of the finest comic writers Britain has ever produced — and as a result of Granada TV's splendid dramatisation in the late 1970s, most people know him only for *Brideshead Revisited* — probably his least successful novel from a literary point of view. Long before he wrote *Brideshead* in 1945, he had produced a string of comic classics as well as giving life to such memorable characters as Paul Pennyfeather, Lady Metroland, Basil Seal, Captain Grimes and Margot Beste-Chetwynde. Twentieth-century English literature would have been poorer without him.

Waugh's books represent a special challenge to modern first edition enthusiasts. Putting together a set of his later novels published during the 1950s and 60s shouldn't prove too troublesome, but acquiring his earliest titles in reasonable condition can represent a lifetime's work. So how come Waugh attracts so many devoted collectors to spend so much time and money on him? It's not hard to see. His books are quite superb, both from a literary and physical viewpoint. Waugh designed many of his early dust-jackets himself, and even those he had no hand in are a pleasure to own. Many of his most respected titles were issued in luxurious limited editions, although these are out of the scope of this book. Collectors quite happily pay up to £2,000 each for the special editions of his first four novels published simultaneously by Chapman & Hall in 1937 — each title was limited to just 12 copies printed on rag mould-made paper. These editions are out of the reach of the ordinary collector, though (they are usually snapped up by American or Japanese enthusiasts). It's enough of a job putting together a collection of trade firsts!

What makes Evelyn Waugh's early novels in particular so humorous is the fact that to a certain extent the author was writing about himself and his friends. He was capturing the ludicrous exploits of the Bright Young Things of the 1920s. Arthur Evelyn St John Waugh was born on 28 October 1903, in North London, the youngest son of the managing director of Chapman & Hall. After a horrific time at Lancing he studied at Hertford College, Oxford where he formed lifelong friendships with Tom Driberg, Robert Byron, Hugh Lygon, Harold Acton and the notorious Brian Howard. All these friends appeared, thinly disguised, in his novels.

He left Oxford with a third-class degree in 1924, and found it hard to settle to any work. It was a miserable period, made worse by years of drudgery working as a teacher and heightened by his embarrassment at being ever-so-slightly middle class. There is a marvellous story that as a young man Waugh frequently walked miles to post his letters just so they would carry a more prestigious postmark. Things became so bad that he tried to drown himself although his intention to swim out to sea was called off when he found himself amidst a shoal of jellyfish. The only work he enjoyed doing around this time was designing dust-jackets for Chapman & Hall.

Evelyn Waugh's first literary efforts were uninspiring affairs, but they are phenomenally valuable today. As a precocious thirteen-year-old he privately printed his *The World to Come: A Poem in Three Cantos*. It's unlikely that more than a handful of copies were produced (in fact, its existence was unknown for many years), and the only copy collectors are ever likely to see is the one which surfaced in the British Library a few years ago. If a copy was offered for sale it wouldn't surprise many pundits if it sold for at least £10,000, perhaps very much more. His second offering is hardly less scarce. In 1926 a friend printed twenty-five copies of Waugh's essay *PRB: An Essay on the Pre-Raphaelite Brotherhood*. The slim volume was issued without a dust-jacket, but even so copies can sell for around £2,000 – £5,000 in fine condition. In 1988 a copy with neither jacket nor spine was offered for £1,300! With a book so scarce, copies in almost any condition fetch amazing prices. Perhaps it's time for an enterprising publisher to produce facsimile editions of these works.

Very good copies of Evelyn Waugh's early novels are hard but not impossible to find today. *Decline and Fall* was published by Chapman & Hall in September, 1928, and set the tone for all his later titles. Waugh designed the jacket showing its hero in four states of downward descent (from student to priest, via bridegroom and convict), as well as providing several humorous line drawings to illustrate the novel. It's not unknown for copies in reasonable condition to sell for at least £600 today — fine copies might fetch as much as £1,000 if the conditions are right. Equally scarce are first editions of his second novel, *Vile Bodies*, which appeared in January 1930. This is probably Waugh's funniest title, a savage but generally affectionate portrait of the Bright Young Things. Again, Waugh designed the yellow jacket featuring a cartoon of a racing car, and copies sell for around the same as *Decline and Fall*. Needless to say, copies without these marvellous jackets are worth a fraction of their potential price, but they are still sought after — few copies survive complete with their jackets.

Waugh was one of the most successful novelists of the 1930s, and a run through his titles shows why. *Black Mischief*, *A Handful of Dust* and *Scoop* all appeared then, as did *Mr Loveday's Little Outing*, three travel books and a biography of Edmund Campion. All these titles are scarce, but it's safe to say that the novels are the most sought after. All three were issued in the familiar brown-purple speckled cloth boards (which seems to have aged well in most cases), but finding copies in clean jackets is by no means easy. *Black Mischief*'s plain buff jacket with the title printed in bold black lettering on the front cover is particularly prone to soiling, and *Scoop*'s jacket is rarely seen these days. It is a wonderfully original design. *Scoop*, of course, tells the story of how a country diarist instead of a successful novelist with the same name is sent to cover 'a promising little war' in a remote African republic by the *Daily Beast*. The jacket makes great play on this newspaper theme. Against a red background is a pastiche of a newspaper story providing the book's blurb and a photograph of the author. Presentable copies with this jacket sell for up to £200. Copies without the jacket fetch in the region of £20 – £30.

Another beautiful jacket is that issued with Waugh's short novel, *The Loved One* (Chapman & Hall, 1948), a humorous study of the American way of death. Stuart Boyle's wonderful line drawing is one of the most attractive jackets on any novel, particularly impressive because the whole volume is printed on very thin paper and produced in conformity with wartime economy standards. Because the print-run for the book was high, collectors should accept nothing less than fine copies, although these aren't easy to find because they tear easily. They shouldn't cost more than £25 today. Incidentally, this book edition wasn't the 'true' first edition of *The Loved One*. It originally appeared as a whole issue of Cyril Connolly's literary journal *Horizon* in February 1948. Waugh completists will want both. This edition of *Horizon* will cost around £10.

No Waugh collection is complete without the *Sword of Honour* trilogy: *Men at Arms* (1952), *Officers and Gentlemen* (1955), and *Unconditional Surrender* (1961). This moving account of Guy Crouchback's progress through the Second World War is one of the masterpieces of modern fiction, and certainly Waugh's best work. All three titles were bound in a resilient royal blue cloth and issued in an attractive series of dust-jackets designed by Val Biro, a prolific and talented illustrator. Acquiring the three volumes throws up one of the curiosities of book collecting. If you can manage to find three fine copies separately they will cost little more than £20 – £30 each, but a ready-made set in truly fine condition will set you back at least £150. Incidentally, Biro also designed the wonderful dust-jacket for *The Ordeal of Gilbert Pinfold*, Waugh's harrowing fictional account of his mental breakdown. It appeared in 1957.

Waugh is best known for his fiction, of course, but he also produced some excellent travel books, all of which are collectable today. Predictably, it is the earliest titles such as *Labels* and *Remote People* which cause most problems, but few are very easy. Even his 1960 offering, *A Tourist in Africa* has become scarce. Just five years ago it was easy to pick up for around £20 — now it would cost at least double that.

Mention has already been made of Waugh's habit of issuing his works in very limited special editions. The ordinary collector can usually ignore these, but there are two titles which were issued in limited edition print-runs only. In 1942 Chapman & Hall issued *Work Suspended: Two Chapters of an Unfinished Novel* in an edition of just 500 copies, and in 1963 Waugh's last novel, *Basil Seal Rides Again* or *The Rake's Progress* was published in an edition of 750 signed copies. This is a particularly attractive volume with illustrations by Kathleen Hale, the author of *Orlando, the Marmalade Cat* books. By the time Evelyn Waugh died at his large Somerset home on 10 April 1966, he had secured his reputation as one of the leading writers of the century. He was collectable even then, and little has happened to change that over the last quarter of a century.

Title	No dj	In dj
The World to Come: A Poem in Three Cantos verse (privately printed, 1916)	£10,000+	n/a
PRB: An Essay on the Pre-Raphaelite Brotherhood non-fiction (privately printed, 1926)	£3,000 – £5,000	n/a
Rossetti biography (Duckworth, 1928)	£50 – £100	£500 – £600
Decline and Fall novel (Chapman & Hall, 1928)	£50 – £100	£600+
Labels travel (Duckworth, 1930)	£40 – £60	£200 – £300
Vile Bodies novel (Chapman & Hall, 1930)	£40 – £60	£600+
Remote People travel (Duckworth, 1931)	£30 – £50	£200 – £300
Black Mischief novel (Chapman & Hall, 1932)	£30 – £50	£200 – £300
An Open Letter to his Eminence the Cardinal Archbishop of Westminster (privately printed, 1933)	£2,000+	n/a
A Handful of Dust novel (Chapman & Hall, 1934)	£30 – £40	£200 – £300
Ninety-Two Days travel (Duckworth, 1934)	£30 – £40	£200 – £300
Edmund Campion biography (Longman, 1935)	£40 – £60	£200 – £300
Mr Loveday's Little Outing short stories (Chapman & Hall, 1936)	£50 – £100	£200 – £300
Waugh in Abyssinia travel (Longman, 1936)	£40 – £60	£200 – £300
Scoop novel (Chapman & Hall, 1938)	£20 – £30	£150 – £200
Robbery Under Law travel (Chapman & Hall, 1939)	£40 – £60	£200 – £300
Put Out More Flags novel (Chapman & Hall, 1942)	£20 – £25	£50 – £100

Title	No dj	In dj
Work Suspended: Two Chapters of an Unfinished Novel fragment (Chapman & Hall, 1942) *limited to 500 copies*	£30 – £50	£100 – £150
Brideshead Revisited novel (Chapman & Hall, 1945)	£10 – £20	£100 – £150
When the Going Was Good travel (Duckworth, 1946)	£20 – £30	£100 – £150
Scott-King's Modern Europe novella (Chapman & Hall, 1947)	–	£20 – £30
The Loved One novel (Chapman & Hall, 1948)	–	£20 – £25
Helena novel (Chapman & Hall, 1950)	–	£20 – £25
The Holy Places essay (Queen Anne Press, 1952)	£10 – £20	£50 – £60
Men at Arms novel (Chapman & Hall, 1952)	–	£20 – £30
Love Among the Ruins novel (Chapman & Hall, 1953)	–	£20 – £30
Officers and Gentlemen novel (Chapman & Hall, 1955)	–	£20 – £30
The Ordeal of Gilbert Pinfold novel (Chapman & Hall, 1957)	–	£20 – £30
Ronald Knox biography (Chapman & Hall, 1959)	–	£20 – £25
A Tourist in Africa travel (Chapman & Hall, 1960)	–	£40 – £45
Unconditional Surrender novel (Chapman & Hall, 1961)	–	£20 – £30
Basil Seal Rides Again novel (Chapman & Hall, 1963) *limited to 750 signed copies*	£40 – £50	£100+
A Little Learning autobiography (Chapman & Hall, 1964)	–	£20 – £25

Title	No dj	In dj
The Diaries of Evelyn Waugh (Weidenfeld & Nicolson, 1976)	–	£20 – £30
A Little Order journalism (Methuen, 1977)	–	£10 – £20
The Letters of Evelyn Waugh (Weidenfeld & Nicolson, 1980)	£10 – £20	–
The Essays, Articles and Reviews of Evelyn Waugh (Methuen, 1983)	–	£10 – £20

HENRY WILLIAMSON

There always seems to have been some doubt that Henry Williamson was one of the valid and significant voices of twentieth-century literature. Slighted and dismissed by some of his critics as 'just another nature writer', or scorned for the unpopular political stance he took during the thirties and forties (he supported Hitler and Oswald Mosley's *British Union of Fascism* movement), his reputation as a writer was considerably diminished. Yet he was the author of over twenty novels, including his fifteen volume sequence, *A Chronicle of Ancient Sunlight*, chosen by Anthony Burgess in 1984 as one of the best Ninety-Nine Novels in English since 1939.

However, it was the celebrated Proust scholar, George Painter, who, in the late fifties, identified the 'underground' army of readers who had supported and championed Williamson over the years; buying, reading and collecting his books, despite lofty criticism by the establishment and Williamson's apparent exclusion from the glittering prizes.

Today that readership has emerged from the underground and is prepared to be counted. The Henry Williamson Society boasts over 600 members. Perhaps his work is now being read and judged by a generation that appreciates Williamson's attitude to the farm, the land and its wild creatures in an era when conservation has become a major issue: a generation that, however, mystified by Williamson's awkward political leanings, does not necessarily believe his entire *oeuvre* to be poisoned with fascist indoctrination.

Williamson was born in 1895 and grew up in a south London suburb. He went to Colfe's school in Blackheath and, after just a year as a clerk in a City office, joined the army and went to serve in France for five years. Those years on the Western Front were to prove pivotal in Williamson's development. His entire adult character was forged on the battlefields of the Western Front; in an astonished realisation of the innocence of his enemies (as personified in the celebrated Christmas Truce in which he took part) — were sown the seeds of deep compassion that permeates so much of his work and, perhaps, the pro-German attitude that was to prove so disastrous to his reputation twenty-five years later.

After demob, Williamson spent some time on the fringes of Fleet Street, writing nature sketches and Light Car Notes for Bernard Falk at the *Weekly Dispatch*. At night he worked secretly and by candlelight upon the book — the testament — 'that would solve the world's problems and end man's un-understanding — while, at the same time, awakening it to the unheralded prophet in its midst'. But Williamson never published *A Policy of Reconstruction*, although it was the genesis of his first sequence of four novels *The Flax of Dream* (1921–1928). In fact, more of Williamson's writing was discarded than was ever published. A constant reviser and corrector of work, he let no opportunity pass to rework his material: probably utilising the wastepaper basket better than any of his contemporaries.

Friction at the family home in South London forced Williamson to review his situation. During 1919 he became the tenant of a cottage in a tiny Devon village. He decided he would make it his permanent home and, indeed, until his death in 1977, he always had a home in North Devon.

During this period (1921) his first novel was published by Collins. *The Beautiful Years* was book one of his 'Willie Maddison' tetralogy. Collins published the next two volumes within three years, but by the time he had completed the final volume, Jonathan Cape and Putnams were publishing his work.

The years 1921–1928 were arguably the most significant period of his writing. In that time he published the first faltering versions of the 'Willie Maddison' books as well as the subsequent, revised versions, the early nature sketches of *The Lone Swallows* (1922), and unsurpassed animal and hunting sketches of *The Peregrine's Saga* (1923) and *The Old Stag* (1926). The remarkable *Tarka the Otter* (1927) was published by himself in a small edition and followed rather grudgingly by a subsequent trade edition from a suspicious Putnams (yet the book was soon to be lauded as the 1928 Hawthornden Prize winner and greeted as a classic of its genre by later generations). Finally, in 1928, came *The Pathway*, the last of the 'Willie Maddison' books, a sophisticated and masterly novel.

His reputation then was as great as it has ever been. The Hawthornden Prize carried as much razzmatazz in the twenties as the Booker Prize does today. His photograph was in every newspaper and editors jostled to print his sketches and stories. Even across the Atlantic he was achieving slight success, with American editions of all his books in print.

The accolades continued. He was just in time to climb aboard the Great War books bandwagon with *The Patriot's Progress* (1930), which the artist William Kermode had anticipated as being a vehicle for his series of lino-cuts, with captions written by Williamson. In the event, Williamson's contribution dominated and engulfed the illustrations. Whilst not yet capable of approaching his experiences during the war as he dared hope he one day might, Williamson nevertheless produced such a powerful indictment of war that Arnold Bennett, reviewing the novel in his newspaper column, was compelled to admit to being completely outclassed as a descriptive writer.

During the thirties Williamson's drive and inspiration appeared to desert him. The two books of nature essays, country sketches and stories that life in his Devon village inspired — *The Village Book* (1930) and *The Labouring Life* (1932) — are quite excellent and representative of some of his finest work. At the time they were not great sellers. Perhaps his choice of material was unwise: another collection of essays, stories and short pieces, *The Linhay on the Downs* (1934), was just as poorly received.

His anonymous novel *The Gold Falcon* (1933), whilst initially quite successful — as well as rather controversial as critics and reviewers attempted (mostly unsuccessfully) to uncover the author's identity — proved to be flawed and rather uncomfortable. Equally unremarkable was *The Star Born* (1933), supposedly the 'celestial fantasy' written by Willie Maddison, central character of *The Flax of Dream* series. Whilst attractively illustrated by a rather bemused C.F. Tunnicliffe, it was probably a book that Williamson should have thought twice about publishing — or even writing.

On Foot in Devon (1933) and *Devon Holiday* (1935) were skylarking potboilers that helped pay a few bills but did little for his reputation. However, also in 1935, in a remarkable display of brinkmanship with new publishers Faber & Faber — and after months of kicking and screaming against the tyranny of writing for a living — Williamson once again confounded his critics and came up with another magnificent best-seller. This was *Salar the Salmon*, which many compare favourably with *Tarka*, and not a few consider an even better book.

Nevertheless Williamson was by now disillusioned with Devon and the writing life. *Salar* had been a dreadful burden and the golden days of 1930 seemed years away. The family was large and growing all the time and Williamson was tired and restless: he needed uplifting. He naively encouraged a change in his own fortunes by alienating a large number of his readers when Faber put out a one-volume edition of *The Flax of Dream* in 1936. Williamson's answer to a Europe vibrating to the sound of jackboots was to include, in his preface to the new edition, a salute to the great man across the Rhine.

Europe's future, he felt, was in its agricultural policy and perhaps his own soul could be saved by hard, manual labour serving the land. He moved the family from Devon to a near-derelict farm on the North Norfolk coast and set about the task of renewing both himself and the farm. *The Story of a Norfolk Farm* was published in 1941, in the same year that he published a short memoir of his friend Lawrence of Arabia, *Genius of Friendship: T.E. Lawrence*.

Wartime subsidies ensured success for the farming venture, but Williamson was still very unsettled. He returned alone to Devon, where he remarried and began the task he had long been preparing for — a novel showing the rise and fall of modern Europe through one family unit and his main character (roughly based in part upon himself and some of his own experiences) would be another Maddison: Phillip, cousin of Willie who had drowned twenty years earlier at the denouement of *The Pathway*.

Eventually Macdonald accepted the first book, *The Dark Lantern*, which they published in 1951. By the time Williamson had taken Phillip Maddison through five years of war and through love affairs, best-sellers, farm life and political diatribes between the wars, eighteen years and fifteen volumes had elapsed. *A Chronicle of Ancient Sunlight* is uneven and flawed, but within it is some magnificent work and several of the novels can stand by themselves against any other contemporary work.

Having published over fifty books, Henry Williamson died aged 82 in 1977.

Collecting his books is not easy but neither is it impossible and, once formed, the collection will prove a very handsome library, for much of Williamson's work was published during the twenties and thirties — an acme of fine commercial book production and at least two of his publishers, Jonathan Cape and Faber & Faber, could be relied upon to produce exceedingly good quality books.

At the same time, a Williamson library is enhanced by the many deluxe and signed editions that were a feature of this era of publishing. Altogether Williamson produced fifteen such deluxe editions, from the magnificent privately printed *Tarka the Otter* (1927), limited to 100 signed copies bound in full vellum, printed for the author and sold by him, to the miserable *The Scandaroon* (1972), limited to

250 signed copies in a horrid gilt-blocked rexine and foisted onto an unsuspecting world by Macdonald.

To put together a Williamson collection with fine jackets (where applicable) is an expensive proposition, for books of the twenties and thirties in such state are very much at a premium. Copies of the early *Flax of Dream* novels published by Collins are practically unknown in their jackets.

Quite a few of his books were only ever published in one edition and others were so thoroughly rewritten that both first and subsequent editions require to be collected. This also enhances prices, particularly of less fine copies, for then the collector is competing with the reader for elusive texts.

The novels of *A Chronicle of Ancient Sunlight* have become scarce over the years and a mint set of the fifteen first editions now commands in excess of £600, many of the individual books fetching up to £60–£70 — if in mint condition. Even the second edition that Macdonald eventually published during the mid-1980s (and which, by a lack of vision, was allowed to be remaindered for less than £20 a set) is becoming less easy to locate.

Title	No dj	In dj
The Beautiful Years	£100	–
novel (Collins, 1921)		
revised edition (Faber, 1929)	£10	£25
also limited edition of 200 copies	£75	n/a
The Lone Swallows	£45	n/a
essays (Collins, 1922)		
revised illustrated edition (Putnam, 1933)	£15	£30
Dandelion Days	£120	–
novel (Collins, 1922)		
revised edition (Faber, 1930)	£10	£25
also limited edition of 200 copies	£75	n/a
The Peregrine's Saga	£45	£185
stories (Collins, 1923)		
revised illustrated edition (Putnam, 1934)	£15	£30
The Dream of Fair Women	£120	–
novel (Collins, 1924)		
revised edition with a Valediction (Faber, 1931)	£10	£25
also limited edition of 200 copies	£75	n/a

Title	No dj	In dj
The Old Stag	£15	£35
stories (Putnam, 1926)		
revised illustrated edition (Putnam, 1933)	£15	£30
Tarka the Otter	£350	n/a
novel (privately printed 100 copies, 1927)		
another edition 1,000 copies (Putnam, 1927)	£150	n/a
another edition (Putnam, 1927)	£30	£60
revised edition (Putnam, 1928)	£15	£30
illustrated edition (Putnam, 1932)	£10	£35
The Pathway	£25	£50
novel (Cape, 1928)		
deluxe limited edition of 200 copies (1931)	£75	n/a
The Ackymals	£150	n/a
story (Windsor Press, San Francisco, 1929)		
225 copies		
The Linhay on the Downs	£30	£45
two stories (Woburn Books, 1929)		
530 copies		
The Wet Flanders Plain	£200/£75	n/a
(Beaumont Press, 1929) *400 copies of which 80 on*		
parchment vellum, signed		
revised edition (Faber, 1929)	£20	£50
The Patriot's Progress	£15	£45
novel (Bles, 1930)		
also limited edition of 350 copies	£150	n/a
The Village Book	£15	£30
stories and essays (Cape, 1930)		
also limited edition of 504 copies	£75	£100
The Wild Deer of Exmoor	£100	n/a
privately printed (1931)		
75 copies		
trade edition (Faber, 1931)	£15	£40
The Labouring Life	£15	£40
stories and essays (Cape, 1932)		
also limited edition of 122 copies	£100	£135

Title	No dj	In dj
The Gold Falcon	£25	£50
anonymous novel (Faber, 1933)		
revised edition with acknowledged authorship (Faber, 1947)	£10	£20
On Foot in Devon	£15	£35
(Maclehose, 1933)		
The Star Born	£30	£50
(Faber, 1933)		
also limited edition of 70 copies	£225	n/a
revised illustrated edition (Faber, 1948)	£10	£15
The Linhay on the Downs	£15	£40
essays (Cape, 1934)		
Devon Holiday	£20	£40
stories (Cape, 1935)		
Salar the Salmon	£20	£60
novel (Faber, 1935)		
illustrated edition (Faber, 1936)	£70	£120
new illustrated edition (Faber, 1948)	£10	£20
The Flax of Dream	£15	£35
1. The Beautiful Years		
2. Dandelion Days		
3. The Dream of Fair Women		
4. The Pathway		
revised version (Faber, 1936)		
Goodbye West Country	£30	£50
autobiographical writing (Putnam, 1937)		
The Children of Shallowford	£20	£50
autobiographical writing (Faber, 1939)		
revised edition (Faber, 1959)	£10	£20
As the Sun Shines	£5	£10
prose selections (Faber, 1941)		
Genius of Friendship: T.E. Lawrence	£25	£60
memoir (Faber, 1941)		
another edition (Henry Williamson Society, 1988)	£10	n/a
The Story of a Norfolk Farm	£25	£60
autobiographical writing (Faber, 1941)		

Title	No dj	In dj
The Sun in the Sands autobiographical writing (Faber, 1945)	£8	£15
Life in a Devon Village **1. The Labouring Life** **2. The Village Book** revised selections (Faber, 1945)	£8	£12
Tales of a Devon Village **1. The Labouring Life** **2. The Village Book** revised selections (Faber, 1945)	£8	£12
The Phasian Bird novel (Faber, 1948)	£8	£15
Scribbling Lark children's (Faber, 1949)	£15	£35
The Dark Lantern book 1 in sequence of 15 forming Chronicle of Ancient Sunlight (MacDonald, 1951) *revised edition (Panther Books, 1962)*	£20 £5	£45 –
Donkey Boy book 2 in sequence of 15 forming Chronicle of Ancient Sunlight (MacDonald, 1952) *revised edition (Panther Books, 1962)*	£20 £8	£60 –
Young Phillip Maddison book 3 in sequence of 15 forming Chronicle of Ancient Sunlight (MacDonald, 1953) *revised edition (Panther Books, 1962)*	£20 £8	£60 –
Tales of Moorland and Estuary stories (MacDonald, 1953)	£15	£35
How Dear is Life book 4 in sequence of 15 forming Chronicle of Ancient Sunlight (MacDonald, 1954) *revised edition (Panther Books 1963)*	£20 £5	£45 –
A Fox Under My Cloak book 5 in sequence of 15 forming Chronicle of Ancient Sunlight (MacDonald, 1955) *revised edition (Panther Books, 1963)*	£35 £10	£75 –

Title	No dj	In dj
The Golden Virgin book 6 in sequence of 15 forming Chronicle of Ancient Sunlight (MacDonald, 1957)	£15	£40
revised edition (Panther Books, 1963)	£5	–
Love and the Loveless book 7 in sequence of 15 forming Chronicle of Ancient Sunlight (MacDonald, 1958)	£15	£40
revised edition (Panther Books, 1963)	£5	–
A Clear Water Stream autobiographical writing (Faber, 1958)	£10	£20
A Test to Destruction book 8 in sequence of 15 forming Chronicle of Ancient Sunlight (MacDonald, 1960)	£20	£45
revised edition (Panther Books, 1964)	£5	–
The Henry Williamson Animal Saga Tarka, Salar and other stories (MacDonald, 1960)	£10	£25
The Innocent Moon book 9 in sequence of 15 forming Chronicle of Ancient Sunlight (MacDonald, 1961)	£15	£35
revised edition (Panther Books, 1965)	£5	–
In the Woods a chapter of autobiography: St Alberts Press (for The Aylesford Review, 1961) *950 copies*	£20	£35
50 copies	£120	n/a
It Was the Nightingale book 10 in sequence of 15 forming Chronicle of Ancient Sunlight (MacDonald, 1962)	£10	£25
revised edition (Panther Books, 1965)	£5	–
The Power of the Dead book 11 in sequence of 15 forming Chronicle of Ancient Sunlight (MacDonald, 1963)	£10	£18
revised edition (Panther Books, 1966)	£5	–
The Phoenix Generation book 12 in sequence of 15 forming Chronicle of Ancient Sunlight (MacDonald, 1965)	£10	£18
revised edition (Panther Books, 1967)	£5	–

Title	No dj	In dj
A Solitary War book 13 in sequence of 15 forming Chronicle of Ancient Sunlight (MacDonald, 1966)	£10	£25
revised edition (Panther Books, 1969)	£5	–
Lucifer Before Sunrise book 14 in sequence of 15 forming Chronicle of Ancient Sunlight (MacDonald, 1965)	£10	£18
The Gale of the World book 15 in sequence of 15 forming Chronicle of Ancient Sunlight (MacDonald, 1969)	£25	£60
Collected Nature Stories (MacDonald, 1970)	£8	£25
The Scandaroon novel (MacDonald, 1972)	£5	£10
also limited edition of 250 copies	£40	n/a

P.G. WODEHOUSE

Anyone who has read books like *Heavy Weather, Right Ho, Jeeves* or *Leave it Psmith* will immediately understand why P.G. Wodehouse is probably the most collectable author in the whole field of modern first editions. Titles like Stephen Spender's *Nine Experiments by S.H.S.* or James Joyce's first book of poems, *Chamber Music*, might fetch much higher prices than individual Wodehouse titles, but I can think of no other author who inspires such devotion in collectors; no other author whose entire output is so eagerly sought after. His quintessential English humour; his superb and economic handling of dialogue; and the overwhelming good-naturedness of his books truly make him the master.

Wodehouse collecting mania only really began around ten years ago — up to the start of the 1980s it was quite possible to pick up first editions of most Wodehousiana for just a few pounds each. Then the boom really started. Almost overnight everybody seemed to discover Wodehouse's appeal. Prices rocketed, and suddenly it became very, very hard to find very good copies in their dust-jackets of anything but the most recent titles. This collectability has increased steadily over the past few years, and there seems absolutely no indication whatsoever that this will change. No Wodehouse book is cheap today — in fact, many are downright expensive — but not one is a waste of money. As well as giving hours and hours of sheer and unadulterated enjoyment, they also represent a fairly sound investment for the future. Collect Wodehouse . . . many people have immeasurably heightened their enjoyment of life by doing so.

Collecting Wodehouse's books can be a lifetime's work, though. As far as I know there isn't a single complete collection of firsts anywhere in the world. It will certainly prove expensive as many of his earliest titles often fetch four figures at auction, despite being issued in quite large print-runs. Obviously, the premium prices are reached for copies complete with clean bright dust-jackets, but these are becoming scarce today, particularly the books published before the Second World War, and even copies without jackets or reprints *with* jackets fetch very good prices today. So if you can't find pristine firsts, look out for fine reprints. If you can afford to pay extra for copies with nice dust-jackets, please don't scrimp — Wodehouse's colourful jackets are some of the most attractive and humorous ever designed. They add immeasurably to a book's overall aesthetic appeal.

Pelham Grenville Wodehouse (most of his life he was nicknamed 'Plum') was born in Guildford in 1881, the son of a civil servant who became a judge in Hong Kong. After a seemingly idyllic education at Dulwich College, London, and an otherwise tedious childhood (he was looked after by a succession of aunts — the prototypes for some of his most severe characters and the bane of Bertie Wooster's life), Wodehouse embarked on a career with the Hong Kong and Shanghai Bank. This was soon abandoned for literature, though; around the turn of the century he began writing short stories for boys' magazines, and magazines like *Strand* and *Punch*. Before long he established himself as a talented story teller.

It is no surprise, then, that Wodehouse's first few books were boys' tales, written quickly and published at the rate of one or two a year. His first novel was *The Pothunters* published by A. & C. Black in 1902 in blue cloth with silver gilt design, and *not* with a pictorial cover — this is a later edition (even that edition fetches good prices on the second-hand market). Other titles from this early period include *A Prefect's Uncle* (1903), *The Gold Bat* (1904), and *The Head of Kay's* (1905), all of which were published by the A. & C. Black company complete with plates. Many (but not all) Black volumes were initially issued in dust-jackets but despite much bibliographical research it hasn't been established if *all* these volumes were adorned with jackets (as they were intended for the juvenile market it's likely some weren't). *A Prefect's Uncle* (see below) was in fact issued with a coarse brown jacket reproducing the front cover design, as was *William Tell Told Again* (this design reproduced one of Philip Dadd's plates from the book). Is it safe to assume that these other A. & C. Black books had similar jackets?

Whatever the case, no copies with jackets have come up for auction in the last ten years or so, and I don't really think it's a vital point for collectors — most of the boards were brightly designed by the books' illustrators, for example, *The Gold Bat* featuring a rather aggressive boxing match. Also attractive are the red cloth boards of *A Prefect's Uncle*, stamped in black and blue with a design showing a young boy with his luggage being met by his uncle. These titles may be scarce, but most Wodehouse collectors are fussy coves, don't you know, and after spending years tracking down titles, aren't prepared to accept shaky or soiled copies. Such copies rarely sell for more than £150 — compare this with the price of very good examples!

Before long Wodehouse turned to humorous writing, and he proved himself a natural master. Many regard him as the greatest humorist of this or any other century. It's hard to disagree with them and even harder to read his books without laughing out loud. To start with, I think his most humorous writing appeared in the weekly 'By the Way' column in *The Globe* newspaper written with Herbert Westbrook. In 1908 *The Globe*'s publishers issued a collection of pieces from the column entitled *By the Way Book: A Literary Quick Lunch For People Who Have Got Five Minutes To Spare* and this is without doubt the rarest item in the whole Wodehouse canon, although there is no acknowledgement of his authorship. Few collectors are even aware of its existence. 'Profusely Illustrated', it was priced one shilling and issued in soft red and brown wrappers featuring a design of steam locomotives and vintage cars. It's almost impossible to find today. Few copies ever reach auction in any kind of condition, and knowledgeable dealers are sure to ask at least £3,000. But because so few people associate it with Wodehouse, it might just be possible to find it in jumble sales or even on bookdealers' bargain shelves for just a few pounds. Who knows? It's the stuff of collectors' dreams.

Wodehouse's novels and collections of short stories from the 1910s and 20s are almost impossible to find in dust-jackets, a huge shame because it was in these books that immortal characters like Bertram Wilberforce Wooster, his enigmatic manservant Jeeves, Aunt Agatha, Psmith (pronounced with a silent p as in pshrimp), Ukridge, Lord Emsworth and his beloved pig, and the Empress of Blandings first appeared. Throughout the next fifty years Wodehouse used all these characters and hundreds more in a succession of dazzling books. During the 1910s most of his books were published by Newnes or Methuen, but during the 1920s and for half a century after, Wodehouse was published by Herbert Jenkins. Jenkins's jackets are quite superb — beautifully drawn and coloured period characters drawn from the novels. The design for *The Inimitable Jeeves* is typical: an alarmed Bertie in the midst of a posse of cats overlooked by a sardonic and superior Jeeves. Like all Jenkins's jackets from this period a message on the front cover advises readers to turn to the rear for a summary of the story. *The Inimitable Jeeves* appeared on 17 May 1923 bound in sage cloth with a design stamped in dark green. As with all the books from this period it's not *too* uncommon without this jacket (they all seem to have survived reasonably well) and could be found for around £50. Copies with the jacket in a collectable state will sell for £200, at the very least. A good thing about these jackets is that although most were discarded, those that have survived tend to be in reasonably good condition — the ink Herbert Jenkins used seems resistant to fading and sunning.

An important thing to remember about these early titles with jackets is that they really have no upper limit for prices — they are so scarce that dealers can ask whatever price they want. The laws of supply and demand apply here rigorously, and with so many devoted collectors all over the world throwing lots of money after so few collectable copies, it's little wonder prices can go through the roof. Wherever I've quoted high values in the listing you should bear in mind it could fetch double that!

Even Wodehouse volumes from the 1930s fetch high prices. Titles like *Thank You Jeeves, Right Ho Jeeves, Hot Water, Laughing Gas* or *Heavy Weather* are all hard to find in their jackets, but they're well worth searching for, especially *Heavy Weather* with its flapper girl and black pig on the cover. Again copies aren't particularly scarce without the jacket, but complete copies invariably sell for at least £250, often much more from specialist dealers. Bibliographical details of these and other titles are available in David Jasen's *A Bibliography and Reader's Guide to the First Editions of P.G. Wodehouse* (Barrie & Jenkins, 1971), itself a collectable volume. However, even this impressive volume has been superseded. Eileen McIlvaine's *P.G. Wodehouse: A Comprehensive Bibliography* (James Heinemann, 1991) is a masterly piece of research and a veritable labour of love. Not only does this give complete details of all the master's books and reprints but also details his plays, short stories, published music and even reproduces some of his correspondence. But the highlight must be the coloured illustrations including hitherto unseen dust-jackets. What a treat! This handsome volume currently retails at a princely £75. Buy it: it will appreciate considerably in due course.

In the mid-1930s Wodehouse went to live in France — a disastrous move. When the Germans invaded France in 1940, Wodehouse was interned but later released; he rather naively agreed to make broadcasts to Britain. Although they were totally innocuous in nature, Wodehouse attracted the sort of notoriety reserved for Lord Haw Haw or Ezra Pound, and for many years his reputation in Britain was tarnished. After the war he went to live in America where he remained for the rest of his life, eventually becoming an American citizen.

Wodehouse never lost his readers though, and even after the war he remained a best-seller. From this point on first editions are easier to find, although it is really only the better copies which attract the highest prices. *Joy in the Morning* (1947) might cost around £100 with a clean jacket, but *Jeeves and the Feudal Spirit* (1954), *Pigs Have Wings* (1952) and *Cocktail Time* (1958) will cost much less. These titles are slimmer and seem sturdier than those issued in the twenties and thirties, and between £40 and £60 should be enough to secure genuinely fine copies free of bumps, nicks or inscriptions. When displayed, they look quite beautiful with their colourful jackets designed by the likes of Sax and Frank Ford. Wodehouse's novels from the 1960s and 1970s look shabby beside them, but these are still very affordable as the print-runs were particularly high.

There are also a few collectable omnibus editions of Wodehouse's works. In 1934 Methuen issued *Library of Humour: P.G. Wodehouse*, and Jenkins produced *Mulliner Omnibus* and *Weekend Wodehouse* in 1935 and 1939. These can cost around £300 with their colourful jackets. Probably the most interesting jacket of all appeared on Wodehouse's only collection of humorous essays, *Louder and Funnier*. Published in 1932 by Faber, this volume had a beautifully intricate yellow-buff jacket designed by Rex Whistler. Only those copies bound in yellow cloth are true first editions — any copies in green cloth were a later issue for the Faber Library series. The true first can sell for up to £500.

Titles from the 1950s and 1960s are much easier to acquire, particularly the more famous books like *Jeeves and the Feudal Spirit, French Leave, Something Fishy, Service With a Smile* and *A Pelican at Blandings*. Despite some repetition of plots and dialogues, Wodehouse was still a marvellously funny writer, and his readership was widening all the time. His ninetieth birthday was marked with the publication of *Much Obliged, Jeeves* in 1971, complete with an attractive jacket by Osbert Lancaster, showing the masterly valet lighting a ninetieth-birthday cake.

Title	No dj	In dj
The Pothunters novel (A. & C. Black, 1902)	£500 – £1,000	–
A Prefect's Uncle novel (A. & C. Black, 1903)	£500 – £1,000	–
Tales of St Austin short stories (A. & C. Black, 1903)	£400 – £800	–
The Gold Bat novel (A. & C. Black, 1904)	£400 – £800	–
William Tell Told Again novel (A. & C. Black, 1904)	£300 – £500	–

Title	No dj	In dj
The Head of Kay's novel (A. & C. Black, 1905)	£400 – £600	–
Love Among the Chickens novel (George Newnes, 1906)	£50 – £100	£500 – £800
The White Feather novel (A. & C. Black, 1907)	£300 – £500	–
Not George Washington (Cassell, 1907) *written with Herbert Westbrook*	£50 – £100	£300 – £500
The Globe by the Way Book essays (Globe, 1907) *paperback. A facsimile edition in a slip-case was* *published by Heinemann and Sceptre in 1985*	£3,000 – £5,000 £40 – £50	– –
The Swoop novel (Alston Rivers, 1909) facsimile edition (Heinemann, 1993)	£750+ £25	– –
Mike novel (A. & C. Black, 1909)	£300 – £500	–
A Gentleman of Leisure novel (Alston Rivers, 1910)	£450+	–
Psmith in the City novel (A. & C. Black, 1910)	£200+	–
The Prince and Betty novel (Mills and Boon, 1912)	£450+	–
The Little Nugget novel (Methuen, 1913)	£450+	–
The Man Upstairs short stories (Methuen, 1914)	£450+	–
Something Fresh novel (Methuen, 1915)	£450+	–
Psmith Journalist novel (A. & C. Black, 1915)	£150+	–
Uneasy Money novel (Methuen, 1917)	£450+	–
Piccadilly Jim novel (Herbert Jenkins, 1918)	£200+	–

Title	No dj	In dj
The Man With Two Left Feet short stories (Methuen, 1917) *featuring the first appearance of Jeeves and Bertie* *in 'Extricating Young Gussie'*	£400+	–
My Man Jeeves short stories (George Newnes, 1919)	£200+	£750+
A Damsel in Distress novel (Herbert Jenkins, 1919)	£50 – £100	–
The Coming of Bill novel (Herbert Jenkins, 1920)	£50 – £100	£400+
Jill the Reckless novel (Herbert Jenkins, 1921)	£50 – £100	£400+
Indiscretions of Archie stories (Herbert Jenkins, 1921)	£50 – £100	£400+
The Clicking of Cuthbert short stories (Herbert Jenkins, 1922)	£50 – £100	£400+
The Girl on the Boat novel (Herbert Jenkins, 1922)	£50 – £100	£400+
The Adventures of Sally novel (Herbert Jenkins, 1923)	£50 – £75	£400+
The Inimitable Jeeves short stories (Herbert Jenkins, 1923)	£40 – £60	£400+
Leave it to Psmith novel (Herbert Jenkins, 1923)	£40 – £60	£400+
Ukridge short stories (Herbert Jenkins, 1924)	£40 – £60	£400+
Bill the Conqueror novel (Herbert Jenkins, 1924)	£30 – £50	£400+
Carry On, Jeeves! short stories (Herbert Jenkins, 1925)	£30 – £50	£400+
Sam the Sudden novel (Methuen, 1925)	£30 – £50	£400+
The Heart of a Goof short stories (Herbert Jenkins, 1926)	£30 – £50	£400+

Title	No dj	In dj
The Small Bachelor novel (Methuen, 1927)	£30 – £50	£400+
Meet Mr Mulliner short stories (Herbert Jenkins, 1927)	£30 – £40	£400+
Money for Nothing novel (Herbert Jenkins, 1929)	£30 – £40	£400+
Mr Mulliner Speaking short stories (Herbert Jenkins, 1929)	£30 – £40	£400+
Summer Lightning novel (Herbert Jenkins, 1929)	£30 – £40	£400+
Very Good, Jeeves short stories (Herbert Jenkins, 1930)	£30 – £40	£300+
Big Money novel (Herbert Jenkins, 1931)	£30 – £40	£300+
If I Were You novel (Herbert Jenkins, 1931)	£30 – £40	£300+
Jeeves Omnibus anthology (Herbert Jenkins, 1931)	£20 – £30	£300+
Louder and Funnier essays (Faber, 1932)	£20 – £30	£500+
Doctor Sally novel (Methuen, 1932)	£30 – £40	£300+
Hot Water novel (Herbert Jenkins, 1932)	£30 – £40	£300+
Mulliner Nights short stories (Herbert Jenkins, 1933)	£30 – £40	£300+
Heavy Weather novel (Herbert Jenkins, 1933)	£30 – £40	£300+
Library of Humour: P.G. Wodehouse anthology (Methuen, 1934)	£20 – £30	£300+
Thank You, Jeeves novel (Herbert Jenkins, 1934)	£30 – £40	£300+
Right Ho, Jeeves novel (Herbert Jenkins, 1934)	£30 – £40	£300+

Title	No dj	In dj
Enter Psmith novel (A. & C. Black, 1935)	£10 – £20	£300+
Mulliner Omnibus anthology (Herbert Jenkins, 1935)	£20 – £30	£300+
Blandings Castle and Elsewhere short stories (Herbert Jenkins, 1935)	£20 – £30	£300+
The Luck of the Bodkins novel (Herbert Jenkins, 1935)	£20 – £30	£300+
Young Men in Spats short stories (Herbert Jenkins, 1936)	£20 – £30	£300+
Laughing Gas novel (Herbert Jenkins, 1936)	£20 – £30	£300+
Lord Emsworth and Others short stories (Herbert Jenkins, 1937)	£20 – £30	£300+
Summer Moonshine novel (Herbert Jenkins, 1938)	£20 – £30	£300+
The Code of the Woosters novel (Herbert Jenkins, 1938)	£20 – £30	£300+
Weekend Wodehouse anthology (Herbert Jenkins, 1939)	£20 – £30	£300+
Uncle Fred in the Springtime novel (Herbert Jenkins, 1939)	£20 – £30	£300+
Eggs, Beans and Crumpets short stories (Herbert Jenkins, 1940)	£20 – £30	£300+
Quick Service novel (Herbert Jenkins, 1940)	£20 – £30	£100 – £150
Money in the Bank novel (Herbert Jenkins, 1946) *his first novel after his disastrous war. Many of the* *following titles appeared first in America*	£20 – £30	£80 – £100
Joy in the Morning novel (Herbert Jenkins, 1947)	£10 – £20	£80 – £100
Full Moon novel (Herbert Jenkins, 1947)	£10 – £20	£50 – £80

Title	No dj	In dj
Spring Fever novel (Herbert Jenkins, 1948)	£10 – £15	£50 – £80
Uncle Dynamite novel (Herbert Jenkins, 1948)	£10 – £15	£50 – £80
The Mating Season novel (Herbert Jenkins, 1949)	£10 – £15	£50 – £80
Nothing Serious short stories (Herbert Jenkins, 1950)	£10 – £15	£50 – £80
The Old Reliable novel (Herbert Jenkins, 1951)	£10 – £15	£50 – £60
Barmy in Wonderland novel (Herbert Jenkins, 1952)	£10 – £15	£50 – £60
Pigs Have Wings novel (Herbert Jenkins, 1952)	£5 – £10	£40 – £50
Ring for Jeeves novel (Herbert Jenkins, 1953)	£5 – £10	£50 – £60
Performing Flea letters (Herbert Jenkins, 1953)	£5 – £10	£40 – £50
Bring on the Girls! autobiography (Herbert Jenkins, 1954)	£5 – £10	£40 – £50
Jeeves and the Feudal Spirit novel (Herbert Jenkins, 1954)	£5 – £10	£40 – £50
French Leave novel (Herbert Jenkins, 1956)	–	£40 – £50
Over Seventy autobiography (Herbert Jenkins, 1957)	–	£30 – £40
Something Fishy novel (Herbert Jenkins, 1957)	–	£40 – £50
Cocktail Time novel (Herbert Jenkins, 1958)	–	£30 – £40
A Few Quick Ones short stories (Herbert Jenkins, 1959)	–	£30 – £40
Jeeves in the Offing novel (Herbert Jenkins, 1960)	–	£30 – £40

Title	No dj	In dj
Ice in the Bedroom novel (Herbert Jenkins, 1961)	–	£30 – £40
Service With a Smile novel (Herbert Jenkins, 1963	–	£30 – £40
Stiff Upper Lip, Jeeves novel (Herbert Jenkins, 1963)	–	£30 – £40
Frozen Assets novel (Herbert Jenkins, 1965)	–	£20 – £30
Galahad at Blandings novel (Herbert Jenkins, 1965)	–	£20 – £30
Plum Pie short stories (Herbert Jenkins, 1966)	–	£20 – £25
The World of Jeeves anthology (Herbert Jenkins, 1967)	–	£20 – £25
Company for Henry novel (Herbert Jenkins, 1967)	–	£20 – £25
Do Butlers Burgle Banks? novel (Herbert Jenkins, 1969	–	£20 – £25
A Pelican at Blandings novel (Herbert Jenkins, 1969)	–	£20 – £25
The Girl in Blue novel (Barrie & Jenkins, 1970)	–	£10 – £20
Much Obliged, Jeeves novel (Barrie & Jenkins, 1971)	–	£10 – £20
The World of Mr Mulliner anthology (Barrie & Jenkins, 1972)	–	£10 – £20
Pearls, Girls and Monty Bodkin novel (Barrie & Jenkins, 1972)	–	£10 – £20
The Golf Omnibus anthology (Barrie & Jenkins, 1973) *the best stories from* The Heart of a Goof, The Clicking of Cuthbert *etc*	–	£10 – £20
Bachelors Anonymous novel (Barrie & Jenkins, 1973)	–	£10 – £20

Title	No dj	In dj
The World of Psmith anthology (Barrie & Jenkins, 1974)	–	£10 – £20
Aunts Aren't Gentlemen novel (Barrie & Jenkins, 1974)	–	£10 – £20
The World of Ukridge anthology (Barrie & Jenkins, 1975)	–	£10 – £20
The World of Blandings anthology (Barrie & Jenkins, 1977)	–	£10–20
Vintage Wodehouse anthology (Barrie & Jenkins, 1977)	–	£10 – £20
Sunset at Blandings novel (Chatto & Windus, 1977) *his last, unfinished work*	–	£10 – £20
Wodehouse on Wodehouse autobiographical anthology (Hutchinson, 1980)	–	£10 – £20
Tales from the Drones Club anthology (Hutchinson, 1982)	–	£10 – £20
Wodehouse Nuggets anthology (Hutchinson, 1982)	–	£10 – £20
The World of Uncle Fred anthology (Hutchinson, 1983)	–	£10 – £20
Sir Agravaine short story (Blandford Press, 1984) *illustrated version of tale from* The Man Upstairs	–	£10 – £15
The World of Wodehouse Clergy anthology (Hutchinson, 1984)	–	£10 – £20
The Hollywood Omnibus anthology (Hutchinson, 1985)	–	£5 – £10
The Parrot verse (Hutchinson, 1987)	–	£5 – £10

The publisher acknowledges the kind assistance relating to the values of Wodehouse first editions, provided by Nigel Williams who is an expert in this subject.

VIRGINIA WOOLF

Virginia Woolf is considered by many to have been a writer who has made a significant and major contribution to twentieth-century literature. Whatever her literary merits, there can be little doubt that she is extraordinarily collectable, with very good copies of her famous novels fetching several hundred pounds each. Rather surprisingly, these are not as hard to acquire as one might at first imagine — they seem to come up for auction or in specialist dealers' shops reasonably frequently. The same cannot be said for titles like *Street Haunting, On Being Ill*, or the special signed editions of *Orlando*, which take years to track down.

Woolf has her followers, but her books are also sought after by collectors keen to acquire books published by the Hogarth Press, Leonard and Virginia Woolf's own company. Hardly surprising really — the Hogarth Press not only revolutionised book design but they were responsible for publishing classic titles like T.S. Eliot's *The Waste Land* and the early works of Katherine Mansfield, Christopher Isherwood, William Plomer and even Sigmund Freud. With both Woolf and Hogarth collectors pursuing these books, the prices will always keep high — a good thing if you already own them; not so good if you're just starting your collection.

Don't despair though. Since Virginia Woolf's death in 1941 the legend surrounding her life and the whole Bloomsbury industry has meant that twice as many books again have been issued posthumously — everything from unfinished fragments to her juvenile diary. One almost expects to see an edition of her complete laundry lists, like Woody Allen's literary creation. Readers never seem to tire of Woolf and Bloomsbury though, and while the legends continue, you can expect her popularity among collectors to grow.

Virginia Woolf came from an eminently literary family. A recent forebear was William Makepeace Thackeray, and her father was Sir Leslie Stephen. Virginia herself was born as Virginia Stephen on 25 January 1882. After the death of her father in 1904 she settled with her sister Vanessa (Bell) in Bloomsbury, becoming part of the famous 'group' including Lytton Strachey, Clive Bell, Leonard Woolf, Roger Fry and John Maynard Keynes, spurning conventional wisdom on sexual, social and artistic mores. It was hardly surprising that she eventually turned to writing herself. To begin with she wrote criticism for *The Times Literary Supplement* and other journals, but eventually she graduated to writing fiction.

Her first novel was *The Voyage Out* (originally called *Melymbrosia*), published by her half-brother Gerald Duckworth on 26 March 1915. With a more conventional narrative than her more famous novels, 2,000 copies of *The Voyage Out* were issued at 6s. each, bound in moss-green cloth and issued with a grey-green dust-jacket printed in blue. Copies with these jackets are extremely scarce today — much better to settle for one without. Although copies without jackets tend to be a little rubbed, they do turn up for between £300 and £400. This was followed by *Night and Day*, her longest work, on 20 October 1919. 2,000 crown octavo volumes bound in dark grey cloth were issued with a white jacket printed in black. Again, these jackets rarely surface. If one does it will increase the book's value by at least ten times.

Before *Night and Day* appeared, though, three slim booklets had been published by the Woolfs' own press. After marrying Leonard in 1912 and suffering a series of mental breakdowns, the couple formed the Hogarth Press as a therapeutic hobby for Virginia: they couldn't have known then that it would emerge as a highly influential publishing house. The Hogarth Press's first 'booklet' was *Two Stories* (featuring Virginia's 'The Mark on the Wall' and Leonard's 'The Three Jews') issued in an edition of 150 copies in July 1917. This 34-page booklet featured four rather crudely printed woodcuts by Dora Carrington and was bound in Japanese paper wrappers. It's extremely scarce today, and horribly prone to tearing or staining. Just three years ago a rather soiled copy was sold at auction for £2,800.

The Mark on the Wall was published as a separate booklet in June, 1919, priced 1s. 6d. 1,000 copies of this 12-page booklet bound in off-white printed wrappers were issued. The previous month *Kew Gardens* appeared and 150 copies of this demy octavo booklet were published by the Press on 12 May 1919, priced at 2s. It was issued in off-white wallpaper wraps hand-coloured in blue, brown and orange, and featured two woodcuts by Vanessa Bell. Again, this is prone to soiling and it isn't unknown for copies to sell for four figures.

Thankfully no other Woolf title achieves such high prices although *Monday or Tuesday* (7 April 1921) often sells for hundreds of pounds despite being issued in an edition of 1,000 copies. It had a Vanessa Bell cover. From this point on, all Virginia Woolf's major works were issued in hard covers and the print-runs steadily increased as the business developed into a mainstream publisher. *Jacob's Room* (27 October 1922; 1,200 copies) is scarce but it is only the 40 specially signed copies reserved for Hogarth Press's top subscribers that sell for the very best prices. Last year Lytton Strachey's own copy complete with a nicked and darkened dust-jacket sold for $2,200. One unsigned copy appears to have been auctioned for £1,800, but this seems to be one of those wildly silly prices occasionally thrown up in auctions rather than an accurate reflection of what the book usually sells for.

All Virginia Woolf's main novels were issued in attractive dust-jackets designed by her sister Vanessa Bell, and the presence of these jackets can affect prices considerably. The Hogarth Press seem to have used a particularly fragile type of paper for these jackets and most copies that have survived tend to be chipped, although they keep their delicate colours well. *Mrs Dalloway* (14 May 1925; 2,000 copies), *To the Lighthouse* (5 May 1927; 3,000 copies), *Orlando* (11 October 1928; 5,080 copies), *The Waves* (8 October 1931; 7,113 copies) and *The Years* (15 March 1937; 18,142 copies) are all as scarce as their print-runs would suggest. Very good copies of *Mrs Dalloway* with their original rust cloth unstained but without their cream jacket (printed in black and yellow) can cost as much as £100; an amount which should be enough to buy a first edition of *The Years* (pale jade green cloth) *with* its cream, black and brown jacket, albeit in slightly chipped or soiled condition.

Virginia Woolf also wrote much non-fiction, most notably two 'series' of criticism called *Common Readers*. Both are hard to come by today, particularly the first (1925) which featured a Bell design on grey cloth-backed boards. Much easier to obtain are a number of Hogarth Press pamphlets such as *Mr Bennett and Mrs Brown* (1924), *A Letter to a Young Poet* (1932), and *Walter Sickert: A Conversation* (1934). The Press published numerous pamphlets by rising writers, including Stephen Spender and John Betjeman but Virginia's own efforts are probably the most collectable. They were issued in soft wrappers with typical Hogarth designs on the front covers and it is hard to find clean, bright copies for less than £20. Many dealers might ask as much as £40 or even £50 for *Mr Bennett and Mrs Brown*.

Virginia Woolf also produced several very collectable limited editions. *Street Haunting* was originally published by the Westgate Press but printed by the influential Grabhorn Press in San Francisco in May, 1930. 500 numbered and signed copies bound in grey paper boards patterned in gold and blue with a blue leather spine were issued, some of which were distributed in Britain in February, 1931, by Simpkin Marshall priced £1.11s.6d. Because it was never published separately in Britain (although it did appear in *The Death of the Moth* seventeen years later), copies are very scarce and could set you back £300–£400. Incidentally, some copies appear to have been issued with a glassine jacket.

Two other important limited editions are *On Being Ill* (Hogarth Press, 1930) and *Beau Brummell*, 500 copies of which were published in New York, although 250 signed and numbered copies were distributed by Douglas Cleverdon of Bristol. Much scarcer, though, is *On Being Ill*. 250 numbered and signed copies with vellum-backed cloth boards, marbled endpapers and a Vanessa Bell jacket were published. In 1989 an unopened copy was auctioned to a dealer for £600, no doubt to be passed on to an eager customer for £700–£800.

Prone to breakdowns and periods of instability, Virginia Woolf suffered with mental problems all her life. With the onset of the Second World War things proved too much to bear and on the 28 March 1941, she left the house at Rodmell in Sussex and drowned herself in the river at the bottom of the garden. It's a measure of the Woolf legend that more of her books have appeared since then than when she was actually alive. Most of these have been previously unfinished or unreleased snippets (easily obtainable if you can afford them), but much more interesting are the six volume set of her letters and the five volume set of her revealing diaries. The letters and diaries are amongst her very best work — no other writer has revealed so much about herself or, conversely, left herself open to so much probing or analysis. Both sets can sell for as much as £100–£150 in fine condition although individual volumes shouldn't cost more than £15–£20 each.

Virginia Woolf has been attacked for ignoring the harsh realities of life in favour of a leisured and self-indulgent exploitation of emotions and ethereal feelings. These criticisms ignore her huge contribution to the development of modern literature.

Title	No dj	In dj
The Voyage Out novel (Duckworth, 1915)	£300 – £400	£2,000+
Two Stories stories (Hogarth Press, 1917) *included* The Mark on the Wall	£2,500 – £3,000	n/a
Kew Gardens story (Hogarth Press, 1919)	£1,000 – £1,500	n/a
The Mark on the Wall story (Hogarth Press, 1919) *first separate publication*	£500 – £600	n/a
Night and Day novel (Duckworth, 1919)	£100 – £200	£500 – £1,000
Monday or Tuesday short stories (Hogarth Press, 1921)	£200 – £300	£400 – £600
Jacob's Room novel (Hogarth Press, 1922) *40 signed special copies*	£200 – £300 £1,000 – £2,000	£500 – £700 n/a
Mr Bennett and Mrs Brown essay (Hogarth Press, 1924)	£20 – £40	n/a
The Common Reader criticism (Hogarth Press, 1925)	£40 – £50	£100 – £150
Mrs Dalloway novel (Hogarth Press, 1925)	£50 – £100	£200 – £300
To the Lighthouse novel (Hogarth Press, 1927)	£50 – £100	£200 – £300
Orlando: A Biography novel (Hogarth Press, 1928)	£50 – £75	£200 – £250
A Room of One's Own essay (Hogarth Press, 1929) *preceded by special signed limited edition of* *492 copies*	£30 – £40 £400	£100 – £150 n/a
Street Haunting essay (Westgate Press S.F., 1930) *limited to 500 signed copies*	£300 – £400	n/a
On Being Ill essay (Hogarth Press, 1930) *limited to 250 signed copies*	£400 – £600	n/a

Title	No dj	In dj
Beau Brummell essay (Rimington & Hooper, New York, 1930) *limited to 500 signed copies*	£300 – £400	n/a
The Waves novel (Hogarth Press, 1931)	£20 – £40	£100 – £150
A Letter to a Young Poet essay (Hogarth Press, 1932)	£30 – £40	n/a
The Common Reader — Second Series criticism (Hogarth Press, 1932)	£30 – £40	£100 – £150
Flush: A Biography 'novel' (Hogarth Press, 1933)	£20 – £30	£50 – £100
Walter Sickert: A Conversation essay (Hogarth Press, 1934)	£30 – £40	n/a
The Roger Fry Memorial Exhibition (privately printed in Bristol 1935) *limited to 125 copies*	£150 – £200	n/a
The Years novel (Hogarth Press, 1937)	£20 – £30	£100 – £150
Three Guineas essay (Hogarth Press, 1938)	£10 – £20	£40 – £50
Reviewing essay (Hogarth Press, 1939)	£20 – £30	n/a
Roger Fry: A Biography (Hogarth Press, 1940)	£15 – £20	£40 – £50
Between the Acts novel (Hogarth Press, 1941)	£10 – £20	£40 – £50
The Death of the Moth essays (Hogarth Press, 1942)	£10 – £20	£40 – £50
A Haunted House short stories (Hogarth Press, 1943)	£10 – £20	£40 – £50
The Moment and Other Essays (Hogarth Press, 1947)	£10 – £20	£30 – £40
The Captain's Death Bed essays (Hogarth Press, 1950)	£10 – £20	£30 – £40

Title	No dj	In dj
A Writer's Diary (Hogarth Press, 1953)	£10 – £20	£40 – £50
Virginia Woolf and Lytton Strachey: Letters (Hogarth Press, 1956)	£10 – £15	£30 – £40
Granite and Rainbow essays (Hogarth Press, 1958)	£10 – £15	£30 – £40
Contemporary Writers essays (Hogarth Press, 1965)	£5 – £10	£10 – £20
Collected Essays Vol I (Hogarth Press, 1966)	–	£10 – £20
Collected Essays Vol II (Hogarth Press, 1966)	–	£10 – £20
Nurse Lugton's Golden Thimble short story (Hogarth Press, 1966) *with illustrations by Bloomsbury colleague Duncan Grant*	£5 – £10	£20 – £30
Collected Essays Vol III (Hogarth Press, 1967)	–	£10 – £20
Collected Essays Vol IV (Hogarth Press, 1967)	–	£10 – £20
Mrs Dalloway's Party short story (Hogarth Press, 1973)	–	£10 – £20
The Flight of the Mind: The Letters of Virginia Woolf 1882–1912 (Hogarth Press, 1975)	–	£10 – £20
Moments of Being autobiographical fragments (Sussex University Press, 1976)	–	£10 – £20
The Question of Things Happening: The Letters of Virginia Woolf 1912–1922 (Hogarth Press, 1976)	–	£10 – £20
Freshwater comedy (Hogarth Press, 1976)	–	£10 – £15
The Diary of Virginia Woolf Volume I 1915–1919 (Hogarth Press, 1977)	–	£10 – £20

Title	No dj	In dj
Books and Portraits essays (Hogarth Press, 1977)	–	£10 – £15
A Change of Perspective: The Letters of Virginia Woolf, 1923–1928 (Hogarth Press, 1977)	–	£10 – £20
The Pargiters novel (Hogarth Press, 1977) *revised version of* The Years	–	£10 – £15
The Diary of Virginia Woolf Volume II, 1920–1924 (Hogarth Press, 1978)	–	£10 – £20
A Reflection of the Other Person: The Letters of Virginia Woolf, 1929–1931 (Hogarth Press, 1978)	–	£10 – £20
The Sickle Side of the Moon: The Letters of Virginia Woolf 1932–1935 (Hogarth Press, 1979)	–	£10 – £20
The Diary of Virginia Woolf Volume III 1925–1930 (Hogarth Press, 1980)	–	£10 – £20
Leave the Letters Till We're Dead: The Letters of Virginia Woolf 1936–1941 (Hogarth Press, 1982)	–	£10 – £20
The Diary of Virginia Woolf Volume IV 1931–1935 (Hogarth Press, 1982)	–	£10 – £20
The London Scene essay (Hogarth Press, 1982)	–	£10–£15
The Diary of Virginia Woolf Volume V 1936–1941 (Hogarth Press, 1984)	–	£10 – £20
A Passionate Apprentice early diaries (Hogarth Press, 1990)	–	£5 – £10

ULTRA MODERNS

One of the recent trends in collecting modern first editions has been the huge upsurge of interest in books by relatively young authors; books published as recently as ten or twenty years ago. It is a startling phenomenon. If these 'ultra-modern firsts' can reach three figure sums just a few years after publication, what hope is there for the young collector trying to find future collectable authors today? Wodehouse enthusiasts might have been buying his books for decades at cheap prices until the recent upsurge. How will the young collector operating on a budget be able to afford any modern firsts at all? If things go too far, there will simply be no one affordable to collect. Perhaps the growing popularity of paperbacks and pulp fiction is a result of this state of affairs.

There are numerous young authors whose books are avidly collected, and far too many to cover here. In this chapter we deal with just three, Martin Amis, Bruce Chatwin and William Boyd, but we could have included thirty-three more. It was very hard (and purely arbitrary) to have to leave out collectable giants like Salman Rushdie, Angela Carter, Ian McEwan and Paul Theroux; unfortunately lack of space made it necessary. We hope the omissions can be rectified in a sequel to this volume.

As the son of Kingsley, it's hardly surprising Martin Amis would pursue a literary career but I don't think his father could have foreseen just how successful Amis *fils* would be. If he isn't currently outselling his father, he must be very close to it. Martin Amis was born in Oxford in 1949 and educated at a series of schools before attending Oxford University where he studied English. Perhaps because of his father's name he found his way into print reasonably easily — his first novel, *The Rachel Papers*, was published by Jonathan Cape who were handling Kingsley's books at the time.

That is not to imply that *The Rachel Papers* didn't deserve publication — it most certainly did: the story of Charles Highway's attempts to sleep with an older woman remains one of his freshest and liveliest novels to date. It is certainly his most collectable: indeed, it is one of the most highly sought after modern books on the market with truly pristine copies selling for up to £250, a remarkable sum considering it could be picked up for just a few pounds no more than five years ago. *The Rachel Papers* was published in 1973. No doubt some collectors might be prepared to pay around £100–£150 for a copy in a dirty or nicked jacket but anything less than that is virtually worthless.

Dead Babies, his second novel issued in 1975, is hardly less scarce. It seems that collectors seemed to wise up to Amis shortly before demand rocketed. The most acceptable copies of these books are tucked away on collectors' shelves, only to be released at high prices very occasionally. A depressing and disturbing tale, *Dead Babies* commands prices up to £100–£150 today, although I personally wouldn't be surprised to see the odd copy sell for much more at a book fair or auction. All these early Martin Amis titles were issued in dull uniform dust-jackets though this doesn't detract from their importance. When you are offered an early Martin

Amis, check the book thoroughly. Make sure the corners aren't bumped or knocked and go over the jacket with a magnifying glass. Nicks, slight abrasions, minor discolouration, even the tiniest of tears could take tens of pounds off its real value. Incidentally, if you are ever offered a paperback called *Dark Secrets* this isn't a new Amis title; it's simply a retitled reprint of *Dead Babies*.

From this point on, Amis's books get easier to acquire and none should cost more than £25 in exceptional condition. The only one which might cause some problems is the collection of essays published as a Hutchinson paperback in 1982 as *Invasion of the Space Invaders*. It's not too hard to find but truly fine copies are becoming increasingly scarce. Most copies offered for sale have dog-eared corners. This book was illustrated by Martin Amis's brother Philip. The other scarcity from the later period is the London Limited Edition of *London Fields*, by far the best novel of 1989, a book that should have won the Booker Prize. In their infinite wisdom the Booker judges even failed to nominate it to the shortlist.

Over the last year or two the young novelist William Boyd has become almost as collectable as Amis *fils*. Despite being under forty, he has established himself as one of the most currently popular authors. Readers of his humorous novels eagerly await each new publication and one thrills to think what he will have achieved in years to come. Born in Ghana in March 1952, he was exposed to the Biafran crisis as a young boy. It's hardly surprising that his best work from his first book *A Good Man in Africa* to the latest *Brazzaville Beach* is set on this continent. William Boyd was educated at Gordonstoun (Prince Charles's old school) and Nice University, before pursuing an academic career at Glasgow and Oxford University. He eventually gave this up when he started making money from his writing.

Boyd's first novel, the black comedy *A Good Man in Africa*, was published by Hamish Hamilton in 1981 and must rate as one of the most collectable books to appear in the 1980s. It seems Boyd became popular overnight and all available copies of the book in their comic dust-jacket were snapped up, making them scarce. Only 1,500 copies were printed and, as most of these would have been destined for public libraries, it's not surprising that fine copies can command prices of £200–£250 today. This title is very hard to find in fine condition. Hamish Hamilton used a very poor quality paper for this book and most copies seem to have developed browned pages. An imperfect copy could still set you back £150.

Boyd's 1981 collection of short stories is similarly scarce. In fact, only 1,200 copies of *On the Yankee Station* were issued (according to Boyd himself), so it should be even harder to find than the first title. As well as being an accomplished author, Boyd has also written some memorable screenplays, two of which were published as *School Ties* by Hamish Hamilton in 1985. Only 1,000 copies of this book were released, so don't be surprised if you are asked for around £50 for a pristine copy. Incidentally, Penguin issued a simultaneous paperback edition of *School Ties*. Even this book can fetch up to £10 today.

Bruce Chatwin was a novelist/travel writer of the kind that only Britain seems able to produce. Our record in this field is long and proud and includes names like Daniel Defoe, Robert Louis Stevenson, and more recently, Jonathan Raban. Since Bruce Chatwin's death in 1989, booksellers have reported a huge increase of interest in his books and this has been reflected in the prices asked.

Chatwin was born in Sheffield in 1940 and educated at Marlborough (where previous alumni had included John Betjeman, Louis MacNiece, and art-historian Anthony Blunt). After a short spell working at Sotheby's where he indulged in his fascination for antiques, he embarked on a wandering life visiting ancient settlements and writing travel pieces for *The Sunday Times*.

His first travel book, *In Patagonia*, was published in a photographically illustrated dust-jacket in 1977 and is extremely scarce today. Fine copies have been known to sell for around £150 and even nicked copies can command three figure asking prices. Many years later Chatwin returned to the remote South American area with Paul Theroux (who had already written *The Old Patagonian Express*) and the pair produced *Patagonia Revisited*, a slim volume with illustrations by Kyffin Williams. This was published in a limited edition of 250 numbered copies by Russell in 1985, shortly before a trade edition was released. Both copies are highly sought after today.

In Patagonia was a travel book; Chatwin has also produced a few highly thought of novels. The best are probably *On the Black Hill* (1982) and *Utz* (1988). *On the Black Hill* has become increasingly hard to find in genuinely fine condition over the past two or three years. It used to be common for under £10. Now it would fetch near to £30. *Utz*, on the other hand, shouldn't give too many problems at around £10–£15. The limited edition of *Patagonia Revisited* was issued with a transparent acetate jacket over its patterned boards. Even this needs to be in place if it is to realise its best price. Don't be put off by dealers telling you it didn't have a jacket.

Here are a few more authors who should become collectable. Jonathan Gash, the creator of that lovable rogue antique dealer Lovejoy, is a name that immediately springs to mind, largely because of the superb BBC adaptation of the books starring Ian MacShane. The television series and the sheer readability of the books brings to mind Colin Dexter and his Inspector Morse series — and look what's happened to them in collecting circles. Start acquiring these soon. Two more names are the spy novelist Ted Allebury (a rival to John le Carré perhaps) and John Gardiner, the chap who has taken over the James Bond mantle from Ian Fleming. These are grossly undervalued at the moment. Two names that were being bandied around a couple of years ago, Clive James and Tom Sharpe, have failed to live up to their collectability promise until now. Is it time for that to change now? We shall have to wait and see.

Unfortunately, neither of the big two names for 'tomorrow's stars' are British — a sad state of affairs! But for the sheer delight their books bring, the superb writing style and (this is important) the attractive dust-jacket designs, you can do no worse than invest in sets of books by Peter Carey and Garrison Keillor. Neither author has been prolific it's true, but there are signs now that more and more cognoscenti are sniffing out really fine firsts from both writers.

It's not hard to see why. When the Booker Prize went to Carey's *Oscar and Lucinda* in 1988 it was probably the only time the nation's literati had agreed with the judges. It is a superb saga of early Australian life, a rambling picaresque tale, sad, funny and surreal. His earlier title *Illywhacker* should have won the prize too and how can anybody ignore a collection of short stories entitled *The Fat Man in History*? If you haven't read Peter Carey yet, do so. Then phone up your local dealer and reserve everything he has in stock!

Garrison is another superb writer, an American humorist in the classic tradition of Mark Twain and James Thurber. He was born in Anoka, Minnesota in 1942 and, after graduating from the University of Minnesota, he began a long radio career. From 1974 to 1987 he was the host of the live radio show *A Prairie Home Companion*, featuring music, jokes, sketches and his famous Lake Wobegon story. Lake Wobegon is a small Minnesotan town peopled by slow Norwegian Lutherans. Nothing much happens in Lake Wobegon but that is its charm. Keillor's Wobegon stories read just as if he was telling them on the radio — he has a superb command of narrative and a gentle, homely way of telling a story. According to the *Observer*, Keillor is 'the funniest author alive'.

He began writing short stories for *The New Yorker* and *The Atlantic* in the 1970s. The first collection, entitled *Happy to Be Here*, was published in America in 1981. It didn't appear in Britain until 1986 shortly before his most famous book, *Lake Wobegon Days*, became a best-seller. Since then he has produced *Leaving Home*, a collection of Lake Wobegon stories, and *We Are Still Married*, a collection of stories, poems and occasional pieces. Obviously the American editions are preferable but most collectors will be more than happy with first UK editions. The dust-jacket for the first UK editions of these (and Peter Carey's Faber books) were all designed by the talented Pierre le Tan. They are instantly recognisable.

Title	No dj	In dj

MARTIN AMIS

The Rachel Papers novel (Jonathan Cape, 1973)	£100 – £150	£200 – £250
Dead Babies novel (Jonathan Cape, 1975)	£50 – £80	£100 – £150
Success novel (Jonathan Cape, 1978)	£20 – £25	£30 – £40
Other People novel (Jonathan Cape, 1981)	£10 – £15	£15 – £20
Invasion of the Space Invaders essays (Hutchinson, 1982) *only issued as a paperback*	£8 – £10	£10 – £15
Money novel (Jonathan Cape, 1984)	£10 – £15	£20 – £25

Title	No dj	In dj
The Moronic Inferno essays (Jonathan Cape, 1986)	£10 – £15	£15 – £20
London Fields novel (Jonathan Cape, 1989)	–	£15 – £20

WILLIAM BOYD

A Good Man in Africa novel (Hamish Hamilton, 1981)	£100 – £150	£200 – £250
On the Yankee Station short stories (Hamish Hamilton, 1981)	£80 – £100	£150 – £200
An Ice Cream War novel (Hamish Hamilton, 1982)	£15 – £20	£20 – £30
Stars and Bars novel (Hamish Hamilton, 1984)	£10 – £15	£15 – £20
School Ties screenplays (Hamish Hamilton, 1985) *issued simultaneously as a Penguin paperback*	£20 – £30	£40 – £50
The New Confessions novel (Hamish Hamilton, 1987)	–	£10 – £20
Brazzaville Beach novel (Sinclair Stevenson, 1990)	–	£10 – £15

BRUCE CHATWIN

In Patagonia travel (Jonathan Cape, 1977)	£80 – £100	£120 – £150
The Viceroy of Ouidah narrative (Jonathan Cape, 1980)	£15 – £20	£20 – £30
On the Black Hill novel (Jonathan Cape, 1982)	£15 – £20	£20 – £30
Patagonia Revisited travel (Russell, 1985) *written with Paul Theroux. Russell also issued a limited* *edition of 250 numbered copies*	£15 – £20 –	£20 – £30 £60 – £80
The Songlines novel (Jonathan Cape, 1987)	–	£20 – £30

Title	No dj	In dj
Utz novel (Jonathan Cape, 1988)	–	£10 – £15
What Am I Doing Here? occasional pieces (Jonathan Cape, 1989) *published posthumously*	–	£10 – £15

PETER CAREY

Title	No dj	In dj
The Fat Man in History short stories (Faber, 1980) *This is actually two separate collections in one,* The Fat Man in History *and* War Crimes, *first published* *by the University of Queensland Press in Australia in* *1979*	£15 – £20	£20 – £30
Bliss novel (Faber, 1981)	£10 – £15	£15 – £20
Illywhacker novel (Faber, 1985)	£10 – £15	£20 – £25
Oscar and Lucinda novel (Faber, 1988)	£10 – £15	£15 – £20

GARRISON KEILLOR

Title	No dj	In dj
Happy To Be Here short stories (Faber, 1986)	£10 – £15	£15 – £20
Lake Wobegon Days novel (Faber, 1986)	£10 – £15	£15 – £20
Leaving Home short stories (Faber, 1988)	–	£10 – £15
We Are Still Married short stories (Faber, 1989)	–	£8 – £10

THE ANGRY YOUNG MEN

Not all collectors seek to acquire all the work of just one author: occasionally bibliophiles like to seek out examples of a particular genre for instance, or important poetic titles. One of the most popular sub-areas is the extraordinary batch of novels published towards the end of the 1950s and the early 60s, commonly dubbed the work of the 'Angry Young Men' (sometimes called either working-class or 'regional' novels). The appearance of these titles within a few years of each other was a spontaneous outburst of aggressive working-class self-assertiveness, and the literary world had never seen anything like it. It shook the establishment and has left its indelible mark on literature today. For the first time in the history of English fiction (and drama) it was acceptable to portray ordinary and, to a certain extent, ugly lives in literature.

From a collecting point of view, this is an ideal area to concentrate on. Confined, compact, relatively recent and accessible, this range of titles is large enough to take time to acquire and has a nice mixture of scarce and not-so scarce titles. Furthermore, condition is all-important and the presence of dust-jackets doubly so, so these titles are a good introduction to collecting modern firsts in general: a microcosm of collecting modern firsts, if you like. But it's not that simple. What is interesting about this area of modern fiction is that few collectors want all the books by these authors. Invariably the seminal titles of Alan Sillitoe, John Osborne, Stan Barstow, Lynn Reid Banks, Shelagh Delaney etc are their *very* first publications, and their most important. Most writers develop from their early books into maturity. This may well be the case with Barstow et al, but it is not how the reading and collecting public see it. Each of these has had to live with the enormous success of their first titles, and all (commercially speaking) have failed. There are very few Sillitoe completists — most just want his first two books and ignore his more recent titles; similarly with John Braine — most just want his classic *Room at the Top*. The same is exactly true of all these authors, regardless of how they have developed as individual writers. And, indeed, virtually all these writers are still working and publishing today.

A few unique factors combined to bring about this rash of 'angry' literature. As well as a general loosening of censorship restrictions on both fiction and drama (the famous *Lady Chatterley's Lover* Penguin case was in 1960 and it was as much a product as a cause of the general trend), post-war English society was going through fundamental changes. Thanks largely to improved education and the evolution of the welfare state it is an indelible fact that the working class were becoming less working class: for the first time in English history it was possible for the lower classes to rise up the social scale a notch or two. This is the essence of this particular strand of fiction. The angry young men in the novels — the Arthur Seatons, Albert Argyles and Joe Lamptons are destructively angry, enviously angry, all keen to use the system to their ends, and ultimately to move up within it. Unlike another similar but much earlier novel, Walter Greenwood's *Love on the Dole* (Jonathan Cape, 1933), these titles allowed the protagonists to have opportunities. They weren't hopeless.

There had been angry writers and realistic novels before, of course, but the titles from the 1950s were new and exciting compared to Gissing's books, for example, or Maugham's *Liza of Lambeth*. The main difference is that the hero of the early titles (and, come to that, D.H. Lawrence's 'earthy' characters) were actually heroes — the heroes of Sillitoe's or John Braine's books are essentially anti-heroes. This was a totally new development in literature. They were disillusioned, cynical and keen to use whatever means they could to achieve their own, often shallow, ends.

Disregarding two early prototypes which have already been discussed in these pages (Kingsley Amis's *Lucky Jim* and Iris Murdoch's *Under the Net*) this new movement burst onto the scene in May 1956 when John Osborne's *Look Back in Anger* opened at the Royal Court Theatre in London to astonished and admiring reviews. The very same week also saw the publication of Colin Wilson's pseudo-existentialist and enormously influential philosophical work, *The Outsider*. Both writers came from the same kind of background. John James Osborne was born in 1929 into a lower-middle-class family, and had spells as a journalist and rep actor before he began writing plays in 1950. Colin Wilson was two years younger. He left school at sixteen, passed through a series of menial jobs, and even spent time sleeping rough on Hampstead Heath during particularly hard times. Today he is one of Britain's most intellectual and prolific authors, with a huge output on a wide range of subjects. One of the interesting things about all these writers is the absence of any prolonged education amidst the dreaming spires; most were born in Yorkshire and attended local grammar schools.

These two works seemed to open the floodgates for similar books. Within the next few years no fewer than seven seminal titles appeared, all of which are still in print today. John Braine (born in Bradford in 1922) worked as a librarian for several years before the phenomenal success of his first novel, *Room at the Top* (Eyre & Spottiswoode, 1957), enabled him to earn a living with his pen. Alan Sillitoe's first two prose works did much the same for him.

Alan Sillitoe was born in Nottingham in 1928, one of five children of a usually unemployed labourer. He started work at the age of fourteen in a local bicycle factory before serving in the RAF in Malaya. He began to write when he was demobilised with tuberculosis and forced into eighteen months' convalescence. He met Robert Graves who encouraged him to write a novel about Nottingham. The result was *Saturday Night and Sunday Morning* (W.H. Allen, 1958), featuring Arthur Seaton, who was a truly working class character and unlike John Braine's Joe Lampton, who tried to climb the social ladder by marrying well. Seaton's philosophy is summed up in the wonderfully evocative line: 'I'm me, and nobody else; and whatever people think I am, that's what I'm not, because they don't know a bloody thing about me.'

Both these books were filmed early on and both are very hard to find today. Needless to say copies without jackets are virtually worthless, and the price varies depending on the jacket's condition. A genuinely fine copy of *Room at the Top* could sell for as much as £50, whereas a similar copy of Sillitoe's classic will sell for twice that. Chipped or faded jackets could reduce the value of the book by around a half. Both authors tried to capitalise on these early successes by producing sequels. They sold relatively well, but collectors seem to ignore them. However, Sillitoe has two other collectable titles. His very first publication was a collection of verse entitled *Without Beer or Bread* (Outpost Publications, 1957) issued in printed wrappers (£50–£80), and his first collection of short stories, *The Loneliness of the Long Distance Runner* (W.H. Allen, 1959) could fetch much the same. Incidentally, the first paperback versions of these two Sillitoe books sold over a million copies each in their Pan editions.

Other early follow-ups included Brendan Behan's *Borstal Boy* (Hutchinson, 1958), the savage tale of a young offender; Shelagh Delaney's (born in Salford in 1939) seminal play, *A Taste of Honey* (Methuen, 1959), Keith Waterhouse's humorous classic *Billy Liar* (Michael Joseph, 1959); and the Guyana-born E.R. Braithwaite's moving tale of black-white relations in a London school, *To Sir, With Love* (Bodley Head, 1959). What is interesting about all these books is that the titles seem to have become part of the English language; everyday phrases that can be applied to so many situations. Another very collectable title from this period is David Storey's *This Sporting Life* (Longmans, 1960). Along with Keith Waterhouse, Storey has probably emerged as the best of these angry young talents. David Malcolm Storey was born in Wakefield in 1933, the third son of a miner. After an education at the Slade School of Fine Art, he worked in a variety of jobs including as a professional footballer, teacher and farmworker — experiences which are reflected in his works. Fine copies of his first novel can fetch as much as £120. The early 1960s saw a few more desirable titles in this genre, particularly Lynn Reid Banks's *The L-Shaped Room* (Chatto & Windus, 1960), and Bill Naughton's *Alfie* (MacGibbon & Kee, 1966); adapted into the marvellous film starring Michael Caine shortly after. One of the most attractive features of these books is the fact that most were made into important British films — there was a whole spate of them during the 1960s. One of the best was a film adaptation (by Keith Waterhouse) of Stan Barstow's *A Kind of Loving* starring Alan Bates and June Ritchie. Occasionally, the film rights to the novel were sold long before the book was even published. This certainly happened with Jack Trevor Story's *Live Now, Pay Later* also starring June Ritchie, this time with Ian Hendry and Liz Fraser, because a still from the filmed version appears on the rear of the first edition's red, white, black and purple dust-jacket (designed by Anne Hickmott). Incidentally, this particular title has two first editions. To cash in on the success of the film the Penguin paperback edition appeared simultaneously with the Secker & Warburg hardback. Both copies fetch good prices today.

Title	No dj	In dj
The L-Shaped Room by Lynne Reid Banks novel (Chatto & Windus, 1960)	£10 – £15	£20 – £30
A Kind of Loving by Stan Barstow novel (Michael Joseph, 1960)	£10 – £15	£20 – £30
Borstal Boy by Brendan Behan novel (Hutchinson, 1958)	£15 – £20	£25 – £30
Room at the Top by John Braine novel (Eyre & Spottiswoode, 1957)	£20 – £30	£40 – £50
To Sir, With Love by E.R. Braithwaite novel (Bodley Head, 1959)	£10 – £15	£15 – £20
A Taste of Honey by Shelagh Delaney play (Methuen, 1959)	£5 – £10	£10 – £20
Alfie by Bill Naughton novel (MacGibbon & Kee, 1966)	£20 – £25	£30 – £40
Look Back in Anger by John Osborne play (Faber, 1957)	£20 – £25	£40 – £50
The Entertainer by John Osborne play (Faber, 1957)	£15 – £20	£20 – £30
The Birthday Party by Harold Pinter play (Encore, 1959) *new edition published as* The Birthday Party and Other Plays *(Methuen, 1960)*	£20 – £30	£40 – £50
The Caretaker by Harold Pinter play (Faber, 1960) *pictorial wrappers*	£5 – £10	£10 – £15
Cathy Come Home by Jeremy Sandford 'faction' (Pan, 1967) *paperback original based on Sandford's television play*	£3 – £5	£4 – £6

Title	No dj	In dj
Without Beer or Bread by Alan Sillitoe verse (Outpost Publications, 1957) *paper wrappers*	£40 – £50	£50 – £80
Saturday Night and Sunday Morning by Alan Sillitoe novel (W.H. Allen, 1958)	£50 – £80	£80 – £100
The Loneliness of the Long Distance Runner by Alan Sillitoe short stories (W.H. Allen, 1959)	£40 – £50	£50 – £80
This Sporting Life by David Storey novel (Longmans, 1960)	£50 – £60	£100 – £120
Flight into Camden by David Storey novel (Longmans, 1961)	£50 – £60	£100 – £120
Live Now, Pay Later by Jack Trevor Story novel (Secker & Warburg, 1963) *simultaneously published as Penguin paperback*	£15 – £20 £4 – £6	£25 – £30
Billy Liar by Keith Waterhouse (Michael Joseph, 1959)	£40 – £50	£50 – £80
The Outsider by Colin Wilson philosophy (Gollancz, 1956)	£40 – £50	£50 – £80
Ritual in the Dark by Colin Wilson novel (Gollancz, 1960)	£20 – £30	£30 – £40
Adrift in Soho by Colin Wilson novel (Gollancz, 1961)	£10 – £15	£15 – £20

SOME MISCELLANEOUS WRITERS

To finish this book it could be useful to present a checklist of some random volumes. As pointed out before, even the most die-hard Wodehousian or Greene devotee occasionally buys books by other authors. Few stick to collecting just one person alone: it would prove a tedious collection to say the least. The books listed are those every decent collection should have in it to give it breadth and interest. Nobody collects all W.H. Davies's books, but a collection of modern firsts without *The Autobiography of a Super Tramp* would be a poor show indeed. The same can be said of Richard Adams's *Watership Down* or Laurie Lee's *Cider with Rosie*. Of course, there have been more important books as literary creations in the twentieth century but these seem to be on most collectors' wants lists.

The choice is the publishers, and they'll look forward to receiving sackfuls of mail suggesting alternatives and additions. But what I've really tried to do is put together a realistic and *practical* list; not one that 99 per cent of collectors will ever have a chance of acquiring. Samuel Beckett's *Whoroscope* and W.H. Auden's handprinted *Poems* may be the heights that collectors aspire to, but aspire in vain. Whenever copies of these pamphlets do come up for auction (and it's not very often) they could sell for five-figure sums, particularly the latter.

The list includes only those titles that are desirable, accessible and affordable to most collectors. Some titles may cost you a few hundred pounds but they are out there somewhere, just waiting to be snapped up. It also includes some widely differing titles covering several genres: children's books, science fiction, verse, literary criticism, biography and autobiography, and philosophy.

Title	No dj	In dj
Watership Down by Richard Adams novel (Rex Collings, 1972)	£30 – £50	£250 – £350
Zuleika Dobson by Max Beerbohm novel (Heinemann, 1911) *More famous as a caricaturist perhaps, but this book displays the incomparable Max's sparkling personality to its best*	£100 – £150	n/a
Trent's Last Case by E.C. Bentley detective novel (Nelson, 1913) *Possibly the greatest detective novel ever written*	£60 – £100	n/a

Title	No dj	In dj
Eating People Is Wrong by Malcolm Bradbury novel (Secker & Warburg, 1959)	£5 – £10	£50 – £60
Fahrenheight 451 by Ray Bradbury sci-fi novel (Hart-Davis, 1954)	£10 – £15	£100 – £150
The Collected Poems of Rupert Brooke (Sidgwick & Jackson, 1918) *Brooke has more collectable volumes, but this is an* *essential overview of the quintessentially English poet*	£20 – £30	£50 – £60
A Clockwork Orange by Anthony Burgess novel (Heinemann, 1962)	£15 – £20	£200 – £300
The Long Goodbye by Raymond Chandler detective novel (Hamish Hamilton, 1953) *The definitive Chandler, but thankfully not the scarcest*	£10 – £20	£40 – £50
Enemies of Promise by Cyril Connolly criticism/autobiography (Routledge, 1938)	£30 – £40	£50 – £80
The Naked Civil Servant by Quentin Crisp autobiography (Jonathan Cape, 1968) *No library should be without it*	–	£30 – £40
The Enormous Room by E.E. Cummings novel (Jonathan Cape, 1928)	£60 – £100	£150–200
The Autobiography of a Super-Tramp by W.H. Davies (Fifield, 1908) *Issued in 'fluffy' greyish boards. Beware the reprint* *issued in green cloth. At first sight it looks like a first* *edition*	£50 – £80	n/a
The Ginger Man by J.P. Donleavy novel (Neville Spearman, 1956) *The infamous Olympia Press issued an earlier edition* *in, 1955 (up to £200) but most collectors will be more* *than happy with this version. It is much more attractive*	£5 – £10	£50 – £80

Title	No dj	In dj
Rebecca by Daphne du Maurier novel (Gollancz, 1938)	£5 – £10	£60 – £100
Justine by Lawrence Durrell novel (Faber, 1957) *This and the three titles below form Durrell's* *Alexandria Quartet*	£10 – £15	£100 – £150
Balthazhar by Lawrence Durrell novel (Faber, 1958)	–	£50 – £80
Mountolive by Lawrence Durrell novel (Faber, 1939)	–	£50 – £80
Clea by Lawrence Durrell novel (Faber, 1960)	–	£30 – £40
Old Possum's Book of Practical Cats by T.S. Eliot verse (Faber, 1939) *Dust-jacket designed and illustrated by Eliot, the Old* *Possum, himself*	£50 – £80	£150 – £200
The African Queen by C.S. Forester novel (Heinemann, 1935)	£20 – £30	£50 – £80
The Day of the Jackal by Frederick Forsyth novel (Hutchinson, 1972) *Classic thriller*	–	£40 – £50
Cold Comfort Farm by Stella Gibbons novel (Longman, 1932)	£30 – £40	£50 – £80
The Wind in the Willows by Kenneth Grahame children's (Methuen, 1908)	£50 – £80	£150 – £200
Love on the Dole by Walter Greenwood novel (Jonathan Cape, 1933) *One of the very earliest working class novels with* *any guts and conviction*	£20 – £30	£40 – £50

Title	No dj	In dj
The Diary of a Nobody by George and Weedon Grossmith comic diary (Arrowsmith, 1892)	£80 – £120	n/a
The Well of Loneliness by Radclyffe Hall novel (Jonathan Cape, 1928)	£10 – £20	£30 – £40
The Go-Between by L.P. Hartley novel (Hamish Hamilton, 1953) *Beware the virtually identical Book Society edition*	–	£20 – £30
Catch-22 by Joseph Heller novel (Jonathan Cape, 1962)	£10 – £20	£40 – £60
For Whom the Bell Tolls by Ernest Hemingway novel (Jonathan Cape, 1941) *Again, not the scarcest Hemingway, but probably the one that most people would recognise him by*	£20 – £30	£50 – £80
Goodbye Mr Chips! by James Hilton novel (Hodder & Stoughton, 1934) *Originally issued as a supplement to The British Weekly. The first book edition features a wonderful jacket and illustration by Bib Pares. Impressive typography and page layout.*	£15 – £20	£60 – £80
A High Wind in Jamaica by Richard Hughes novel (Chatto & Windus, 1929) *Neglected by both readers and collectors*	£10 – £20	£40 – £60
Brave New World by Aldous Huxley novel (Chatto & Windus, 1932)	£20 – £30	£150 – £200
Three Men in a Boat by Jerome K. Jerome novel (Arrowsmith, 1889) *A bit early for a modern first, perhaps but like Sherlock Holmes and Diary of a Nobody, it had to be included*	£100 – £150	n/a

Title	No dj	In dj
Ulysses by James Joyce novel (Egoist Press, 1922) *First British edition, limited to 2,000 numbered copies.* *This seminal novel was first published in Paris by The* *Shakespeare Press.*	£250 – £350	n/a
Bodley Head issued a new edition in 1936 but it wasn't *until 1986 that the book first appeared as Joyce actu-* *ally wrote it*	£150 – £200	n/a
On the Road by Jack Kerouac novel (Andre Deutsch, 1958) *The Bible of the Beat Generation, and the book that* *launched a million cross-country car journeys. The* *dust-jacket to the second edition was designed by Len* *Deighton*	£10 – £15	£80 – £100
One Flew Over the Cuckoo's Nest by Ken Kesey novel (Methuen, 1963)	£10 – £15	£50 – £60
Cider with Rosie by Laurie Lee autobiography (Hogarth Press, 1959)	–	£20 – £30
The Apes of God by Wyndham Lewis novel (Nash & Grayson, 1931) *First trade edition, and the one in reach of most* *collectors.*	£30 – £40	£50 – £80
The Arthur Press had published a signed limited edition *a year before*	£200+	n/a
Gentlemen Prefer Blondes by Anita Loos novel (Brentano's, 1926)	£20 – £30	£40 – £50
Under the Volcano by Malcolm Lowry novel (Jonathan Cape, 1947)	£20 – £30	£60 – £100
Gone with the Wind by Margaret Mitchell novel (Macmillan, 1936)	£50 – £80	£150 – £200
Lolita by Vladimir Nabokov novel (Putnam, 1958)	–	£30 – £40

Title	No dj	In dj
The Poems of Wilfred Owen (Chatto & Windus, 1931)	£30 – £40	£50 – £80
Ariel by Sylvia Plath verse (Faber, 1965) *Posthumous title from the Bitter Flame*	£10 – £15	£30 – £40
Gamesmanship by Stephen Potter comic manual (Rupert Hart-Davis, 1947) *The first of four titles in this very popular series. The others are Lifemanship (1950), One-Upmanship (1952), and Supermanship (1958).*	£5 – £10	£20 – £30
The Good Companions by J.B. Priestley novel (Heinemann, 1929)	£15 – £20	£50 – £60
Angel Pavement by J.B. Priestley novel (Heinemann, 1930) *Something of a 'swings and roundabouts' author. Very popular in the, 1960s and, 1970s. Then he fell out of favour during the Thatcher years. Today, though, dealers report an upsurge of interest from collectors, particularly these two famous titles*	£10 – £15	£40 – £50
Hadrian the Seventh by Frederick Rolfe novel (Chatto & Windus, 1904) *The classic hate novel from the embittered Catholic Baron Corvo. He designed the wonderfully ornate boards*	£150 – £200	n/a
The History of Western Philosophy by Bertrand Russell philosophy (Allen & Unwin, 1945) *Everything you ever wanted to know about thinkers and what they thought. . . Most copies seen have a jacket printed on what looks like military maps — part of the war-time economy measures for publishing*	£10 – £15	£30 – £40
Memoirs of a Fox-Hunting Man by Siegfried Sassoon autobiography (Faber, 1928)	£30 – £40	£150 – £200
Memoirs of an Infantry Officer by Siegfried Sassoon autobiography (Faber, 1930)	£10 – £15	£50 – £80

Title	No dj	In dj
Sherston's Progress by Siegfried Sassoon autobiography (Faber, 1936) *A very collectable trilogy*	£5 – £10	£40 – £50
Novel on Yellow Paper by Stevie Smith novel (Jonathan Cape, 1936) *An important novel, and very scarce in a nice jacket*	£50 – £80	£250 – £350
One Day in the Life on Ivan Denisovich by Alexander Solzhenitsyn novel (Gollancz, 1963)	–	£30 – £40
The Prime of Miss Jean Brodie by Muriel Spark novel (Macmillan, 1961)	–	£30 – £40
Eminent Victorians by Lytton Strachey biography (Chatto & Windus, 1918) *The book that ended the Victorian era and changed the nature of biography.*	£50 – £80	£100 – £150
Under Milk Wood by Dylan Thomas play (Dent, 1954) *By far the most collectable post-war play — perhaps pre-war too?*	£5 – £10	£60 – £80
A Standard of Behaviour by William Trevor novel (Hutchinson, 1958) *All his books are becoming extremely popular just now — this is the first*	£40 – £50	£150 – £200
Cat on a Hot Tin Roof by Tennessee Williams play (Secker, 1956)	–	£30 – £40
The Day of the Triffids by John Wyndham sci-fi novel (Michael Joseph, 1951)	£10 – £20	£80 – £100

INDEX

We wish to thank those publishers who contributed information for this book and allowed us to reproduce their dust jackets. We would also like to offer apologies to any publisher that we were unable to trace or contact before this book went into print.